The English Springer Spaniel Handbook

BY

LINDA WHITWAM

Copyright © 2022 Linda Whitwam and Canine Handbooks

All rights reserved

ISBN: 979-8781887293

Copyright

© 2022 **Linda Whitwam and Canine Handbooks.** All rights reserved. No part of this document, text, title, digital book, audio book, series, images, graphics or style may be reproduced or transmitted in any form or by any means: electronic, mechanical, photocopying, recording or otherwise, without prior written permission of the author. For permission to reproduce any element of this book contact caninehandbooks@gmail.com

I am deeply grateful to the passionate experts who have shared their extensive first-hand knowledge and love for the beautiful English Springer Spaniel throughout these pages. This book, the 18th in The Canine Handbooks series, would definitely not have been possible without them.

Specialist Contributors

LOUISE SCOTT

LESLEY FIELD

CHRIS BRANDON-LODGE

LYNNE LUCAS

LISA CARDY

HAJA VAN WESSEM

DR VICKY PAYNE, MRCVS

DR MARIANNE DORN, MRCVS

and

FRANCIE NELSON

Other Main Contributors

Special thanks to: The English Springer Spaniel Club, English Springer Spaniel Health, Southern English Springer Spaniel Society (SESSS), Cynthia Turvey and Northern English Springer Spaniel Rescue (NESSR), and holistic vet Dr Sarah Skiwski, DVM.

(Contributors' details appear at the back of the book)

Table of Contents

1. Meet the Springer 6
2. History of the Springer 12
3. Breed Standard 20
    - Basic Differences Between the US and UK 29
4. Finding Your Puppy 32
    - Family and Children 34
    - Spotting Bad Breeders 39
    - Choosing a Healthy English Springer Spaniel 44
    - Advice from Breeders 46
5. Bringing Puppy Home 49
    - Where Should the Puppy Sleep? 54
    - Vaccinations and Worming 58
6. Crate and Housetraining 65
    - Using A Crate 65
    - Housetraining 70
    - Bell Training 75
    - Breeders on Crates and Housetraining 76
7. Feeding a Springer 78
    - Feeding Options 83
    - Springer Feeding Tips 85
8. Springer Traits 94
    - Typical English Springer Spaniel 95
    - 10 Ways to Avoid Unwanted Behaviour 99
    - Separation Anxiety 100
9. Basic Training 107
    - Training Tips 110
    - Collar and Lead (Leash) Training 119
    - Harnesses and Collars 121
    - Dealing with Common Problems 122
10. Gundog Training 128
    - The Next Steps 130
    - Professional Help 132

11. Exercise and Socialisation	139
Socialisation	145
12. English Springer Spaniel Health	150
Health Certificates for Puppy Buyers	151
Joints	158
Eyes	160
Fucosidosis (Fuco)	165
Phosphofructokinase Deficiency (PFK)	165
The Heart	172
Canine Cancer	174
13. Skin & Allergies	179
Types of Allergies	180
Ear Infections	192
Some Allergy Treatments	194
The Holistic Approach	197
14. Grooming	200
Grooming Techniques and Equipment	203
15. The Facts of Life	210
Neutering - Pros and Cons	213
16. Springer Rescue	225
17. Caring for Older Springers	233
Helping Your Dog To Age Gracefully	236
What the Experts Say	238
Contributors	241
Useful Contacts	242
Disclaimer	243

Author's Notes: I have alternated between "he" and "she" in chapters to make this book as relevant as possible for all owners.

The English Springer Spaniel Handbook uses British English, except where Americans have been quoted, when the original US English has been preserved.

1. Meet the Springer

English Springer Spaniels have established themselves as firm favourites with families and are devoted to their beloved humans. They are also sporting dogs par excellence.

Their beautiful eyes, floppy ears, athletic physique and undeniable good looks, coupled with intelligence and a good-natured temperament, have captured hearts and minds all over the world. And there are few more appealing things on this Earth than English Springer puppies.

But don't expect a lapdog; what you're getting is a bundle of happy energy. With his ever-wagging tail, zest for life and love of a job or challenge, The English Springer is The Busy Optimist of the Canine World.

Heritage

There are hundreds of breeds registered with Kennel Clubs worldwide and all of them are different, but the English Springer Spaniel is truly unique; no two dogs are the same.

Originally developed to flush, or *spring*, birds out of the undergrowth for the waiting guns, the English Springer is the tallest and fastest of all the land Spaniels - and first choice gundog for many sportsmen and women.

Over 200 years ago, the Springer and Cocker Spaniels were the same breed, with both types being born into the same litter. It wasn't until 1892 that they were designated completely separate breeds.

The smaller dogs, which hunted woodcock, were Cocker Spaniels and the larger dogs were Springer Spaniels.

Ten years later, the UK Kennel Club recognised the English Springer Spaniel and the Welsh Springer Spaniel as two separate breeds. The Welsh is slightly smaller with red, rather than liver or black, markings.

These days the English Springer is often to be found relaxing at home with his family. Well-socialised Springers make super family pets, get along with everybody, form deep bonds with their owners and children, and do well with other dogs in the home.

Although they may get on very well with your pet cat in the house, once they are out and about it can be a different story! Some Springers still have a strong prey drive/hunting instinct and, especially as puppies, will chase anything small and moving - including the kids!

As Springers are also bred to retrieve game, don't be surprised if yours brings you slippers, socks, the mail or other "gifts," which he will undoubtedly present with pride - and if he gets a rub or a treat as well for his efforts, he is doubly pleased!

Page 6 THE ENGLISH SPRINGER SPANIEL HANDBOOK

A Lot of Dog in a Medium Package

English Springers are first and foremost pack animals that thrive on being with other animals or people. Sometimes described as "Velcro" dogs, they stick to your side and love to be involved in whatever's going on. These are not dogs that enjoy their own company for long periods.

Although they need their own quiet space to rest, these versatile dogs thrive on having a job to do, a game to play or a challenge - after all, they were originally bred to work, and many still retain much of that working instinct.

Springers are best suited to active families, as they have a high **drive** - a need for physical and mental exercise. The UK Kennel Club recommends more than two hours exercise a day.

Many take part and excel at shoots and Field Trials, while others spend their weekends trying to win prizes at Agility, Flyball, Obedience, conformation shows and other canine competitions. Whatever the challenge, this breed is up for it! If you have the time, these are great ways for your dog to channel his energy and enjoy himself.

The Springer approaches life with happiness, enthusiasm and bags of energy. He loves pleasing his owners and is a very honest dog: WYSIWYG - what you see is what you get!

There are very few, if any, bad temperament traits inherent in this breed. If your Springer starts showing signs of poor behaviour, it is often down to a lack of training, exercise, socialisation, or all three.

Teaching the **Recall** is very important as English Springers have an instinctive desire to run free - and you want yours to come back to you.

They also have an incredibly strong sense of smell, which is why they are used as sniffer dogs. Unfortunately, if they are not properly trained, their ears switch off when their nose kicks in!

A well-trained, athletic Springer instinctively covering the ground at top speed, his nose picking up every scent, then returning to his owner after a single call or whistle, is a truly impressive sight - and the envy of many other dog owners.

Photo: A working-type English Springer Spaniel

Some Springers are sensitive dogs that can pick up on your mood, others are bomb-proof! But none of them respond well to heavy-handed training or handling.

They are one of the most **"biddable"** (willing to accept instruction) of all breeds. Springers were bred to follow commands and they do respect authority. This, along with their intelligence and great desire to please you, means you have a willing student and - provided you put in the time and are kind but firm where necessary - a star pupil!

They are a hardy breed that love going out in all weathers - including snow. Most of them love swimming and are pretty good at it. They are also long-lived, with a typical lifespan of 12 to 14 years – a UK ESS Breed Health Survey recorded one that lived to 20!

Different Types

There are two main types of English Springer Spaniel: those bred from working bloodlines and those bred from show bloodlines - known as *field* and *bench* in the US. In the UK, the great majority of English Springer Spaniels are working-type, or a mixture of working and show-type, also known as dual-purpose.

Although they are all regarded as the same breed with the same Breed Standard, there are some differences. The show type is designed for the show ring, so has a longer, thicker coat with more feathering. He tends to be slightly larger and heavier than the working type, with longer ears.

The beauty of the show Springer has long been recognised in America. English Springer Spaniels have won the third-most **Best in Show** awards at the annual Westminster Kennel Club Dog Show (equivalent to the UK's Crufts) with six titles.

Photo: Two American-bred show English Springer Spaniels.

For some inexplicable reason, the English Springer has yet to win Best in Show at Crufts. Perhaps they are just more renowned for their working abilities in the UK, where they are generally regarded as a gundog second to none.

The working type is designed for going on shoots (hunting), so he has less coat and feathering (longer hair on the legs, chest, belly, ears and tail).

Tail docking is the norm for English Springers in the US, but is only allowed in the UK on evidence that a Springer puppy is likely to become a working dog. The theory is that it's kinder to the dog, as a long, feathered tail gets caught more easily in the undergrowth. However, there are plenty of active working Springers with tails.

The AKC (American Kennel Club) says this about the breed in general: "The English Springer Spaniel is a sweet-faced, lovable bird dog of great energy, stamina, and brains. Sport hunters cherish the duality of working Springers: handsome, mannerly pets during the week, and trusty hunting buddies on weekends. Built for long days in the field, English Springer Spaniels are tough, muscular hunters...

"Bred to work closely with humans, Springers are highly trainable people-pleasers. They crave company and are miserable when neglected. Polite dogs, Springers are good with kids and their fellow mammals. They are eager to join in any family activity. Long walks, games of chase and fetch, and swimming are favorite pastimes of these rugged spaniels."

Regardless of type, all English Springer Spaniels come in one of three different coat colour combinations: liver-and-white (the most common), black-and-white, and either of these with tan markings, usually on the cheeks and eyebrows.

The One and Only...

They'll make you laugh - and they might make you cry when they're driving you nuts as puppies, or disappearing at full speed into the undergrowth after a rabbit, deaf to your frantic calls! But whatever life throws at you, your English Springer Spaniel will be there for you through thick and thin.

Three Kennel Club Assured Breeders, both English Springer Spaniel Breed Health Co-ordinators, three veterinary surgeons, several people who train working Springers and shoot with their dogs, one rescue organisation, and an international show judge and American breeder who has produced multiple champions have all added their 100s of years of combined expertise to this book.

And it's fair to say that they know a thing or two about English Springer Spaniels!

English-bred show-type Springers Chaos (Sh. Ch. Meadowdale Chaos) behind his daughter Flame (Flaming Whirlwind Of Meadowdale), pictured enjoying a trip to Ireland. Owned by Jane Eyeington. Photo by Lesley McCourt.

Here is what a few of them had to say about the uniqueness of the one and only English Springer Spaniel:

Lynne Lucas, Traxlerstarr Spaniels, Surrey, England, a breeder for the past decade: "What makes my Springers unique? I could go on forever!

"They are highly intelligent, easy to train, affectionate and loyal. They understand everything you say to them (but can have a selective understanding if they wish!). They are energetic, but also couch potatoes - although mine aren't allowed on the furniture.

"They love to wallow in mud and swim in freezing water, but are very reluctant to go out to pee in the rain!

"I hold conversations with my girls and I know that they understand every word; we chat on walks all the time."

Louise Scott, long-time Springer owner and Joint UK English Springer Spaniel Health Co-ordinator: "They are affectionate, lovable, loyal, devoted, happy, funny, mischievous, engaging, intelligent (mostly!).

"They are great family dogs, versatile (suited to many different activities), neither too big nor too small, generally healthy and long-lived.

"Any of those characteristics could be used to describe a whole host of breeds. What makes English Springers unique? Well for me, it's the fact that all of those qualities are combined within this single, most beautiful breed.

"Amusing anecdotes...where do I start? Many years ago, our first English Springer, Ben, was in the garden with us one day as we were chatting to our neighbour over the fence. The neighbour was holding his prize-winning racing pigeon and regaling us with the story of his latest success.

"He made the mistake of leaning over the fence (which wasn't very high) to show us the pigeon more closely....at which point Ben (who had been quietly sitting next to us listening intently to the conversation) jumped up and, before any of us could blink, the pigeon found itself in Ben's mouth.

"He then proceeded to do a quick lap around the garden with the pigeon, before returning to us and calmly giving it back to my husband.

"The neighbour nearly had a heart attack and my husband and I nearly died of embarrassment, but the pigeon, I'm happy to say, was completely unharmed and none the worse for wear.

"We spent the next 10 minutes apologising profusely to our neighbour, although if I'm honest I had a secret inner pride that our completely untrained, show-bred English Springer Spaniel had demonstrated a 'soft mouth' and the instincts of a proper gundog!"

Veterinary surgeon and breeder of Quincegrove Working English Springer Spaniels, Vicky Payne, MRCVS: "Springers are hard-working, happy dogs, and my first rather headstrong Springer, Quincy, taught me an awful lot about training dogs!

"He wasn't perfect, but the Guns loved him as he would always find them some game. Once I sent him for a 'dead' bird in a patch of bramble, but he ran off along a ditch and would not come back.

"The Guns searched for the pheasant, which they were sure was stone dead, to no avail. After 10 minutes Quincy returned soaked to the skin with a rather angry 'runner' (live bird) in his mouth. Trust your dog!

"Because it is so important to encourage puppies to retrieve, I always go through a stage with my youngsters where they are constantly bringing me things. My current puppy, Cafferty, tells me when it is time to go for a run by bringing me my trainers.

"Rumer, my Open Field Trial bitch, treats me as her PA (personal assistant). I often feel I am just there to drive her to shoots and to carry the birds she has retrieved. I feel under pressure when I shoot for her as she will make a little grunt if I miss!"

Chris Brandon-Lodge: "Some years ago our lovely bitch, Linnet, made her mark on the occasion of a small supper party.

"There were just five of us and we had cooked a shoulder of venison which was in the bottom oven of the Aga with the door pushed closed, but not fastened, to keep it hot while we ate the starter.

"In due course, I asked my husband to start carving the venison. A minute later he was back holding up a 7-shaped bone with a few strands of meat clinging to it. 'Do you mean this?' he said with a grin - to gasps from the guests and laughter from my elderly father.

"Linnet had opened the extremely hot door and in a very short space of time scoffed the lot, despite the meat being hot. The most annoying thing was she had no ill effects from it whatsoever!

"But what to give the guests? Fortunately, the day before I had been on a Press Open Day at the local abattoir and came away with several sirloin steaks, which filled the bill nicely.

"English Springer Spaniels are very food-orientated and soon become overweight if their diet is not carefully controlled and they don't get enough exercise.

"They are very loyal dogs and eager to please; very focused on their personal human. Bear in mind that my experience is based on a line of working-cross-show Springers, but they are easy to train and generally obedient.

"My old Millie was pure working stock and the best temperament I have known, which has come on down the line."

Brains and Beauty: A portrait of Fudge (Fenaybrook Chocolate Fudge of Fernlin), bred by Pat Guy and owned by Lesley Field.

Lesley, Joint Breed Health Co-ordinator with Louise, said: "We called her Fudge for obvious reasons - she had a brown head with no white markings. She was a sheer delight to live with. Her favourite game was to retrieve stones and bring them to me. Wherever and whenever they were thrown for her to retrieve, she would find the exact same one.

"Not many of my English Springer Spaniels ever barked much, but when she did it was the deepest bark I have ever heard from an English Springer - she sounded more like a Rottweiler! She was like Velcro and was a constant companion and friend to everyone."

A Final Few Words...

And finally, we asked our experts to sum up the English Springer Spaniel in a few words:

- People pleaser - whatever job you give him to do, he's up for it!
- Natural mud magnets
- Happy dogs with great personalities
- Velcro, they will stick by you through thick and thin
- Not for the faint-hearted...!
- Loyal, energetic, loving
- Spirited but adaptable; loads of energy, but as happy in work as snoozing in a warm bed
- Happy, loyal and energetic
- Hard-working happiness
- Loyal, intelligent, active, friend
- Simply the best!

Arm yourself with a good pair of boots, a waterproof coat, lots of time and patience and a sense of humour.

Then read on to learn how to understand, train and take best care of these wonderful dogs for the rest of their lives, and how to successfully build a deep bond that will become one of the most important things in your life - and certainly theirs.

2. History of the Springer

By Haja van Wessem

Origins

Without a doubt the Spaniel is one of the oldest breeds in history. Its origins date back over a thousand years and the breed has been recorded for posterity in literature, law and art. It is generally thought that the name *'Spaniel'* derives from the word Spain - or Hispania as it used to be called.

Between 910 and 948 Wales was ruled by King Hywel Dda (Hywel the Good), who drew up a new legal code. The Spaniel was at that time already present in Wales, brought, some say, by the Spanish clan of Ebhor or Ivor many centuries before.

In King Hywel's 10th century *Book of Laws, (pictured),* mammals were divided into three categories: Birds, Beasts and Hounds, and the Hounds had three subdivisions:

- Hounds for the Scent
- Greyhounds
- Spaniels

The Greyhound and Spaniel were the favourite hunting dogs for many generations.

King Hywel also laid down in his Book of Laws that *"The Spaniel of the King is a pound of value."*

FACT ▶ In the year AD 948, a pound could buy several wives, slaves, horses, oxen, turkeys and geese! So the Spaniel was certainly a dog of both high reputation and value at that time.

During the Crusades of 1095 to 1291, noblemen were often accompanied by huntsmen and their dogs. These dogs interbred with local dogs in the Arabian countries and the noblemen brought these crossbreeds back to their own country.

These dogs became very popular with the Royals because of their excellent hunting abilities and were also regarded as status symbols; their owners had, after all, fought for their religion.

Between the 10th and 15th centuries, these crossbreeds produced offspring with excellent hunting qualities. They spread out over the continent and developed in different ways, according to the country where they lived and the work they were asked to do.

In France they became *Epagneuls* (French for Spaniel), in Germany **Wachtelhunde**, in the Netherlands **Spioen,** and in Britain they were **Spaniels.**

Mention of a Spaniel is made in Geoffrey Chaucer's (1343-1400) **Canterbury Tales**. The Tales are about a group of pilgrims travelling together who pass the time by each telling a story, the themes of which are courtly love, treason, avarice and adultery.

The Wife of Bath's Tale is about a woman who had been married five times (very unusual in those days) and who was looking for Husband Number Six.

The storyteller compared her with a Spaniel: *"She coveteth every man that she may se: for as a spaynel she wol on hym lepe."*

Hunting scenes and dogs became popular subjects for paintings between the 17th and 20th century, many of them featuring Spaniels of various sizes and types.

....

Early Hunting

A contemporary of Chaucer, Gaston III, Count of Foix, owned an estate in south west France. Between 1350 and 1390 he was the leader of a band of adventurers who travelled from the Pyrenees to Scandinavia.

Between his travels he stayed on his estate, Orthez, where he dedicated himself to his three passions: weapons, love and hunting.

In 1387, at over 50 years of age and finding himself too old for warfare and love, he decided to devote himself solely to the hunt.

Between 1387 and 1391 he wrote a book on hunting, **Livre de Chasse**, which was translated into English by Edmund de Langley as *The Book of Hunting.*

It contained beautiful images *(pictured)* and was one of the first books on hunting.

De Foix, who also used the name Gaston Phébus, referred to the Spaniel: *"Another kind of hound there is that be called hounds for the hawk and Spaniels, for their kind cometh from Spain, notwithstanding that there are many in other countries. A good Spaniel should not be too rough, but his tail should be rough."*

In 1486 the first list of domesticated dogs appeared in **The Book of St. Albans.** The book was probably meant as teaching material for the pupils of the school in the Hertfordshire town. Dame Juliana Berners, *(pictured, below)*, said to be Prioress of the nearby St. Mary of Sopwell Convent, is considered to be the author.

In the chapter on hunting, she writes: *"Thyse ben the names of houndes, fyrste there is a Grehoun, a Bastard, a Mengrell, a Mastiff, a Lemor, a Spanyel, Raches, Kenettys, Teroures, Butchers' Houndes, Myddyng dogges, Tryndel-taylles, and Prikherid currys, and smalle ladyes' poppees that bere awaye the flees."* The last part refers to small lapdogs to fend off the fleas of their mistress!

In 1570, Dr John Keye (or Kaye) published **De Canibus Britannicis** in Latin under his pseudonym, Dr Caius. Later it was translated into English as *Treatise of English Dogges*. Dr Caius described four kinds of dogs:

- *Venatici* - for the hunt of big game
- *Aucupatorii* - for the hunt of small game
- *Delicati* - such as Toy Spaniel or Comforter
- *Rustici* - such as the Pastoralis (herding dog) and the Villaticus (mastiff)

The First Springing Spaniels

Dr Caius subdivided *Aucupatorii* into land spaniels and "Spaniells which findeth game on the water." He named this group *Hispaniolus.*

He describes them as white with red markings or the rarer solid black or red. There is also reference in literature of the time to: *"A spaniel dog with floppy ears, the chest, belly and feet white, picked out with black, the rest of the body black."*

The land spaniels were praised for their work of springing game for the hounds and hawks to chase.

During Henry VIII's reign (1509-1547), large parties were held at the court with great feasts and the demand for game was inexhaustible. Partridge, quail, pheasant, rabbit and hare were caught with the snare, but demand surpassed supply.

Huntsmen began to look for other means to catch the game and they discovered the use of the net. A dog flushed the game from its cover, sat down and the huntsman threw a net over the game and the dog.

FACT The dogs they used with the net were called *'setting'* or *'sitting spaniels'* and are the ancestors of our modern Setters. The dogs that were used to flush the game were called *'springing spaniels.'* This did not mean that the dogs had to spring, but rather that it was their job to make the game spring from its cover.

With the invention of matchlock, wheellock and flintlock firearms, netting disappeared and the game was shot. The setting spaniels were used to find the game and point it and the springing spaniels proved to be especially talented at flushing game for the shooters.

The early 17th century sportsman Richard Surflet said: *"The spaniel is gentle, loving and courteous to man more than any other dog, of free untiring laborsome ranging, beating a full course over and over, which he does with a wanton playing taile and a busie labouring noise, neither desisting nor showing less delight in his labours at night than he did in the morning."*

This is as true today as it was 400 years ago. The 21st century Spaniel is indeed loving, happy, eager to please his owner and, given half a chance, busy from morn till night with a constantly wagging tail.

In the 18th century, the term **springing spaniel** was gaining ground as a description, not of a particular variety but of the group of gundogs that sprung their game.

All land spaniels came under this heading and the varieties we now know as Welsh and English Springers, Field, Cocker, Clumber and Sussex Spaniels were all originally springing spaniels.

The highly-prized hunting properties of these spaniels - namely their highly-developed sense of smell and talent for finding and flushing the game - contributed to their popularity in the late 1800s. The Sandringham kennels of King Edward VII in Norfolk contained many fine Springers that were known for some time as Norfolk Spaniels.

FACT Not only in Norfolk but also in other parts of England, all parti-coloured spaniels were known as *Norfolk Spaniels* until after 1900 when they all became Springer Spaniels.

The Land Spaniel was divided into two sizes; the smaller being the **Cocking Spaniel** (forerunner of today's Cocker Spaniel), so-named because they were used to flush woodcock. In his 1803 book ***"The Sporting Dictionary and Rural Repository of general information upon every subject appertaining to The Sports of the Field,"*** author William Taplin wrote:

"Spaniel is the name of a dog of which there are different kinds; and even these have been so repeatedly crossed that, unless it is in the possession of sportsmen who have been careful in preserving the purity of the breed perfectly free from casual contamination, the well-bred genuine cocking Spaniel is difficult to obtain."

Development of the Breed

The Boughey family of Aqualate in Shropshire, England, are regarded as instrumental in the development of the English Springer Spaniel. The Bougheys carefully developed their distinct bloodline and kept a detailed studbook tracing each dog's ancestry right up to 1930. The first dog to appear in the Aqualate register was Mop I, born in 1812.

The early Springer types had a look of the Clumber Spaniel about them. They were broader, heavier and their coat was curlier.

In 1885 the Spaniel Club was founded. The first field trial was held in 1899 on Mr William Arkwright's estate in Derbyshire. However, it was not an English Springer that won, but a Clumber Spaniel. A year later it was an English Springer Spaniel by the name of Tring who took the top honours.

In 1902 The Kennel Club recognised the English Springer Spaniel as a specific variety of spaniel and individual breed. The Spaniel Club drew up the Breed Standard and submitted it to The Kennel Club for approval. The following year, Sir Thomas Boughey bred Ch. Velox Powder (later owned by Mr C. Eversfield of Denne Springers), who went on to win 20 field trial stakes. His pedigree went right back through the Aqualate Stud Book to Mop I.

This same year saw the first winner in the show ring when Beechgrove Will, a five-year-old liver and white dog owned by F. Winton Smith became the first English Springer Spaniel to be awarded a Challenge Certificate. Will was awarded his Championship in 1906. Harry Jones' Fansome became the first female to win a Championship.

In 1913, the first Springer to become a Field Trial Champion was Rivington Sam, **pictured.** Sam was the grandsire of Field Trial Champion Rex of Avendale, who features in the pedigrees of many of our modern English Springers.

World War I (1914-1918) put paid to dog showing for over a decade. Then, in 1921, The English Springer Spaniel Club was founded. It is now referred to as *'The Parent Club'* due to its position as the oldest of the eight UK breed clubs.

The Springer enjoyed increasing popularity - the early pioneers held strongly to the view that the English Springer was basically a working dog, and their aim was to breed for working abilities as well as breed conformation.

Until 1920 the breed fanciers were not much interested in showing. Still, Springers did well because alongside their happy, gentle nature and devotion to their owners, these dogs were not only much-loved pets, they were also good at bringing home a rabbit - an important food for many country families between the two wars. Notable stud dogs of the early days were Ch. Velox Powder, Ch. Rivington Sam, Ch. Rex of Avendale and many others. Notable breeders were Mr C.A. Philips (Rivington) and Mr H.S. Lloyd.

Although their usefulness in the field and field trial competitions attracted far more attention than conformation shows, the number of Springers participating in shows was growing. However, the outbreak of World War II in 1939 once again put an end to breeding, shows and field trials, and it was many years before the breed was back to its pre-war quality.

Before the war, a dog could only win the title of Champion if he had won at both conformation shows and field trials. A Field Trial Champion was a dog that had won at Field Trials without having been shown.

In the 1950s, the Kennel Club introduced the title of **Show Champion** for a dog that had won three Challenge Certificates (CCs) at shows, and the title of **Champion** for a dog that had won three CCs AND had also qualified in the field. The title of **Field Trial Champion** was maintained.

Very few dogs have won the title of **Dual Champion,** i.e. a dual champion in both show and field trials, and the Kennel Club's decision to split the titles is regretted by many fans of the breed, as it has resulted in two types of dog: show Springers and working Springers.

Photo: Islay (Ch Melverly Islay Inspired At Lossiedoon) bred by Ray Smith and owned by Diane Scott. Islay has won 8 Challenge Certificates (CCs) and 4 Reserve CCs and was Best of Breed at Crufts in 2015.

Islay then went on to gain her Show Gundog Working Certificate in 2016, making her the breed's first - and still the only - Full Champion in the UK since 1997, a true dual purpose English Springer Spaniel.

Although the aim of the English Springer Spaniel Club has always been to support field and show, it was unavoidable that a distinct working-type English Springer came into being.

There is a tendency in working lines to breed a smaller and lighter dog, whereas the show Springer is heavier in bone and slightly larger with more coat. **(See Francie Nelson's description of today's two types in Chapter 3. Breed Standard, as well as a photo of Islay competing at a show).**

Great Britain has seen and has many top winning English Springers. In the 1970s Sh.Ch Hawkhill Connaught was top dog all breeds in 1972 and 1973. He was bred by Judith Hancock and owned by her in partnership with Jimmy Cudworth. It was the first time in history that an English Springer became top dog all breeds.

Hawkhill Connaught went on to win a total of 50 Challenge Certificates in the 1970s. On the working side, a famous dog is undoubtedly Hales Smut, bred by Keith Erlandson, who sired at least 13 field trial champions. Mr Erlandson's **Gwibernant** prefix is internationally renowned.

More recently, Sh.Ch Wadeson Inspector Wexford, born in 1995, gained fame by holding the breed record with 62 Challenge Certificates, a record which still stands at the time of writing. The bitch Ch Mompesson Remember Me, bred by Mrs F. Jackson, holds the breed record for bitches since 2004 with 55 CCs.

The English Springer Spaniel in America

Early Days

Spaniels can be traced back to 1620 and the landing of the Mayflower, which brought a Mastiff and a Spaniel to New England. Edward Winslow, one of the leaders on the ship, and William Bradford wrote *Journal of the Beginning and Proceeding of the English Plantation settled at Plymouth in New England*, published in 1622, which mentions a spaniel.

When the Pilgrims had been there two months, two of the men, John Goodman and Peter Brown, set out one bitterly cold January day: *"At dinner time (they) took their meat in their hands, and would go walk and refresh themselves. So going a little off they find a lake of water, and having a great mastiff bitch with them and a spaniel, by the water side they found a great deer; the dogs chased him, and they followed so far as they lost themselves and could not find the way back. They wandered all that afternoon being wet, and at night it did freeze and snow."*

Picture: A romanticised painting of the First Thanksgiving by Jean Leon Gerome Ferris (1863–1930)

The two men heard the roars of "lions" and spent a freezing night pacing under a tree, ready to climb up it if the wild beasts attacked. The two men survived and rejoined the other Pilgrims who were onshore, although *"John Goodman was fain to have his shoes cut off his feet they were so swelled with cold."*

The dogs also survived and the spaniel is mentioned again: *"John Goodman went abroad to use his lame feet, that were pitifully ill with the cold he had got, having a little spaniel with him. A little way from the plantation two great wolves ran after the dog; the dog ran to him and betwixt his legs for succor. He had nothing in his hand but took up a stick, and threw at one of them and hit him, and they presently ran both away."*

In the modern era, the English Springer Spaniel has become very popular in the United States. In the 19th and early 20th centuries they were almost entirely used as gundogs, working in swamplands and brambles, just as in Britain.

Later, due to the growing popularity of setters and pointers, their number declined to such an extent that the breed was threatened with extinction.

Thanks to breeders and the Sporting Spaniel Society, the Springer was saved. The Society set out to redevelop the Springer by using the liver-and-white and black-and-white Keepers Spaniels, the Clumber, the old English Water Spaniel, the Sussex, and the setter and spaniel crosses owned by American sportsmen. They succeeded in their attempts and as the breed revived, interest increased and many imports from the UK contributed to a wider genetic base.

The Modern Era

The first official US registration of an English Springer Spaniel was in 1910, and the first show with classes for Springers was in 1923 in Madison Square Garden, New York, followed by the first field trial in 1924.

This year also saw the foundation of the English Springer Field Trial Association, the breed's parent club, and the American Kennel Club's recognition of the breed. The US Breed Standard was drawn up, along with rules for the conduct at field trials.

However, two years earlier on September 30, 1922, The English Springer Spaniel Club of Canada ran the first Spaniel Field Trials near St. Agathe, Manitoba, Canada. There were 26 runners in the three stakes and it lasted about six-and-a-half hours.

The first brace were: *"put down in some nice thick brush, poplar and stunted oak, with considerable under-growth."* The dogs duly performed, with Flora flushing a rabbit and a partridge and Patty a prairie chicken!

One name that is synonymous with the Springer in North America is Mr Eudore Chevrier (1886-1982), **pictured,** the Canadian breed enthusiast known as "The Father of North American Springers."

In the space of three-and-a-half years he imported 250 dogs from England, including several field trial champions. In 1925 he had 600 Springers in his kennels and at the Westminster Show he entered 11 Springers!

Mr Chevrier lived in Winnipeg and was founder of the renowned Avondale Kennels. He was instrumental in the forming the English Springer Spaniel Club of Canada and organising the 1922 Spaniel Field Trial Breeding. He bred literally thousands of Springers over 40 years.

In the years between the two World Wars many of the best English Springers of both show and working strains were exported to the US and Canada. In the 1950s and 1960s many good quality English Springers found their way from Great Britain to the States and since then the breed has prospered.

As in Great Britain, a dog can become a **Field Trial Champion** after having won two All Aged Stakes, and to gain the title of **Champion** the dog has to have a field trial qualification as well as the necessary number of wins at championship shows.

The most famous American breeder is undoubtedly Mrs Julia Gasow, of Michigan, with her **Salilyn** prefix. Her most famous dog was the liver-and-white Ch. Salilyn's Aristocrat, known as Risto, **pictured.**

He won 45 Bests in Show and was number one sire all-time all breeds. He sired 188 champions out of 92 dams - all without the use of frozen sperm!

No dog has had more impact on The Westminster Dog Show. His descendants who won the prestigious Best in Show (BIS) title include Ch. Chinoe's Adamant James (1971, 1972), Ch. Salilyn's Condor (1993) and his daughter Ch. Salilyn 'N Erin's Shameless (2000).

Although an English Springer has never won Crufts in England, the breed has won the third most BIS titles at Westminster - a total of six - and year after year Risto's descendants continue to win at Breed and Group level.

Risto was top dog, all breeds, in 1967, as was his son Adamant James in 1971 and his great-grandson Condor in 1992. His grandsons Ch. Salilyn's Private Stock and Ch. Telltale Royal Stuart and his great-grandson Ch. Salilyn's Classic have each sired more than 100 champions.

Mrs Gasow, with the support of her husband veterinarian Fred Gasow, produced several hundred champions who changed the course of English Springer history. However, it nearly didn't happen…. in the late 1940s a faulty furnace started a fire that burned her first kennel to the ground. Sadly, none of the kennelled dogs survived.

But in a merciful quirk of fate, a few of the Salilyn Springers were boarded at Fred's Clinic awaiting routine check-ups on the night of the fire. Devastated and heartbroken, Mrs Gasow wanted to quit the sport, but her husband urged her to continue and had the facility quickly rebuilt.

Salilyn's greatest days were yet to come. One of the surviving dogs was King Peter of Salilyn, who went on to win many titles and sire champions. "I don't think I knew where this would all go," Mrs Gasow, aged 92, told the Kennel Gazette in 1997: "But I sincerely loved every minute of it."

As in Great Britain, the gap between the American show and working type has widened over the years. Breeders have created a show dog that has its own, very distinct type, and now the difference between English and American Springer Spaniels has become just as notable as the difference between show and working type Springers.

Photos: Two classic heads which highlight the difference between English and American show Springers. Left: the English Sh. Ch. Mompesson Classic Moods, and right: the American Ch. Salilyn's Aristocrat.

American Springers are mostly all "open marked," i.e. black-and-white or liver-and-white without any ticking. They have more coat and are slightly more Cocker-like in type, especially in the head.

Although different in type, the American Springer is without any doubt a beautiful dog in its own right. Some fanciers of both the American and the English type suggested that the American Springer Spaniel be recognised as a separate breed, as has happened with the Cocker Spaniel.

However, the English Springer Spaniel Trial Association, the US parent club, was of the opinion that there were basically few differences and saw no reason to split the breed.

The English Springer is a lovely dog to live and work with. Handsome, affectionate, intelligent and loving, with a reputation second to none in the field, it's no wonder this breed is so popular throughout Europe and North America.

3. Breed Standard

The Breed Standard is a blueprint not only for the ideal appearance of each breed, but also for character and temperament, how the dog moves and what colours are acceptable.

In other words, it ensures that an English Springer Spaniel looks and acts like an English Springer Spaniel, ensuring it is "fit for function, fit for life."

Good breeders strive to breed their dogs to the Breed Standard. Breeders of working Springers also want to ensure that the Springer's natural hunting instincts are passed down through their bloodlines from one generation to the next.

If you are looking to buy a puppy, decide whether a working type or show type would be most suitable, then have a good look at the mother and father - or at least the mother. Purebred puppies usually resemble their parents.

....

The Breed Standard is administered by the Kennel Club in the UK. In the USA it is written by the national breed club (the ESSFTA for English Springer Spaniels) and approved by the AKC (American Kennel Club).

The Kennel Clubs then keep the register of purebred (pedigree) dogs. Dogs entered in conformation shows run under Kennel Club and AKC rules are judged against the Breed Standard.

Breeders approved by the Kennel Clubs agree to produce puppies in line with the Breed Standard and maintain certain welfare conditions.

Responsible breeders select only the finest dogs for reproduction, based on the health, look and temperament of the parents and their ancestors.

English Springer Spaniels were originally bred as hunting dogs. Their job was - and still is – to flush or *spring* game birds from the undergrowth or scrub into the air.

The Springer is in the **Gundog Group** in the UK and **Sporting Group** in the US.

Our photo shows a working-type Springer.

The Kennel Club says this about the Gundog Group: "Dogs that were originally trained to find live game and/or to retrieve game that had been shot and wounded.

"This group is divided into four categories - Retrievers, Spaniels, Hunt/Point/Retrieve, Pointers and Setters - although many of the breeds are capable of doing the same work as the other sub-groups. They make good companions, their temperament making them ideal all-round family dogs."

Points of Concern

In 2014 the UK Kennel Club launched its **Breed Watch Fit For Purpose** campaign. It identified potential faults that could lead to health issues. There are three categories:

1. Breeds with no current points of concern reported
2. Breeds with Breed Watch points of concern
3. Breeds where some dogs have visible conditions or exaggerations that can cause pain or discomfort

The good news is that English Springer Spaniels are classed in Category 1, they are regarded internationally as a healthy breed.

The Kennel Club says: "The English Springer is the highest on the leg of all the Land Spaniels and he shares the same ancestry as the other spaniels. When classification took place, selective breeding for size and colour followed and that stabilised type.

"At one stage the breed was called the Norfolk Spaniel as it was reputed that the Duke of Norfolk developed the breed.

"After the invention of guns, the breed was used to flush game from undergrowth. The liver and white colour is the most popular, but black and white and tri-colours occur in lower numbers.

"The English Springer is the most popular of the spaniels for working in the field."

Our photo shows an English show Springer. Show Springers tend to be larger and heavier than working-type Springers and have more coat.

The KC adds: **Size** - Medium, **Exercise** - More than 2 hours per day, **Size Of Home** - Small house, **Grooming** - More than once a week, **Coat Length** - Medium, **Sheds** - Yes, **Lifespan** - Over 10 years, **Vulnerable Native Breed** - No, **Town Or Country** - Either, **Size Of Garden** - Large garden.

The AKC has this description: "The English Springer Spaniel is a sweet-faced, lovable bird dog of great energy, stamina, and brains. Sport hunters cherish the duality of working Springers: handsome, mannerly pets during the week, and trusty hunting buddies on weekends."

"Built for long days in the field, English Springer Spaniels are tough, muscular hunters standing 19 to 20 inches at the shoulder and weighing between 40 and 50 pounds.

"The double coat comes in several colors and patterns, the ears are long and lush, and the kindly, trusting expression of the eyes is a cherished hallmark of the breed.

"Springers move with a smooth, ground-covering stride. Bred to work closely with humans, Springers are highly trainable people-pleasers. They crave company and are miserable when neglected.

"Polite dogs, Springers are good with kids and their fellow mammals. They are eager to join in any family activity. Long walks, games of chase and fetch, and swimming are favorite pastimes of these rugged spaniels."

UK Breed Standard

Like the English Springer Spaniel himself, the UK Breed Standard is relatively straightforward:

General Appearance - Symmetrically built, compact, strong, merry, active. Highest on leg and raciest in build of all British land Spaniels.

Characteristics - Breed is of ancient and pure origins, oldest of sporting gundogs; original purpose was finding and springing game for net, falcon or greyhound. Now used to find, flush and retrieve game for gun.

Temperament - Friendly, happy disposition, biddable. Timidity or aggression highly undesirable.

Head and Skull - Skull of medium length, fairly broad, slightly rounded, rising from foreface, making a brow or stop, divided by fluting between eyes, dying away along forehead towards occipital bone which should not be prominent. Cheeks flat.

Foreface of proportionate length to skull, fairly broad and deep, well chiselled below eyes, fairly deep and square in flew. Nostrils well developed.

Pictured is the beautiful classic head of Sophie (Sh. Ch. Donarden Madame Butterfly), courtesy of owner-breeders Nicola Dobbin and Grace Donaldson.

Eyes - Medium size, almond-shaped, not prominent nor sunken, well set in (not showing haw), alert, kind expression. Dark hazel. Light eyes undesirable.

Ears - Lobular, good length and width, fairly close to head, set in line with eye. Nicely feathered.

Mouth - Jaws strong, with a perfect, regular and complete scissor bite, i.e. upper teeth closely overlapping lower teeth and set square to the jaws.

Neck - Good length, strong and muscular, free from throatiness, slightly arched, tapering towards head.

Forequarters - Forelegs straight and well boned. Shoulders sloping and well laid. Elbows set well to body. Strong flexible pasterns.

Body - Strong, neither too long nor too short. Chest deep, well developed. Well-sprung ribs. Loin muscular, strong with slight arch and well coupled.

Hindquarters - Hindlegs well let down. Stifles and hocks moderately bent. Thighs broad, muscular, well developed. Coarse hocks undesirable.

Feet - Tight, compact, well rounded, with strong, full pads.

Tail - Previously customarily docked. Docked: Set low, never carried above level of back. Well feathered with lively action. Undocked: Set low, never carried above level of back. Well feathered with lively action. In balance with the rest of the dog.

Gait/Movement - Strictly his own. Forelegs swing straight forward from shoulder, throwing feet well forward in an easy free manner. Hocks driving well under body, following in line with forelegs. At slow movement may have a pacing stride typical of this breed.

Coat - Close, straight and weather resisting, never coarse. Moderate feathering on ears, forelegs, body and hindquarters.

Pictured is full champion Islay (Ch Melverly Islay Inspired At Lossiedoon) bred by Ray Smith and owned by Diane Scott. Photo by Kay Woodward.

Colour - Liver and white, black and white, or either of these colours with tan markings.

Size - Approximate height: 51 cms (20 ins).

Faults - Any departure from the foregoing points should be considered a fault and the seriousness with which the fault should be regarded should be in exact proportion to its degree and its effect upon the health and welfare of the dog and on the dog's ability to perform its traditional work.

Note - Male animals should have two apparently normal testicles fully descended into the scrotum.

*Note for prospective puppy buyers

Size - The Kennel Club breed standard is a guide and description of the ideal for the breed; the size as described does not imply that a dog will match the measurements given (height or weight). A dog might be larger or smaller than the size measurements stated in the breed standard.

US Breed Standard

The AKC Breed Standard is far more detailed regarding the dog's physical appearance:

General Appearance: The English Springer Spaniel is a medium-sized sporting dog, with a compact body and a docked tail. His coat is moderately long, with feathering on his legs, ears, chest and brisket. His pendulous ears, soft gentle expression, sturdy build and friendly wagging tail proclaim him unmistakably a member of the ancient family of Spaniels.

He is above all a well-proportioned dog, free from exaggeration, nicely balanced in every part. His carriage is proud and upstanding, body deep, legs strong and muscular, with enough length to carry him with ease. Taken as a whole, the English Springer Spaniel suggests power, endurance and agility.

He looks the part of a dog that can go, and keep going, under difficult hunting conditions. At his best, he is endowed with style, symmetry, balance and enthusiasm, and is every inch a sporting dog of distinct spaniel character, combining beauty and utility.

Size, Proportion, Substance: The Springer is built to cover rough ground with agility and reasonable speed. His structure suggests the capacity for endurance. He is to be kept to medium size.

Ideal height at the shoulder for dogs is 20 inches; for bitches it is 19 inches. Those more than one inch under or over the breed ideal are to be faulted.

A 20-inch dog, well-proportioned and in good condition, will weigh approximately 50 pounds; a 19-inch bitch will weigh approximately 40 pounds. The length of the body (measured from point of shoulder to point of buttocks) is slightly greater than the height at the withers.

The dog too long in body, especially when long in the loin, tires easily and lacks the compact outline characteristic of the breed.

A dog too short in body for the length of his legs, a condition which destroys balance and restricts gait, is equally undesirable. A Springer with correct substance appears well-knit and sturdy with good bone, however, he is never coarse or ponderous.

Head: The head is impressive without being heavy. Its beauty lies in a combination of strength and refinement. It is important that its size and proportion be in balance with the rest of the dog. Viewed in profile, the head appears approximately the same length as the neck and blends with the body in substance.

The stop, eyebrows and chiseling of the bony structure around the eye sockets contribute to the Springer's beautiful and characteristic expression, which is alert, kindly and trusting.

The *eyes,* more than any other feature, are the essence of the Springer's appeal. Correct size, shape, placement and color influence expression and attractiveness. The eyes are of medium size and oval in shape, set rather well-apart and fairly deep in their sockets. The color of the iris harmonizes with the color of the coat, preferably dark hazel in the liver and white dogs and black or deep brown in the black and white dogs.

Eye rims are fully pigmented and match the coat in color. Lids are tight with little or no haw showing. Eyes that are small, round or protruding, as well as eyes that are yellow or brassy in color, are highly undesirable.

Ears are long and fairly wide, hanging close to the cheeks with no tendency to stand up or out. The ear leather is thin and approximately long enough to reach the tip of the nose. Correct ear set is on a level with the eye and not too far back on the skull.

The *skull* is medium-length and fairly broad, flat on top and slightly rounded at the sides and back. The occiput bone is inconspicuous. As the skull rises from the foreface, it makes a stop, divided by a groove, or fluting, between the eyes. The groove disappears as it reaches the middle of the forehead.

The amount of stop is moderate. It must not be a pronounced feature; rather it is a subtle rise where the muzzle joins the upper head. It is emphasized by the groove and by the position and shape of the eyebrows, which are well-developed.

The *muzzle* is approximately the same length as the skull and one half the width of the skull. Viewed in profile, the toplines of the skull and muzzle lie in approximately parallel planes.

The nasal bone is straight, with no inclination downward toward the tip of the nose, the latter giving an undesirable downfaced look. Neither is the nasal bone concave, resulting in a "dish-faced" profile; nor convex, giving the dog a Roman nose. The cheeks are flat, and the face is well-chiseled under the eyes.

Jaws are of sufficient length to allow the dog to carry game easily: fairly square, lean and strong. The upper lips come down full and rather square to cover the line of the lower jaw, however, the lips are never pendulous or exaggerated. The nose is fully-pigmented, liver or black in color, depending on the color of the coat. The nostrils are well-opened and broad. Teeth are strong, clean, of good size and ideally meet in a close scissors **bite.**

An even bite or one or two incisors slightly out of line are minor faults. Undershot, overshot and wry jaws are serious faults and are to be severely penalized.

Neck, Topline, Body: The *neck* is moderately long, muscular, clean and slightly arched at the crest. It blends gradually and smoothly into sloping shoulders.

The portion of the topline from withers to tail is firm and slopes very gently. The body is short-coupled, strong and compact.

The chest is deep, reaching the level of the elbows, with well-developed forechest; however, it is not so wide or round as to interfere with the action of the front legs. Ribs are fairly long, springing gradually to the middle of the body, then tapering as they approach the end of the ribbed section.

The underline stays level with the elbows to a slight upcurve at the flank. The back is straight, strong and essentially level. Loins are strong, short and slightly arched. Hips are nicely-rounded, blending smoothly into the hind legs. The croup slopes gently to the set of the tail, and tail-set follows the natural line of the croup.

The *tail* is carried horizontally or slightly elevated and displays a characteristic lively, merry action, particularly when the dog is on game. A clamped tail (indicating timidity or undependable temperament) is to be faulted, as is a tail carried at a right angle to the backline in Terrier fashion.

Forequarters: Efficient movement in front calls for proper forequarter assembly. The shoulder blades are flat and fairly close together at the tips, molding smoothly into the contour of the body.

Ideally, when measured from the top of the withers to the point of the shoulder to the elbow, the shoulder blade and upper arm are of apparent equal length, forming an angle of nearly 90 degrees; this sets the front legs well under the body and places the elbows directly beneath the tips of the shoulder blades.

Elbows lie close to the body. Forelegs are straight with the same degree of size continuing to the foot. Bone is strong, slightly flattened, not too round or too heavy. Pasterns are short, strong and slightly sloping, with no suggestion of weakness. Dewclaws are usually removed. Feet are round or slightly oval. They are compact and well-arched, of medium size with thick pads, and well-feathered between the toes.

Hindquarters: The Springer should be worked and shown in hard, muscular condition with well-developed hips and thighs. His whole rear assembly suggests strength and driving power. Thighs are broad and muscular. Stifle joints are strong. For functional efficiency, the angulation of the hindquarter is never greater than that of the forequarter, and not appreciably less.

The hock joints are somewhat rounded, not small and sharp in contour. Rear pasterns are short (about 1/3 the distance from the hip joint to the foot) and strong, with good bone. When viewed from behind, the rear pasterns are parallel. Dewclaws are usually removed. The feet are the same as in front, except that they are smaller and often more compact.

Coat: The Springer has an outer coat and an undercoat. On the body, the outer coat is of medium length, flat or wavy, and is easily distinguishable from the undercoat, which is short, soft and dense. The quantity of undercoat is affected by climate and season. When in combination, outer coat and undercoat serve to make the dog substantially waterproof, weatherproof and thornproof.

On ears, chest, legs and belly the Springer is nicely furnished with a fringe of feathering of moderate length and heaviness. On the head, front of the forelegs, and below the hock joints on the front of the hind legs, the hair is short and fine. The coat has the clean, glossy, "live" appearance indicative of good health. It is legitimate to trim about the head, ears, neck and feet, to remove dead undercoat, and to thin and shorten excess feathering as required to enhance a smart, functional appearance.

The tail may be trimmed, or well fringed with wavy feathering. Above all, the appearance should be natural. Overtrimming, especially the body coat, or any chopped, barbered or artificial effect is to be penalized in the show ring, as is excessive feathering that destroys the clean outline desirable in **a sporting dog. Correct quality and condition of coat is to take precedence over quantity of coat.**

Color: All the following combinations of colors and markings are equally acceptable:
(1) **Black or liver** with white markings or predominantly white with black or liver markings
(2) **Blue or liver roan;**
(3) **Tricolor:** black and white or liver and white with tan markings, usually found on eyebrows, cheeks, inside of ears and under the tail. Any white portion of the coat may be flecked with ticking.

Off colors such as lemon, red or orange are not to place.

Gait: The final test of the Springer's conformation and soundness is proper movement. Balance is a prerequisite to good movement. The front and rear assemblies must be equivalent in angulation and muscular development for the gait to be smooth and effortless. Shoulders which are well laid-back to permit a long stride are just as essential as the excellent rear quarters that provide driving power.

Seen from the side, the Springer exhibits a long, ground-covering stride and carries a firm back, with no tendency to dip, roach or roll from side to side. From the front, the legs swing forward in a free and easy manner. Elbows have free action from the shoulders, and the legs show no tendency to cross or interfere.

From behind, the rear legs reach well under the body, following on a line with the forelegs. As speed increases, there is a natural tendency for the legs to converge toward a center line of travel. Movement faults include high-stepping, wasted motion; short, choppy stride; crabbing; and moving with the feet wide, the latter giving roll or swing to the body.

Temperament: The typical Springer is friendly, eager to please, quick to learn and willing to obey. Such traits are conducive to tractability, which is essential for appropriate handler control in the field. In the show ring, he should exhibit poise and attentiveness and permit himself to be examined by the judge without resentment or cringing.

Aggression toward people and aggression toward other dogs is not in keeping with sporting dog character and purpose and is not acceptable. Excessive timidity, with due allowance for puppies and novice exhibits, is to be equally penalized.

Photo: Two American show-type English Springer Spaniels in Illinois by Lynn M. Stone, naturepl.com

Summary: In evaluating the English Springer Spaniel, the overall picture is a primary consideration. One should look for type, which includes general appearance and outline, and also for soundness, which includes movement and temperament.

Inasmuch as the dog with a smooth easy gait must be reasonably sound and well-balanced, he is to be highly regarded, however, not to the extent of forgiving him for not looking like an English Springer Spaniel.

An atypical dog, too short or long in leg length or foreign in head or expression, may move well, but he is not to be preferred over a good all-round specimen that has a minor fault in movement.

It must be remembered that the English Springer Spaniel is first and foremost a sporting dog of the Spaniel family, and he must look, behave and move in character.

NOTE: Since 2007, it has been illegal to dock dogs' tails in the UK unless they are working (also called *field*) dogs. Some UK Springer Spaniels are working dogs with docked tails, but the tails of pet Springers are not usually docked. However, in the USA it is customary to dock the tail.

The American parent body, the ESSFTA (English Springer Spaniel Field Trial Association), says: "Springer enthusiasts, both field and conformation, dock tails for utilitarian function and to reinforce the breed's moderate, balanced outline, consistent with proper breed type as defined in the standard.

"Conformation, field, and performance English Springers are customarily and routinely docked in the United States. However, English Springers imported to this country from abroad are not. English Springers with natural, undocked tails may be shown according to AKC rules. While an undocked (natural) tail may not be customary in the U.S., it is acceptable."

NOTE: The US Breed Standard describes the English Springer Spaniel as a docked tail breed.

Glossary:

Dewclaw – the extra nail on the upper, inner part of a dog's foot – usually on the front legs

Croup – where the back meets the tail

Hock – joint on a dog's back leg below the stifle (knee); like the ankle joint of a human

Haw - the third eyelid or "nictitating membrane"

Occiput - bony bump seen at the top rear of the skull on some breeds

Pastern – the area below the wrist (front legs) or hock (back legs) but above the foot

Roach – when the back is slightly humped rather than flat

Stop - area between a dog's eyes, below the skull

Withers - the ridge between the shoulder blades

Basic Differences Between the US and UK

By Francie Nelson

Most of us intend our English Springers to be household pets or hunting companions - or both. The breed is well-suited for these purposes on both sides of the Atlantic. When we become the owner of an English Springer, it's fun to learn more about the breed and appreciate its unique features.

English Springers originated, of course, in England. As the old adage says: *"Form follows function."*

The breed's general appearance as a smart, medium sized, bi-or-tri-colored, dog of good substance with a lovely, well chiseled head and intelligent, soft expressive eyes, comes down to us from the early breeders who needed a strong, active, intelligent, and biddable dog to find, flush, and fetch game for the table.

As the breed developed further in England, a written Breed Standard was developed, against which dogs could be evaluated as breeding stock, and/or as competitors in the show ring. The UK Breed Standard came into being early in the twentieth century. Once the US and Canada began importing English Springers, breeders soon followed suit and developed written Standards.

A century later, it is interesting to consider the similarities and differences in the English Springers in the UK and in the US. The English Breed Standard describes the breed without much detail from which the reader can create a visual image.

In contrast, the US Standard is quite specific, and from it we can discern and identify type. *"Type"* is best defined as those traits that make a breed unique and distinct from other breeds.

Pictured left to right: English show Springer, American show Springer, English working Springer.

There are five key elements of the English Springer Spaniel breed type:

- General appearance
- Head and expression
- Color/markings
- Movement
- Behavior

General Appearance and Markings

There was a time, during the early days of importing Springers from the UK to the US when the differences in general appearance were not as marked as they are today.

UK breeders have kept the wide variations in markings, including heavy ticking and spotting, while the US has created a fancier dog with a heavier coat and an absence of ticking and spotting. The difference in markings is probably the most striking.

In recent years, importation from the UK and Scandinavia, and even from Eastern Europe, has brought a bit of colorful variation back to the US.

Other differences in general appearance include size (height). US-bred Springers tend to be of more uniform size, with females about an inch less in height at the withers and about 10 pounds lighter in weight. According to the UK Breed Standard, females are to be the same height as males, so females in particular appear larger in the UK than in the US.

The US Standard still describes the English Springer as a docked-tail breed. Tail docking was banned in England and Wales back in 2007, although Spaniels may still have a docked tail if they are actively working.

Head Type

The correct English Springer head, eye shape, and expression combine to present the most beautiful and unique feature of our breed.

In fact, the US Breed Standard describes English Springer head and expression as the breed's hallmark. The most profound differences between US and UK can be found here.

Though there are many heads of correct proportion in the US, many heads are pleasant but plain, lacking the depth and chiseling that complete a proper Springer. *"Chiseling"* describes what some call *"workmanship."*

Photo of a correct English Springer head and expression: English-bred Calvdale Felon, owned by the author.

The head actually appears to have been modeled with a sculptor's tools; distinct and beautiful bony indentations and protrusions emphasize the brows, cheeks, and skull. Eye shape, placement, and color are also very important.

In both nations, eye shape, size, and color vary. The US excels in eye color; the UK excels in eye shape. UK English Springers are more likely to have correct depth of muzzle when compared to their US counterparts.

Movement

The English Breed Standard contains an important guide to English Springer movement - a phrase that was unfortunately removed from the US Standard decades ago: *"Movement strictly his own."*

This means that proper English Springer movement, like a proper Springer head and expression, can be considered somewhat unique among the sporting (gundog) breeds. It takes a long time to understand and appreciate the unique qualities of movement.

First, all the parts and pieces of a Springer are in proper balance and alignment. Second, there is a freedom and ease because all parts are in balance.

Finally, balance, freedom, and ease create a strong and lasting impression that a proper Springer, trotting with a level back, almost "floats;" showing the slightest hesitation as each of its four feet fall.

This movement is less seen among US English Springers; again, the US breed standard no longer calls for it. It is more frequently seen among UK and other European Springers.

Behavior

Having spent more than half a century in the company of English Springers on both sides of the Atlantic, I am happy to say that the breed's characteristics of behavior and temperament are much the same.

Just as we desire to see a physically moderate and balanced dog, we also strive toward mental moderation and balance, no matter where we may be in the world. Interestingly, we expect a great deal from our Springers, and we always have.

We expect them to be companionable, biddable pets at home, then we expect them to be bold, aggressive seekers of game in the hunting field. Sometimes, certain English Springer behavior characteristics can err toward one end of the spectrum or the other.

Photo: English Springer Spaniel James (Felicity's Diamond Jim) winning Best in Show at the 131st Westminster Kennel Club Dog Show in New York.

The breed's singular behavior characteristic is intelligence. Another characteristic is cheerful, yet deliberate willfulness. Anyone seeking the companionship of an English Springer should be prepared to invest time, attention, and energy into bringing out and rewarding innate intelligence while setting proper boundaries for the breed's more willful tendencies.

This is a happy, friendly, essentially kind and tolerant breed, but its abundant enthusiasm and willful eagerness require training and good, consistent dog management.

About the Author: Francie Nelson, of Minneapolis, Minnesota, USA, got her first English Springer Spaniel in 1969. She went on to breed Springers under two prefixes, CHUZZLEWIT and FANFARE, producing multiple champions, obedience winners, hunting companions, top producers, and the breed's first Obedience Trial Champion.

From the 1980s, Francie held numerous positions, including President, of ESSFTA, the US national (parent) club. She served as a member of the Breed Standard Revision Committee in 1994 and wrote the commentary for the breed's first illustrated Standard. She is one of three founder members of the English Springer Foundation, a charity that raises and grants funds for health and genetic research and breed education.

Francie was approved by the American Kennel Club to judge English Springers In 1991 and has judged most major specialty (championship) shows in the US. She is the first US citizen to judge the breed and award CCs in England.

She still has one English Springer at home, the English import Calvdale Absconder, "Arthur."

4. Finding Your Puppy

Finding a good puppy can be a minefield. If you haven't got yours yet, read this chapter before you commit to anything; it will increase your chances of finding a healthy, happy puppy with a good temperament.

The best way to select a puppy is with your HEAD - not your heart! You'll soon find dozens of English Springer Spaniel puppies advertised, but it requires a bit more time and research to find a first-rate breeder. If you already have your puppy, skip to the next chapter.

With their beautiful eyes, floppy ears, constantly wagging tail and high spirits, there are few more appealing things on this Earth than English Springer Spaniel puppies. If you go to view a litter, the pups are sure to melt your heart and it is extremely difficult — if not downright impossible - to walk away without choosing one.

If you haven't yet chosen your pup and take only one sentence from this entire book, it is this:

FIND AN ETHICAL, KNOWLEDGEABLE BREEDER WHO PRODUCES HEALTHY PUPPIES WITH GOOD TEMPERAMENTS

— even if that means waiting longer than you'd like. It will be worth it in the long run.

Tip: Although the English Springer Spaniel is regarded as a healthy breed, there are still genetic disorders that can be passed down. So, look for a puppy whose parents have been screened for the hereditary diseases for which there is a test. See Chapter 12. Springer Health for details.

Find a breeder who knows English Springer Spaniels inside out and who does not offer lots of different breeds.

After all, apart from getting married or having a baby, getting a puppy is one of the most important, demanding, expensive and life-enriching decisions you will ever make. Spaniels will love you unconditionally - but there is a price to pay. In return for their devotion - you have to fulfil your part of the bargain.

In the beginning, you have to be prepared to devote much of your day to your new puppy. You have to feed her several times a day and housetrain virtually every hour, you have to give her your attention and start to gently introduce the rules of the house. You also have to be prepared to part with hard cash for regular healthcare and pet insurance.

Springer Puppies are high energy and hard work! If you are unable to devote the time and money to a new arrival, if you have a very young family, a stressful life or are out at work all day, then now might not be the right time for a puppy.

English Springer Spaniel puppies demand your attention and thrive on being involved — they are not couch potatoes. If left alone too long, behaviour issues can result. This is a natural reaction and is not the dog's fault; they are simply responding to an environment that is failing to meet their needs.

Pick a healthy pup and they should live for well over a decade if you're lucky - so this is certainly a long-term commitment. Before taking the plunge, ask yourself some questions:

Do I Have Enough Time for a Puppy?

Even a strong-willed puppy will feel a bit lonely at being on their own after leaving mother and littermates for the first time. Spend time with your new arrival to make them feel safe and sound. Ideally, for the first few days you will be around most of the time to help yours settle and to start bonding.

If you work, book time off if you can - although this is more difficult for some of our hardworking American readers who get short vacations - but don't just get a puppy and leave them all alone in the house a couple of days later. Start by leaving them a few minutes a day and gradually build up the time so they don't over-bond with you and develop Separation Anxiety.

Housetraining (potty training) starts the moment your pup arrives home. Then, after the first few days and once he or she's feeling more settled, make time for short sessions of a few minutes of behaviour training. English Springer Spaniel puppies are very lively, curious, playful and greedy with a strong sense of smell, and these traits can lead to mischief if not channelled.

You'll also have to find time to slowly start the socialisation process by taking your puppy out of the home to experience new places, strangers, other animals, loud noises, busy roads, etc. - but make sure you CARRY them until the vaccinations have taken effect.

FACT The importance of socialisation cannot be over-emphasised. Start as soon as possible, as that critical window up to four months of age is when your puppy is at their most receptive to all things new.

Under-socialised dogs bark at the slightest thing and become too noisy; some become too protective of their food, toys or humans. The more positive experiences a Springer is introduced to, the better. Get into the habit of taking your pup for a short walk every day - five minutes once fully vaccinated, increasing gradually to around 10 minutes at four months.

While the garden or yard is fine, new surroundings stimulate interest and help to stop puppies becoming bored.

Gently introducing her to different people will help her to become more relaxed around people. Initially, get people to sit on the floor at her level.

Make time right from the beginning to get your pup used to being handled by all the family and dog-friendly visitors, gently brushed, ears checked, and later having their teeth touched and cleaned.

Tip We recommend you have your pup checked out by a vet within a couple of days of arriving home — many good breeders insist on it - but don't put your puppy on the clinic floor where she can pick up germs from other dogs.

Factor in time to visit the vet's surgery for annual check-ups as well as vaccinations, although most now last several years — check with your vet.

How Long Can I Leave My Puppy?

This is a question we get asked a lot and one that causes much debate among new owners. All dogs are pack animals; their natural state is to be with others. So being alone for long periods is not normal for them - although many have to get used to it.

Another issue is the toilet; English Springer Spaniel puppies have really tiny bladders. Forget the emotional side of it, how would you like to be left for eight hours without being able to visit the bathroom? So how many hours can you leave a dog alone?

FACT > In the UK, canine rescue organisations will not allow anybody to adopt if they are intending to regularly leave the dog alone for more than four or five hours a day.

The English Springer Spaniel was originally bred as a working dog to run all day, and leaving one alone for too long can trigger unwanted behaviour. A bored or lonely Spaniel may display signs of unhappiness such as nuisance barking, peeing/pooping indoors, chewing, resource guarding, getting into things they shouldn't, stubbornness, aggression, disobedience, or just plain switching off.

Tip In terms of housetraining, a general rule of thumb is that a puppy can last without urinating for one hour or so for every month of age, sometimes longer.

So, provided your puppy has learned the basics, a three-month-old puppy should be able to last for around three hours without needing to go. Of course, until housetraining kicks in, young puppies just pee at will!

Family and Children

English Springer Spaniels really do make excellent family pets, with one big proviso: You have to be able and willing to devote enough time to meet your Springer's needs in terms of attention, training, grooming and - once they are fully grown - plenty of exercise.

Spaniel puppies may not be suitable for every family with very young children. Toddlers and young kids are uncoordinated and there can be a risk of injury if not well supervised. Springers can and do form very strong and loving bonds with children - once both have learned respect for each other.

Tip Children (and adults) should be taught how to correctly handle puppies so as not to injure their delicate frames. Encourage youngsters to interact with the dog on the floor, rather than constantly picking them up to cuddle.

Puppies regard children as playmates - just like a child regards a puppy as a playmate. Both are playful and excitable, so it's important to teach them both the boundaries of play. A Springer puppy wouldn't intentionally harm a child, or vice versa, but either could cause injury if they get over-excited.

Your children will naturally be delighted with your new arrival, but kids and puppy should not be left unsupervised until each has learned to respect the other - no matter how well they get along in the beginning.

✓ **Teach your children to be gentle with your dog and your dog to be gentle with your children.**

Lively behaviour and nipping are not aggression; it is normal play for puppies. Put the time in to teach your pup what is acceptable and what is not – and any nipping should be dealt with straight away. See **Training chapters 9 and 10** for more detailed information.

Your dog's early experiences with children should all be positive. If not, a dog may become nervous or mistrustful - and what you want around children is most definitely a relaxed dog that does not feel threatened by a child's presence.

Take things steady in the beginning and your Springer Spaniel will undoubtedly form a deep, lifelong bond your children will remember throughout their lives.

Breeder Chris Brandon-Lodge, of Cottonstones English Springer Spaniels, who has 40 years' experience of the breed, says:

"Springers usually get on well with children and I would certainly sell a puppy to a family with children, but I would use my judgement on that family as to whether I sold them a puppy at all."

Lisa Cardy, of CallisWold English Springer Spaniels, added: "English Springer Spaniels and children go together like cheese and pickle; they were made for each other.

"As long as the nipping stage is managed well by families, the children will not become frightened of pup's teeth. One thing that they should not do is scream and run away, as pup then thinks that this is a good game.

"I do not believe that children under six years old can deal with this situation, so will not home my pups with children so young. Springers are generally very good with children, and gentle. But, like all dogs, they should never be left on their own with small children."

Lynne Lucas, of Traxlerstarr Spaniels: "English Springer Spaniels are the most fantastic dogs for an active family. They are devoted to their owners and have a special bond with children; you wouldn't find a better family dog."

Single People

Many singles own dogs, but if you live alone, getting a puppy will require a lot of dedication on your part. There is nobody to share the responsibility, so taking on an active, people-loving dog like the English Springer Spaniel requires a commitment and a lot of your time if the dog is to have a decent life.

If you are out of the house all day, a Springer is NOT a good choice. They thrive on being involved and get bored quite easily, which can lead to mischief - typical of dogs originally bred to do a job.

Being alone all day is not much of a life for a dog as loving and active as the Springer. However, if you can afford to devote a lot of time on a daily basis to your Springer, then he or she will undoubtedly become your best friend.

Older People

As a general rule, a Springer isn't a great choice for the elderly due to the breed's need for a lot of exercise and mental stimulation. A companion breed would be a better choice than a working breed for most - although there are always exceptions!

Other Pets

However friendly your puppy is, other pets in your household may not be too happy at a new arrival. Socialised Springer Spaniels usually get on well with other animals, but it might not be a good idea to leave your hamster or pet rabbit running loose! The English Springer Spaniel was bred to flush out game and some have strong prey instincts. The pup has first to learn to fit in alongside other pets and if introduced slowly, they will probably become best friends.

Photo: Millie, Maple Harvest of Cottonstones, with her close feline friend Black Sam

Owner Chris Brandon-Lodge says: "Millie was pure working Springer from a very good field trial line, she was five in the photo. She and Sam were devoted to each other, and when she was restless and unhappy before her first whelping, Sam went to lie close beside her in the bed and stayed there until she started. He was a particularly charming cat and I think he actually thought he was a dog! Both were great characters."

Chris added: "It certainly does make a big difference if a Springer is introduced to cats as a puppy. I haven't found Springers to be particularly interested in cats, but squirrels and rabbits will spark a lot of interest - and if the dog's not on the lead, they will probably start to go after them. They never have much chance of catching them!"

Spaniel puppies are naturally extremely curious and playful and will sniff and investigate other pets. They may even chase them in the beginning.

Depending on how lively your pup is, you may have to separate them initially, or put the pup into a pen or crate for short periods to allow the cat to investigate without being pestered by a hyperactive pup who thinks the cat is a great playmate.

This will also prevent your puppy from being injured. If the two animals are free and the cat lashes out, your pup's eyes could get scratched. A timid English Springer Spaniel might need protection from a bold cat - or vice versa. A bold cat and a timid Springer will probably settle down together quickest!

If things seem to be going well with no aggression, then let them loose together after one or two supervised sessions. Take the process slowly; if your cat is stressed or frightened, he may decide to leave. Our feline friends are notorious for abandoning home because the board and lodgings are better down the road...

More than One Dog

Well-socialised English Springer Spaniels have no problem sharing their home with other dogs. Introduce your puppy to other dogs and animals in a positive, non-frightening manner that will give her confidence. Supervised sessions help everyone to get along and for the other dog or dogs to accept your new pup.

If you can, introduce them for the first time outdoors on neutral ground, rather than in the house or in an area that one dog regards as her own. You don't want the established dog to feel they have to protect their territory, nor the puppy to feel she is in an enclosed space and can't get away.

If you are thinking about getting more than one pup, consider waiting until your first puppy is a few months old or an adult before getting a second. Waiting means you can give your full attention to one puppy; get housetraining, socialisation and the basics of obedience training out of the way before getting your second.

Another benefit is that an older well-trained dog will help teach the new puppy some manners.

Tip: Think carefully before getting two puppies from the same litter. Apart from the time and expense involved, you want your new Springer to learn to focus on YOU, and not her littermate.

Owning two dogs can be twice as nice; they will be great company for each other, but bear in mind that it's also double the training, food and vet's bills.

Plan Ahead

Choosing the right breeder is one of the most important decisions you will make. Like humans, your puppy will be a product of her parents and will inherit many of their characteristics. Appearance, size, natural temperament and how healthy your puppy is depends to a large extent on the genes of her parents.

Responsible breeders test their dogs; they check the health records and temperament of the parents and only breed from suitable stock.

Pictured relaxing at home are Stella, who is fully-health tested, and her daughter Esther, bred by Lynne Lucas.

The price of puppies of all breeds has shot up, so it's hard to say what a fair price is for a well-bred pedigree pup.

Factors such as colour, markings and region can also affect price, and you may have to pay more for an English Springer Spaniel with show prospects or ancestors with a proven track record in the field than for a pet Spaniel.

Since Covid, price is no longer a reliable indication of the quality of the pup, but beware of *"bargain"* puppies, these are not top-quality pups. Instead, spend the time to find a reputable breeder and read **Chapter 12. Springer Health** to discover what health certificates to look for before buying.

> **BE PATIENT.** Start looking months or even a year before your planned arrival. Good English Springer Spaniel breeders with health-screened breeding dogs often have a waiting list for their pups, so get your name on a list in good time.

Phone or email your selected breeder or breeders to find out about future litters and potential dates, but don't commit until you've asked lots of questions. A healthy Springer will be your irreplaceable companion for over a decade so why buy one from a general ad?

Would you buy an old car or a house with potential structural problems just because it looked pretty in a website photo or was cheap? The answer is probably no, because you know you'd have stress and expense at some point in the future.

Visit the breeder personally at least once before picking the puppy up – this should be an absolute must in the UK.

NOTE: Some American breeders do not allow the public on to their properties when they have unvaccinated pups. Also, when vast distances are involved, personal visits are not always possible. In these cases speak at length on the phone to the breeder, video call, ask lots of questions and ask to see photos and videos of the pups. Reputable breeders will be happy to answer all your questions - and will have lots for you too.

English Springer Spaniels should be eight weeks old before they leave the breeder. Puppies need this time to physically develop and learn the rules of the pack from their mothers and littermates. In the UK and some US states it is illegal to sell a puppy younger than eight weeks.

Buyer Beware

Good breeders do not sell their dogs on general purpose websites, Gumtree, Craig's List or Freeads, in car parks or somebody else's house. In 2020, the UK Government passed **Lucy's Law** saying:

"**'Lucy's Law'** means that anyone wanting to get a new puppy or kitten in England, Scotland or Wales must now buy direct from a breeder, or consider adopting from a rescue centre instead. Licensed dog breeders are required to show puppies interacting with their mothers in their place of birth. If a business sells puppies or kittens without a licence, they could receive an unlimited fine or be sent to prison for up to six months. The law is named after Lucy, a Cavalier King Charles Spaniel who was rescued from a puppy farm."

There is no such law in the US. And if you are looking at dogs on Pets4Homes in the UK, follow their guidelines carefully, see the pup with the mother and check what health screening has been carried out.

There is a difference between **a hobby breeder** and a **backyard or backstreet breeder**. Both may breed just one or two litters a year and keep the puppies in their homes, but that's where the similarity ends.

In the UK there are many good **hobby breeders.** They often don't have a website and you will probably find out about them via word of mouth.

Good hobby breeders are usually breed enthusiasts or experts; sometimes they show their pedigree dogs. They carry out health tests and lavish care and love on their dogs. They are not professional dog breeders. **NOTE:** While it is often a good sign in the UK, the term *"hobby breeder"* can have negative implications in the USA.

Backyard breeders are often breeding family pets. They have less knowledge about the breed, pay little attention to the health and welfare of their dogs and are doing it primarily for extra cash. They may be very nice people, but avoid buying a dog from them.

FACT All GOOD breeders, professional or hobby, have in-depth knowledge of the English Springer Spaniel. They take measures to prevent potential health issues being passed on to puppies, and are passionate about the breed.

Here are four reasons for buying from a good breeder:

1. **HEALTH:** Like all breeds, English Springer Spaniels have potentially inheritable health issues. Screening breeding stock and NOT mating two dogs whose health screening results mean that, if mated together, there would be a significant risk of producing puppies with certain known inherited disorders.

2. **SOCIALISATION:** Scientists and dog experts now realise that the critical socialisation period for dogs is up to the age of four months. An unstimulated puppy is likely to be less well-adjusted and more likely to have fear or behaviour issues as an adult.

   Good breeders start this process, they don't just leave the puppies in an outbuilding for two or three months. Socialisation is important for all dogs.

3. **TEMPERAMENT:** Good breeders select their breeding stock based not only on sound structure and health, but also on temperament. They will not breed from an aggressive or overly timid dog.

4. **PEACE OF MIND:** Most good breeders agree to take the dog back at any time in her life or rehome her if things don't work out - although you may find it too hard to part with your beloved English Springer Spaniel by then.

Spotting Bad Breeders

Getting a puppy is such an emotional decision - and one that should have a wonderfully positive impact on you and your family's life for a decade or longer. Unfortunately, the high price of puppies has resulted in unscrupulous people producing litters for the money.

This section helps you avoid the pitfalls of getting a puppy from a puppy mill/farm, a puppy importer, dealer or broker (somebody who makes money from buying and selling puppies) or a backyard breeder.

You can't buy a Rolls Royce or a Corvette for a couple of thousand pounds or dollars - you'd immediately suspect that the *"bargain"* on offer wasn't the real deal. No matter how lovely it looked, you'd be right — well, the same applies to English Springer Spaniels.

Become Breeder Savvy

- Websites have become far more sophisticated and it's getting harder to spot the good, ethical breeders from those who are driven by the cash. Avoid websites where there are no pictures of the owners' home or kennels or the dogs in the home
- If the website shows lots of photos of cute puppies with little information about the family, breeding dogs, health tests and environment, click the **X** button
- Don't buy a website puppy with a shopping cart symbol next to them
- See the puppies with their mother face-to-face. If this is not possible due to distances, speak at length on the phone with the breeder and ask lots of questions
- You hear: "You can't see the parent dogs because......" ALWAYS ask to see the parents and, as a minimum, see the mother and how she looks and behaves with the pups. If the pups are really hers, she will interact with them
- Good breeders are happy to provide lots of information and at least one reference before you commit
- If the breeder is reluctant to answer your questions, look elsewhere
- Pressure selling: on the phone, the breeder doesn't ask you many questions and then says: "There are only X many puppies left and I have several other buyers interested." Walk away
- You hear "Our Springer puppies are cheaper because...." Walk away
- At the breeder's, ask to see where the puppy is living. If the breeding dogs are not housed in the family home, they should be in clean kennels, not too hot or cold, with access to grass and time spent with humans
- Ask to see the other puppies from the litter

Photo: Mother and pup in a loving home.

- Be wary if the mother is not with the puppies, but brought in to meet you
- Or if the puppies look small for their stated age
- If the breeder says that the dam and sire are Kennel Club or AKC registered, ask to see the registration papers
- Photographs of so-called "champion ancestors" do not guarantee the health of the puppy

> **Tip:** Look beyond the cute, fluffy exterior. The way to look INSIDE the puppy is to see the parents – or at least the mother with the pups – and check what health screening has been carried out. *"Vet checked"* does NOT mean the pup or parents have passed any health tests

- The person you are buying the puppy from did not breed the dog themselves. Deal with the breeder, not an intermediary
- The only place you meet the puppy seller is a car park, somebody else's house or place other than the puppies' home
- The seller tells you that the puppy comes from top, caring breeders from your own or another country. It is now illegal in the UK to buy a puppy from a third party. i.e. anyone other than the breeder
- Ask to see photos of the puppy from birth to present day
- Be wary of "rare colours" or "rare markings" as it probably means that the puppy you are looking at is not pure Springer
- Price – if you are offered a very cheap puppy, there is usually a reason
- Familiarise yourself with the Breed Standard and what an 8-week-old Springer should look like. Make sure the puppy you are interested in looks and acts like a Springer
- If you get a rescue English Springer Spaniel, make sure it is from a recognised rescue group and not a "puppy flipper" who may be posing as a do-gooder, but is in fact getting dogs (including stolen ones) from unscrupulous sources
- NEVER buy a puppy because you feel sorry for it; you are condemning other dogs to a life of misery
- If you have any doubt, go with your gut instinct and WALK AWAY - even if this means losing your deposit. It will be worth it in the long run

> **Tip:** Bad breeders do not have two horns coming out of their heads! Most will be friendly when you phone or visit - after all, they want to make the sale. It's only later that problems develop.

Puppy Farms and Mills

Unscrupulous breeders are everywhere. That's not to say there aren't some excellent English Springer Spaniel breeders out there; there certainly are. You just have to do your research.

While new owners might think they have bagged a cheap or a quick puppy, it often turns out to be false economy and emotionally disastrous when the puppy develops health problems or behavioural problems due to poor temperament or lack of socialisation.

The UK's Kennel Club says as many as one in four puppies bought in the UK may come from puppy farms - and the situation is no better in North America.

The KC Press release states: "As the popularity of online pups continues to soar:

THE ENGLISH SPRINGER SPANIEL HANDBOOK Page 41

- Almost one in five pups bought (unseen) on websites or social media die within six months
- One in three buys online, in pet stores and via newspaper adverts - outlets often used by puppy farmers – this is an increase from one in five in the previous year
- The problem is likely to grow as the younger generation favour mail order pups, and breeders of fashionable breeds flout responsible steps

"We are sleepwalking into a dog welfare and consumer crisis as new research shows that more and more people are buying their pups online or through pet shops, outlets often used by cruel puppy farmers, and are paying the price with their pups requiring long-term veterinary treatment or dying before six months old." The KC research found that:

- One third of people who bought their puppy online, over social media or in pet shops failed to experience "overall good health"
- Some 12% of puppies bought online or on social media end up with serious health problems that require expensive on-going veterinary treatment from a young age

The Kennel Club said: "Whilst there is nothing wrong with initially finding a puppy online, it is essential to then see the breeder and ensure that they are doing all of the right things. This research clearly shows that too many people are failing to do this, and the consequences can be seen in the shocking number of puppies that are becoming sick or dying."

Marc Abraham, TV vet and founder of Pup Aid, added: "Sadly, if the *"buy it now"* culture persists, then this horrific situation will only get worse. There is nothing wrong with sourcing a puppy online, but people need to be aware of what they should then expect from the breeder.

"For example, you should not buy a car without getting its service history and seeing it at its registered address, so you certainly shouldn't buy a puppy without the correct paperwork and health certificates and without seeing where it was bred."

"However, too many people are opting to buy directly from third parties, such as the internet, pet shops, or from puppy dealers, where you cannot possibly know how or where the puppy was raised. Not only are people buying sickly puppies, but many people are being scammed into paying money for puppies that don't exist, as the research showed that 7% of those who buy online were scammed in this way."

As a canine author, I hear these stories all the time. In fact a good friend of mine was scammed out of a £350 ($460) deposit on a puppy earlier this year.

Visit the UK Kennel Club's **Buying a Dog** section for tips before you buy a puppy. www.thekennelclub.org.uk

....

Where to Find a Good Breeder

1. The Kennel Club in your country. Look for Assured Breeders in the UK at www.thekennelclub.org.uk/search/find-an-assured-breeder and an AKC Breeder of Merit or a Bred with H.E.A.R.T. breeder in the US: https://marketplace.akc.org/puppies/english-springer-spaniel
2. Breed clubs. In the UK there is a list of regional clubs on the ESSC website at: www.englishspringer.org/english-springer-spaniel-uk-breed-clubs/
3. In the USA, visit the ESSFTA website at https://essfta.org for a list of regional clubs.

4. Visit dog shows, shoots or canine events where English Springer Spaniels are participating and talk to participants and breeders.
5. Get a recommendation from somebody who has an English Springer Spaniel that you like - but make sure the breeder health screens her dogs.
6. Ask your vet for details of local, ethical English Springer Spaniel breeders.
7. Search the internet - there are hundreds of breeders out there; use the advice in this chapter to find the right one.
8. If you are in the UK, visit the English Springer Spaniel stand at Discover Dogs during the annual Crufts dog show in early March or Discover Dogs at Excel in London, normally held during November. Visit the Events and Activities section on the Kennel Club website.

Questions to Ask a Breeder

Here's a list of the questions you should be asking:

1. **Can I see the litter with the parents** - or at least the mother? It's important to see the pup in his or her normal surroundings, not brought out of a building and shown to you.
2. **Have the parents been health screened?** Ask to see certificates and what guarantees the breeder is offering in terms of genetic illnesses.
3. **What veterinary care have the pups had so far?** Puppies should have had their first wormings by eight weeks old and possibly their first vaccinations.
4. **Are you an Assured Breeder (UK), Breeder of Merit or Bred With Heart breeder (US) or a member of an English Springer Spaniel breed club?** Not all good English Springer Spaniel breeders are members, but this is a good place to start.
5. **How long have you been breeding Springers?** You are looking for someone with a good track record with the breed.
6. **Can you put me in touch with someone who already has one of your puppies?** ALWAYS contact at least one owner.
7. **How many litters has the mother had?** Females should be 18 months or two years old before their first litter. The UK Kennel Club will not register puppies from a dam that's had more than four litters or is over the age of eight.
8. **What happens to the mother once she has finished breeding?** Are they kept as part of the family, rehomed in loving homes, sent to animal shelters or auctioned off? Do you see any old Spaniels at the breeder's home?
9. **Do you breed any other types of dog?** Buy from a specialist, preferably one who does not have lots of other breeds.
10. **What is so special about this litter?** You are looking for a breeder who has used good breeding stock and his or her knowledge to produce handsome, healthy dogs with good temperaments.

11. **What is the average lifespan of your dogs?** Generally, pups bred from healthy stock tend to live longer.
12. **How socialised and housetrained is the puppy?** Good breeders usually start the socialisation and housetraining process before they leave.
13. **How would you describe the temperament of the parents?** Temperament is extremely important; try to interact with both parents, or at least the mother.
14. **What do you feed your adults and puppies?** A reputable breeder will feed top quality food and advise you to do the same.
15. **Do you provide a written Sale or Puppy Contract?**
16. **Why aren't you asking me any questions?** A good breeder is committed to making a good match between the new owners and their puppies. If (s)he doesn't, then walk away.

Choosing a Healthy English Springer Spaniel

Once you've selected your breeder and a litter is available, you then have to decide WHICH puppy to pick, unless the breeder has already earmarked one for you after asking lots of questions. Here are some pointers on puppy health:

1. Your chosen Springer puppy should have **a well-fed appearance.** She should not, however, have a distended abdomen (pot belly) as this can be a sign of worms or other illnesses. The ideal puppy should not be too thin either - you should be able to feel, but not see, her ribs.
2. **The pup's eyes should be bright and clear** with no discharge or tear stain. Steer clear of a puppy that blinks a lot. (Bordetella and Kennel Cough vaccines can sometimes cause runny eyes and nose for up to 10 days – ask when the litter was vaccinated for these).
3. **Her nose should be cool, damp and clean** with no discharge.
4. **The pup's ears should be clean** with no sign of discharge, soreness or redness and no unpleasant smell.
5. **Check the puppy's rear end** to make sure it is clean and there are no signs of diarrhoea.
6. **The pup's coat should look clean,** feel soft, not matted - and puppies should smell good! The coat should have no signs of ticks or fleas. Red or irritated skin or bald spots could be a sign of infestation or a skin condition. Also, check between the toes of the paws for signs of redness or swelling.
7. **Springers are friendly and alert dogs and puppies should be the same.** They should be relaxed, curious about you and their surroundings, not timid. Be wary if the breeder makes excuses for the puppies' behaviour.
8. **Gums should be clean and pink.**

9. **Choose a puppy that moves freely** without any sign of injury or lameness. It should be a fluid movement, not jerky or stiff, and the pup should have a straight back, not arched.
10. When the puppy is distracted, clap or make a noise behind her - not so loud as to frighten her - to **make sure she is not deaf.**
11. Finally, **ask to see veterinary records** to confirm your puppy has been wormed, possibly her first vaccinations and a vet check.

If you get the puppy home and things don't work out for whatever reason, good breeders will either take the puppy back or find them a suitable home.

Tip: Take your puppy to a vet to have a thorough check-up within 48 hours of purchase. If your vet is not happy with the pup's condition, return her - no matter how painful it may be. Keeping an unhealthy puppy will only lead to further distress and expense.

Puppy Contracts

Most good breeders provide their puppy parents with an official Puppy Contract, also called a Sale Contract. This protects both buyer and seller by providing information on the puppy until he or she leaves the breeder. A Puppy Contract will answer such questions as whether the puppy:

- Is covered by breeder's insurance and can be returned if there is a health issue within a certain time period
- Has been micro-chipped (compulsory in the UK) and/or vaccinated and details of worming treatments
- Has been partially or wholly toilet-trained
- Has been socialised and where he or she was kept
- What health conditions the pup and parents have been screened for
- What the puppy is currently being fed and if any food is being supplied
- Was born by Caesarean section
- And details of the dam and sire

It's not easy for caring breeders to part with their puppies after they have lovingly bred and raised them, and so many supply extensive care notes for new owners, which may include details of:

- The puppy's daily routine
- Feeding schedule
- Vet and vaccination schedule
- General puppy care
- Toilet training
- Socialisation

The Royal Society for the Prevention of Cruelty to Animals (RSPCA) has a free downloadable puppy contract, *pictured,* endorsed by vets and animal welfare organisations; you should be looking for something similar from a breeder. Visit https://puppycontract.org.uk/about-us or type *"AKC Preparing a Puppy Contract"* if you're in the US.

THE ENGLISH SPRINGER SPANIEL HANDBOOK Page **45**

Advice from Breeders

Lynne Lucas: "The pups should be with mum. If mum is not available or any excuses are given as to where she is, do NOT proceed. And if dad is in the house, then he should be available to see. There should be good interaction between mum and pups.

"Any other family members as well as mum and dad should have good temperaments and be keen to meet strangers. A breeder should always be keen to 'show off' their dogs and be proud of them.

"The pups' area should be clean, as should the pups, without any smell of urine or faeces. They should be housed in an appropriate area free from hazards and preferably within the house. If they are in an outside area, it should be heated, and the pups should be keen to meet strangers and not withdrawn.

Photo of Myrtle's boys courtesy of Lynne.

"I always advise new families to come with an open mind, sit down and see which pups choose them; they should be lively and eager to play. There should not be a timeframe on the decision; it can take a while. I allow as much time as needed - sometimes this has run to a few hours.

"A well-bred puppy should be full of play, inquisitive, bright-eyed, clean and keen to meet new people. It is not a worry if they are sleepy if everything else seems to be in order as the pups could just be tired, especially if you are viewing after they have eaten.

"They should play well together, play fighting is also acceptable as they are sorting the hierarchy within the litter. You nearly always get some that are slightly quieter than the rest, but as I always say a quiet pup at four weeks could be a devil at eight, and vice versa.

"A good breeder will want extensive information from you. I ask for work details, address, contact number and family details before I even get into a conversation. If they are not prepared to offer their address so that I can make a few checks, then the enquiry does not go further. If the breeder is not interested in any information from a prospective buyer, it is a bad sign.

"The breeder should be keen to offer as much advice as is requested, answer all questions and have all health certificates to hand for prospective families to view. They should also offer a lifetime of support for the new family as it can be a daunting experience for them. I believe that the parents should be fully health tested to ensure that the breed line continues with pups of the highest quality.

"Do not let your heart rule your head. If you have any doubts, **walk away**. You could be taking on a lifetime of trouble."

Lisa Cardy: "The breeder should be open and knowledgeable about the breed. You should be shown where the pups are sleeping, playing, feeding, etc. and all the paperwork for mum and pups should be available if they are KC registered. You should see mum interacting with puppies and be allowed to hold the puppies.

"Having puppies separated from mum is a bad sign, as is the breeder not having a basic knowledge of the breed or being unsure of the pups' date of birth. Having multiple litters for sale is also a very bad sign, particularly of different breeds.

"Small breeds having large litters is another. For instance, Cavaliers don't have nine puppies - as I have seen advertised!"

Photo: Lilly with a six-week-old puppy, courtesy of Lisa.

"A Springer pup should be bold, confident, playful. Eyes should be bright and coat shiny. They should be happy to come up to you and be happy to be picked up.

"I've heard of LOTS of unscrupulous breeders! There are many signs to look out for and many scams. A lot of litters are imported into this country, put to a lactating bitch and sold as being the pups of that bitch when they aren't.

"Also, people sometimes put two litters together with one mum and sell them as her puppies - usually as the other mother is in a different country. A bitch will feed any pups, not just her own."

Chris Brandon-Lodge: "It's always better to find the breeder first before you are ready to actually get a puppy. Any decent breeder will be happy to let you come and see their animals before a litter is due.

"When you visit a litter it's a good idea to go when they are quite young, as soon as the breeder will allow, so you can see where they have been born and where they are kept. If this isn't possible, go at around six weeks to choose a puppy before collection at eight weeks.

"You should expect the litter to be in warm, clean conditions, either in the breeder's house or, in the case of a commercial breeder, in a suitable whelping room. The bitch should look fit and well, bright-eyed and happy.

"If you are seeing the puppies at six weeks or more, they should be pretty much weaned and the bitch should be around, but not necessarily with them. By eight weeks she should have plenty of condition and though she will still have some milk, her teats should be drying up.

"A good breeder will show you any paperwork you ask to see. Particularly ask about health tests and worming.

"The state of the breeder's home will tell you a lot. Filthy conditions mean poor management. If the puppies are looking thin and undernourished or their coats are dull and staring (hair standing on end or bad condition), it's a bad sign. If the bitch is not available to be seen, beware. ALWAYS see the mother.

"On the other hand, if both dog and bitch are around that is not necessarily a good sign. Obviously, if it is a breeder producing a lot of litters, they may well have their own stud dog. In that case, it is always a good idea to check the pedigree in case of inbreeding.

"If the person selling the puppies is evasive when asked questions or will not show you relevant paperwork, be wary – or if the breeder tries to hassle you into making instant decisions. And any sign of vermin, leave quickly."

Photo: The beautiful Poppy (Cottonstones Ruby) bred by Chris.

"A litter of healthy Springers will be bouncing around and eager to see you, vying for your attention. They will want to play, bite your shoes, pull on your trouser legs and beg to be picked up and cuddled.

"They should be plump with fat tummies and clean coats, glossy on the coloured patches. Look out for any that don't come forward because they may have a problem.

"I have heard of too many stories of unscrupulous breeders. The dog world is a minefield for the unwary, made much worse by the internet.

"There are a lot of people out there bringing in dogs from abroad, particularly Eastern Europe, purporting to be breeders but merely passing them on. Many are in a poor state and often die of a variety of complaints within a few weeks.

"Check out the breeder before you go and be careful if answering adverts online. If the supposed breeder wants to meet you in a car park somewhere to hand over a puppy, forget it. In the world of dogs the words BUYER BEWARE were never more apt."

A good course of action would be something like this:

1. Decide to get an English Springer Spaniel.
2. Decide what type (working or field/show/dual purpose) would best suit you.
3. Do your research and find a good breeder whose dogs are health screened.
4. Decide on a male or female.
5. Register your interest - and WAIT until a puppy becomes available.
6. Pick one with a suitable temperament – a good breeder will help you choose a puppy to fit in with your family and lifestyle.
7. Enjoy a decade or longer with a beautiful, healthy English Springer Spaniel.

Some people pick a puppy based on how the dog looks. If coat colour or size, for example, are very important to you, make sure the other boxes are ticked as well.

5. Bringing Puppy Home

Getting a new puppy is so exciting; you can't wait to bring him home. Before that happens, you probably dream of all the things you are going to do together: going for long walks, playing games, travelling, snuggling down at home together, and maybe even taking part in activities, shoots or shows.

Your pup has, of course, no idea of your big plans, and the reality when he arrives can be a BIG shock! Puppies are wilful little critters with minds of their own and sharp teeth. They leak at both ends, chew anything in sight, constantly demand your attention, nip the kids or anything else to hand, cry and don't pay a blind bit of notice to your commands... There is a lot of work ahead before the two of you develop that unique bond!

Your pup has to learn what you require from him before he can start to meet some of your expectations - and you have to learn what your pup needs from you.

....

Once your English Springer Spaniel puppy lands in your home, your time won't be your own, but you can get off to a good start by preparing things before the big day. Here's a list of things to think about getting beforehand - your breeder may supply some of these:

Puppy Checklist

- ✓ A dog bed or basket
- ✓ Bedding – a Vetbed or Vetfleece is a good choice
- ✓ A piece of cloth (remove buttons, etc) that has been rubbed on the puppy's mother to put in the bed
- ✓ A puppy gate or pen
- ✓ A crate if you decide to use one
- ✓ A collar or puppy harness with ID tag and a lead (leash)
- ✓ Food and water bowls, preferably stainless steel
- ✓ Puppy food – find out what the breeder is feeding and stick with that to start with
- ✓ Puppy treats, healthy ones, carrot and apple pieces are good, no rawhide
- ✓ Newspapers or pellet litter and a bell if you decide to use them for housetraining
- ✓ Poo(p) bags
- ✓ Toys and chews suitable for puppies
- ✓ A puppy coat if you live in a cool climate or it's winter
- ✓ Old blanket for cleaning and drying and partially covering the crate

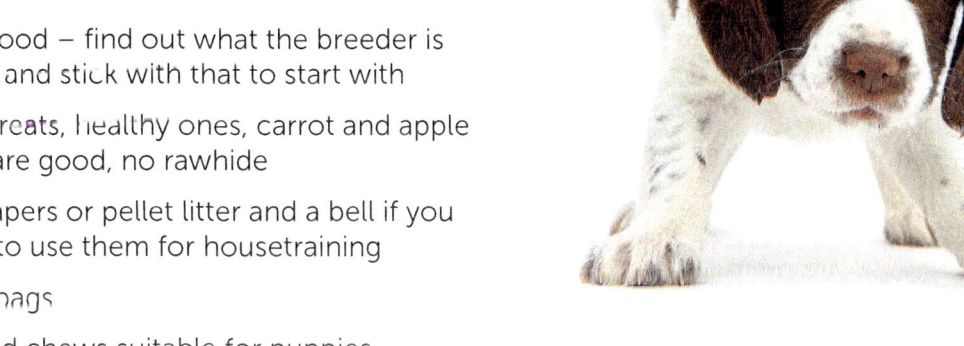

AND PLENTY OF TIME!

Later, you'll also need grooming brushes, flea and worming products and maybe a car grille or travel crate. Many good breeders provide Puppy Packs, which contain some or all of these items:

- ✓ Pedigree certificate
- ✓ Puppy contract
- ✓ Information pack with details of vet's visits, vaccinations and wormings, parents' health certificates, diet, breed clubs, etc.
- ✓ Puppy food
- ✓ ID tag/microchip info
- ✓ Blanket that smells of the mother and litter
- ✓ Soft toy that your puppy has grown up with, possibly a chew toy as well
- ✓ A month's free insurance

FACT By law, all UK puppies have to be microchipped and registered BEFORE they leave the breeder. New owners are legally bound to ensure their puppy's microchip registration is updated with their own details and also to register any change of address or ownership.

Puppy Proofing Your Home

Some adjustments will be needed to make your home safe and suitable. Springer puppies are small bundles of curiosity, instinct and energy when they are awake, with little common sense and even less self-control. They have bursts of energy before running out of steam and spending much of the rest of the day sleeping. As one breeder says: "They have two speeds – ON and OFF!"

They also have an incredible sense of smell and love to investigate with their noses and mouths. Fence off or remove all poisonous or low plants with sharp leaves or thorns, such as roses, that could cause eye injuries.

There are literally dozens of plants harmful to a puppy if ingested, including azalea, daffodil bulbs, lily, foxglove, hyacinth, hydrangea, lupin, rhododendron, sweet pea, tulip and yew.

The Kennel Club has a list of some of the most common ones, type *"Kennel Club poisons in your garden"* into Google. The ASPCA has an extensive list for the USA if you Google *"ASPCA poisonous plants."*

Make sure any fencing planks are extremely close together and that EVERY LITTLE GAP has been plugged; Springer puppies can get through almost anything and they have no road sense whatsoever. Don't leave your puppy unattended in the garden or yard in the beginning.

FACT Dognapping is on the increase. Over 2,000 dogs are now being stolen each year in the UK. The figures are much higher for the US, where the AKC reports increasing dog thefts and warns owners against leaving dogs unattended.

Puppies are little chew machines and puppy-proofing your home involves moving anything sharp, breakable or chewable - including your shoes.

Lift electrical cords, mobile phones and chargers, remote controls, etc. out of reach and block off any off-limits areas of the house with a child gate or barrier, especially as he may be shadowing you for the first few days.

Create an area where your puppy is allowed to go, perhaps one or two rooms, preferably with a hard floor that is easy to clean. Keep the rest of the house off-limits, at least until the pair of you have mastered potty training.

This area should be near the door to the garden or yard for toileting. Restricting the puppy's space also helps him to settle in. He probably had a den and small space at the breeder's home. Suddenly having the freedom of the whole house can be quite daunting - not to mention messy!

You can buy a purpose-made dog barrier or use a sturdy baby gate, which may be cheaper, to confine a puppy to a room or prevent him from going upstairs. Choose one with narrow vertical gaps or mesh, and check that your puppy can't get his head stuck between the bars, or put a mesh over the bottom of the gate initially.

You can also make your own barrier, but bear in mind that cardboard, fabric and other soft materials will definitely get chewed. Don't underestimate your puppy! Young English Springer Spaniels are lively and determined - they can jump and climb, so choose a barrier higher than you think necessary.

You'll then need a bed and/or a crate. A rigid moulded bed that's more difficult for a puppy to damage is a good option initially, with Vetbed or blankets inside for comfort. A luxury soft bed could prove to be an expensive mistake while puppies are still at the chewing stage! Some owners also like to create a penned area for their pup.

Collecting Your Puppy

- Let the breeder know what time you will arrive and ask her not to feed the pup for a couple of hours beforehand - unless you have a very long journey, in which case the puppy will need to eat something.

    He will be less likely to be car sick and should be hungry when he lands in his new home. The same applies to an adult dog moving to a new home

- Ask for an old blanket or toy that has been with the pup's mother – you can leave one on an earlier visit to collect with the pup. Or take one with you and rub the mother with it to collect her scent and put this with the puppy for the first few days. It will help him to settle

- Get copies of any health certificates relating to the parents and a Contract of Sale or Puppy Contract – see **Chapter 4. Finding Your Puppy** for details.

    It should also state that you can return the puppy if there are health issues within a certain time frame. The breeder will also give you details of microchip registration, worming and any vaccinations, as well as an information sheet

- Find out exactly what the breeder is feeding and how much; dogs' digestive systems cannot cope with sudden changes in diet - unless the breeder has deliberately been feeding several different foods to her puppies to get them used to different foods. In the beginning, stick to whatever the pup is used to; good breeders send some food home with the puppy

The Journey Home

Bringing a new puppy home in a car can be a traumatic experience. Your puppy will be sad at leaving his mother, brothers and sisters and a familiar environment. Everything will be strange and frightening and he may whimper and whine or even bark on the way home.

If you can, take somebody with you on that first journey – some breeders insist on having someone there to hold and cuddle the pup to make the journey less stressful for the pup.

Under no circumstances have the puppy on your lap while driving. It is simply too dangerous - a Springer puppy is extremely cute, wriggly and far too distracting. Have an old towel between your travel companion and the pup as he may quite possibly pee, drool or be sick - the puppy, not the passenger! Kitchen towel is also useful, as is a large plastic bag for putting any soiled items in.

If you have to travel any distance, take a crate – a canvas or plastic travel crate with holes in for air flow, or a wire crate he'll use at home. Cover the bottom of the crate with a waterproof material and then put a comfortable blanket on top. You can put newspapers in half of the crate if the pup is partly housetrained.

Don't forget to allow the pup to relieve himself beforehand, and if your journey is more than a couple of hours, take water to give him en route. He may need the toilet, but don't let him outside on to the ground as he is not yet fully vaccinated. As soon as you arrive home, let your puppy into the garden or yard, and when he "performs," praise him for his efforts.

These first few days are critical in getting your puppy to feel safe and confident in his new surroundings. Spend time with the latest addition to your family, talk to him often in a reassuring manner. Introduce him to his den and toys, slowly allow him to explore and show him around the house – once you have puppy-proofed it.

If you've got other animals, introduce them to each other slowly and in supervised sessions on neutral territory - or outdoors where there is space so neither feels threatened - preferably once the pup has got used to his new surroundings, not as soon as you walk through the door.

Gentleness and patience are the keys to these first few days, so don't overwhelm your pup.

Tip: Have a special, gentle puppy voice and use his new name frequently - and in a pleasant, encouraging manner. <u>Never use his name to scold</u> or he will associate it with bad things. The sound of his name should always make him want to pay attention to you as something good is going to happen - praise, food, playtime, and so on.

Settling In

We receive emails from worried new owners. Here are some of their most common concerns:

- My puppy won't stop crying or whining
- My puppy is shivering
- My puppy won't eat
- My puppy is very timid
- My puppy follows me everywhere, he won't let me out of his sight
- My puppy sleeps all the time, is this normal?

These behaviours are quite common at the beginning. They are just a young pup's reaction to leaving his mother and littermates and entering into a strange new world. It is normal for puppies to sleep most of the time, just like babies. It is also normal for some puppies to whine during the first couple of days.

Tip: If you constantly pick up a crying pup, he will learn that your attention is the reward for his crying. Wait until your puppy STOPS crying before giving him your attention.

If your puppy is shivering, check that he's warm enough, as he is used to the warmth of his siblings. If he's on the same food as he was at the breeder's and won't eat, then it is probably just nerves. If he leaves his food, take it away and try it later, don't leave it down all of the time or he may get used to turning his nose up at it.

Make your new pup as comfortable as possible, ensuring he has a warm (but not too hot), quiet den away from draughts, where he is not pestered by children or other pets. Handle him gently, while giving him plenty of time to sleep. Avoid placing him under stress by making too many demands. If your puppy whines or cries, it is usually due to one of the following reasons:

- He is lonely
- He is hungry
- He is cold
- He needs to relieve himself
- He wants attention from you

If it is none of these, then physically check him over to make sure he hasn't picked up an injury. Try not to fuss too much! If he whimpers, reassure with a quiet word. If he cries and tries to get out of his allotted area, he may need to go to the toilet. Take him outside and praise him if he performs.

FACT: English Springer Spaniel puppies from breeders who have already started socialisation and training are often more confident and less fazed by new things. They often settle in quicker than those reared with less human contact and new experiences.

Pictured looking pretty confident at six weeks old is Davey (Davidoff van het Veense Springertje). Photo courtesy of Helma and Rudo van den Brink.

A puppy will think of you as his new mother, and if you haven't decided what to call him yet, "Shadow" might be apt as he will follow you everywhere! But after a few days start to leave your pup for periods of a few minutes, gradually building up the time.

A puppy unused to being left alone can grow up to have Separation Anxiety - see **Chapter 8. Typical Springer Traits** for more information.

Helping a new pup to settle in is virtually a full-time job. If your routine means you are normally out of the house for a few hours during the day, get your puppy on a Friday or Saturday so he has at least a couple of days to adjust to his new surroundings.

A far better idea is to book time off work to help your puppy to settle in, if you can. (Easier to do in the UK than the US). If you don't work, leave your diary free for the first couple of weeks.

> **FACT** Your puppy's arrival at your home coincides with his most important life stage for bonding, so the first few weeks are very important.

The most important factors in bonding with your puppy are TIME and PATIENCE, even if he makes a mess in the house or chews something. Spend time with your English Springer Spaniel pup and you will have the most loyal lifelong friend. This emotional attachment may grow to become one of the most important aspects of your life – and certainly his.

Where Should the Puppy Sleep?

Just as you need a home, so a puppy needs a den; a haven where your pup feels safe. One of the most important things you can do for your young Springer puppy is to ALLOW HIM LOTS AND LOTS OF SLEEP – as much as 18 or 20 hours a day!

Your puppy doesn't know this and will play until he drops, so make sure you put him in his quiet place regularly during the day - even if he doesn't want to go, he will fall asleep and get the rest he needs.

> **Tip** The importance of pups getting enough sleep cannot be overemphasised. Lack of sleep can lead to over-excitement and naughtiness, which will make him harder to train.

Where do you want your new puppy to sleep? In the beginning, you cannot simply allow a pup to wander freely around the house. Ideally, he will be in a contained area at night, such as a pen or a crate. While it is not acceptable to shut a dog in a cage all day, you can keep your puppy in a crate at night until housetrained, and some adult English Springer Spaniels prefer to sleep in a crate - with the door open.

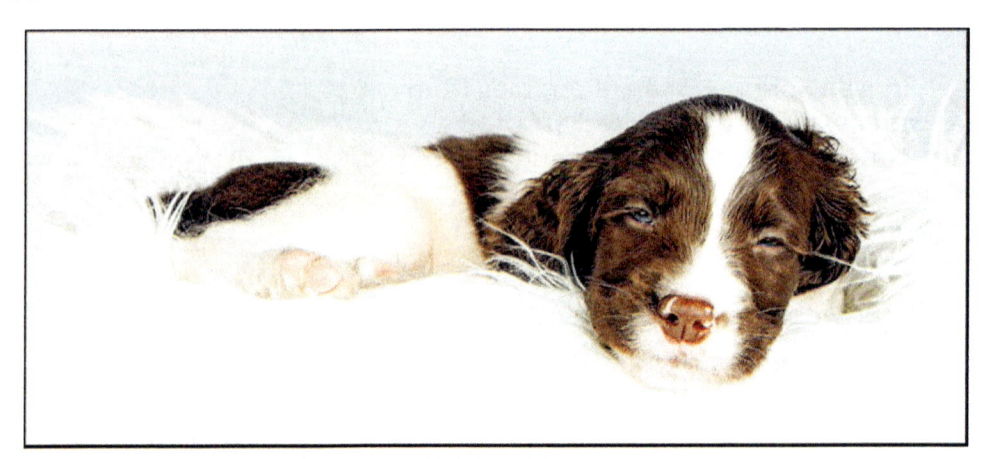

Some breeders recommend putting the puppy in a crate (or similar) next to your bed for the first two or three nights before moving him to the permanent sleeping place. Knowing you are close and being able to smell you may help overcome initial fears.

Others recommend biting the bullet and starting the puppy off in his permanent sleeping place; he will quieten down after a few nights. Ask your own breeder's advice on this one.

Tip It's normal for most puppies to cry for the first night or two. Resist the urge to get up to hold and comfort your pup, who learns that crying equals attention. Invest in a pair of silicone earplugs; they soon settle down.

Young puppies can't go through the night without needing to pee (and sometimes poo); their bodies simply aren't up to it.

Many breeders recommend putting newspapers or pellets in the pup's confined area – but away from his bedding – so he can relieve himself during the night, until he can last for six or seven hours. Set your alarm for an early morning wake-up call and take him out first thing, even before you are dressed. As soon as he wakes, he will want to pee.

Alternatively, we set our alarm and get up with a puppy once in the middle of the night for the first week - lights off, no fuss, quick trip outside - to speed up housetraining. Again, ask your breeder what she recommends for your puppy.

We don't advise letting new puppies sleep on the bed. They are not housetrained. They need to learn their place in the household and have their own quiet place for resting.

It's up to you whether to let yours on the bed or not once housetrained. English Springer Spaniels can sleep almost anywhere and anyhow. They don't need your comfy bed!

And be aware that dogs snuffle, snore, fart and - if not in a crate - pad around the bedroom in the middle of the night and come up to the bed to check you are still there - or see if you want to play! None of this is conducive to a good night's sleep.

Tip A Springer puppy used to being on his own every night (i.e. not in your bedroom) is less likely to develop Separation Anxiety, so consider this when deciding where he should sleep.

While it is not good to leave a dog alone all day, it is also not healthy to spend 24 hours a day together, as a dog can become too dependent. Although this is very flattering for you, it actually means that the dog is nervous and less sure of himself when you are not there. The last thing you want on your hands is an anxious English Springer Spaniel.

The puppy's designated sleeping area should not be too hot, cold or damp and should be free from draughts. Little puppies can be sensitive to temperature fluctuations; if you live in a hot climate, your new pup may need air conditioning in the summertime.

It may surprise American readers to learn that it's not uncommon practice in the UK to contain the puppy in the kitchen or utility room until he's housetrained, and then to allow him to roam around the house at will. There are owners who do not allow their dogs upstairs, but many do.

THE ENGLISH SPRINGER SPANIEL HANDBOOK Page 55

When deciding whether to let your pup upstairs, remember that while he is still growing, his bones are not yet fully developed. Studies have shown that pups who run up and down stairs regularly or jump on and off furniture before their growth plates are fully formed, may be more likely to develop joint problems later in life.

The time any young children spend with the puppy should be limited to a few short sessions a day and supervised. You wouldn't wake a baby every hour or so to play, and the same goes for puppies.

Wait a day or two before inviting friends round to see your handsome new puppy... and even then, don't inundate the puppy with constant visitors. However excited you are, your new arrival needs a few days to get over the stress of leaving mother and siblings and start bonding with you.

While confident, well-socialised puppies may settle in right away, other puppies may feel sad and a little afraid. Make the transition as gentle and unalarming as possible.

After a few sleep-deprived nights followed by days filled with entertaining your little puppy and dealing with chewed shoes, nipping and a few housetraining "accidents," your nerves might be a tiny bit frayed! Try to remain calm and patient... your puppy is doing his best... it just takes a little time for you both to get on the same wavelength.

FACT How you react and interact with each other during these first few days and weeks will help to shape your relationship and your Springer's character for the rest of his life.

Treats and Toys

English Springer Spaniels have an incredibly strong sense of smell, which is why they are used as sniffer dogs; and Springer puppies explore the world with their noses. Once they have found something interesting, they usually want to put it in their mouths, so chew treats and toys are a must. Don't scold a pup for chewing; it's natural for them to chew.

Instead, put objects you don't want chewed out of reach and replace them with chew toys. There are some things you can't move out of puppy's way, like kitchen cupboards, doors, sofas, fixtures and fittings, so try not to leave your pup unattended for any length of time where he can chew something that is hard or expensive to replace.

Tip Avoid giving old socks, shoes or slippers, or your pup will naturally come to think of your footwear as fair game!

You can give an English Springer Spaniel puppy *a raw bone* to gnaw on - NEVER cooked bones as these can splinter.

Avoid poultry and pork bones. Ribs - especially pork ribs - are too high in fat. Knuckle bones are a good choice and the bone should be too big for the puppy to swallow.

Puppies should ALWAYS BE SUPERVISED and the bone removed after an hour or so. Don't feed a puppy a bone if there are other dogs around, it could lead to food aggression.

FACT Raw bones contain bacteria, and families with babies or very young children shouldn't feed them indoors. Keep any bones in a fridge or freezer and always wash your hands after handling them.

Alternatives to real bones or plastic chew bones include natural **reindeer antler** chew toys which have the added advantage of calcium, although they are hard and have been known to crack teeth.

Natural chews preferred by some breeders include ears, dried rabbit pelt and tripe sticks – all excellent for teething puppies - once you have got over the smell!

Tip Rawhide chews are not recommended as they can get stuck in a dog's throat or stomach, but bully sticks *(pictured)* are a good alternative.

Made from a bull's penis(!) they can be a good distraction from chewing furniture, etc. and help to promote healthy teeth and gums. **Bully sticks** are highly digestible, break down easily in the stomach and are generally considered safe for all dogs.

They are made from 100% beef, normally contain no additives or preservatives, come in different sizes and dogs love 'em. **NOTE:** Puppies should be supervised while eating bully sticks or any other treats.

Dental sticks are good for cleaning your dog's teeth, but many contain preservatives and don't last very long with a determined chewer. One that does last is the **Nylabone Dura Chew Wishbone, pictured,** made of a type of plastic infused with flavours appealing to dogs. Get the right size and throw it away if it starts to splinter with sharp edges.

Another long-lasting treat option is the **Lickimat (pictured)**, which you smear with a favourite food. This inexpensive mat will keep your puppy occupied for some time – although they can leave a bit of a mess.

Other choices include **Kong toys,** which are pretty indestructible, and you can put treats - frozen or fresh - or smear peanut butter inside (one without Xylitol, which is highly toxic to dogs) to keep your dog occupied while you are out. All of these are widely available online, if not in your local pet store.

As far as toys go, the **Zogoflex Hurley** and the **Goughnut (pictured)** are both strong and float, so good for swimmers – and you'll get your money back on both if your Spaniel destroys them!

For safety, the Goughnut has a green exterior and red interior, so you can tell if your dog has penetrated the surface - as long as the green is showing, you can let your dog "goughnuts!"

A **natural hemp** or cotton tug rope is another option, as the cotton rope acts like dental floss and helps with teeth cleaning. It is versatile and can be used for fetch games as well as chewing.

FACT Puppies' stomachs are sensitive, so be careful what goes in. Even non-poisonous garden plants can cause intestinal blockages and/or vomiting. Like babies, pups can quickly dehydrate, so if your puppy is sick or has watery poop for a day or two, seek veterinary advice.

Vaccinations and Worming

We recommend having your English Springer Spaniel checked out by a vet soon after picking him up. In fact, some Puppy Contracts stipulate that the dog should be examined by a vet within a couple of days. This is to everyone's benefit and, all being well, you are safe in the knowledge that your puppy is healthy, at least at the time of purchase.

Tip: Keep your pup on your lap away from other dogs in the waiting room as he will not yet be fully protected against infectious diseases.

Vaccinations

Puppies are covered by immunity from their mum until around eight weeks. Then all puppies need immunisation, and currently the most common way of doing this is by vaccination. They receive their first dose at around eight weeks old - although it can be any time from six to nine weeks old.

When you collect your puppy from the breeder, check if he has had his first round of vaccinations.

The second vaccination is done two to four weeks later, typically at 11 to 13 weeks.

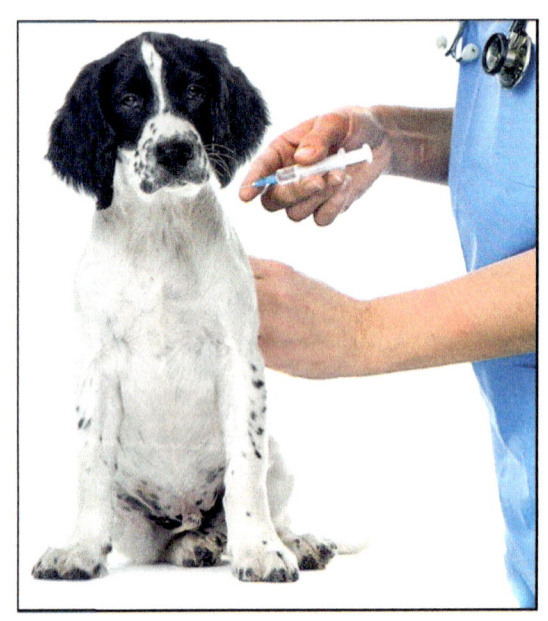

Dr Vicky Payne, UK veterinarian and breeder of Quincegrove Working Springer Spaniels says: "Puppies are considered to be fully protected one to two weeks after their second vaccination (depending on brand). If intranasal Kennel Cough vaccine is given, this provides protection after three weeks.

"The WSAVA suggests an additional DHP vaccine at or after 16 weeks, but this is rarely offered by UK vets unless there is a disease outbreak (except Rottweilers who have weirdly long-acting maternal antibodies!).

"It is not advisable to delay the first vaccine so the second can be after 16 weeks as this severely impacts socialisation and habituation (getting used to new things).

"Speak to your vet to discuss a vaccine protocol which best suits local disease risks and the lifestyle of your puppy."

A booster is then required at six to 12 months.

FACT: An unimmunised puppy is at risk every time he meets other dogs as he has no protection against potentially fatal infectious diseases – and it is unlikely a pet insurer will cover an unvaccinated pup.

It should be stressed that vaccinations are generally safe and side effects are uncommon. If your English Springer Spaniel is unlucky enough to be one of the *very few* that suffers an adverse reaction, here are some signs to look out for; a pup may exhibit one or more of these:

MILD REACTION - Sleepiness, irritability and not wanting to be touched. Sore or a small lump at the place where he was injected. Nasal discharge or sneezing. Puffy face and ears.

SEVERE REACTION - Anaphylactic shock. A sudden and quick reaction, usually before leaving the vet's, which causes breathing difficulties. Vomiting, diarrhoea, staggering and seizures.

A severe reaction is rare. There is a far greater risk of your Springer either being ill or spreading disease if he does not have the injections.

BSAVA (British Small Animal Veterinary Association) recommends the following core vaccinations in the UK:

- CDV (Distemper)
- CPV (Parvo)
- CAV (Adenovirus or Infectious Canine Hepatitis)
- Leptospirosis (often called **Lepto**)

The English Springer Spaniel Health website says: "The Leptospira vaccine is not always considered to be a core vaccination as its use depends on veterinary advice within different parts of the UK and on the environmental and lifestyle risks of individual dogs.

"These include exposure to, or drinking from, rivers, lakes or streams; roaming on rural properties (because of exposure to potentially infected wildlife, farm animals, or water sources); exposure to wild animal or farm animal species; contact with rodents or other dogs. Owners should discuss the most appropriate course of action with their vet."

Many vets also recommend vaccinating against Kennel Cough (Bordetella). Rabies is very rare in the UK; it's more commonly seen in some US states and Europe. When deemed necessary, Rabies vaccines start at 12 weeks.

Veterinarian Sam Goldberg adds: *"I also recommend puppies have at least one course of Fenbendazole (marketed in the UK as Panacur) as it also covers Giardia, which we see commonly in puppies with diarrhoea."*

Google *"AKC puppy shots"* for a list of recommended vaccinations. In-depth information on core vaccinations for the US can be found on the World Small Animal Veterinary Association website, search online for *"WSAVA dog vaccinations"* or visit: https://wsava.org/wp-content/uploads/2020/01/WSAVA-Vaccination-Guidelines-2015.pdf (skip to Page 17).

WSAVA states: "Core vaccines for dogs are those that protect against canine distemper virus (CDV), canine adenovirus (CAV) and the variants of canine parvovirus type 2 (CPV-2)... with the final dose of these being delivered at 16 weeks or older and then followed by a booster at six or 12 months of age."

Puppies in the US also need vaccinating separately against Rabies after 16 weeks, but this varies by state. There are optional vaccinations for Coronavirus (C) and - depending on where you live and if your dog is regularly around woods or forests - Lyme Disease.

Bordetella (Kennel Cough) is another non-core vaccine. It can be given intranasally, by tablet or injection, with boosters recommended for dogs deemed to be at high risk, e.g. when boarding or showing.

- Boosters for Distemper, Parvo and Canine Hepatitis are recommended no more often than every three years
- Boosters for Leptospirosis are every year

The current Lepto vaccine only protects against certain types of the many different variants of the Leptospira bacteria. However, having your dog vaccinated does decrease their risk of becoming sick with Lepto. The Lepto vaccination should not be given at the same time as Rabies.

NOTE: Some dogs have been known to have bad reactions to the Lepto 4 vaccine, although Springers are not thought to be a particularly susceptible breed.

The ESS Health website says: "There is much debate over whether to give the Lepto 2 or Lepto 4 vaccine. The newer Lepto 4 vaccine protects dogs against two additional strains of the Leptospira disease that have been identified as an area of concern for higher risk groups of dogs or those travelling abroad.

"It can also be said that Lepto 2 still provides a suitable cover for most dogs, it just depends on what you, as an owner, and your vet think is the most appropriate vaccine to give for your dog."

Diseases such as Parvo and Kennel Cough are highly contagious and you should not let your new arrival mix with other dogs - unless they are your own and have already been vaccinated - until a week after his last vaccination, otherwise he will not be fully immunised.

Parvovirus can also be transmitted by the faeces of many animals, including foxes.

Tip: Avoid taking your new puppy to places where unvaccinated dogs might have been, like the local park. This does not mean that your puppy should be isolated - far from it.

This is an important time for socialisation. It is OK for the puppy to mix with other dogs that you absolutely know are up-to-date with their vaccinations and appropriate boosters. Perhaps invite a friend's dog round to play in your garden or yard to begin the socialisation process.

The vet should give you a record card or send you a reminder when a booster is due, but it's also a good idea to keep a note of the date in your diary.

Tests have shown that the Parvovirus vaccination gives most animals at least seven years of immunity, while the Distemper jab provides immunity for five to seven years. In the US, many vets now recommend that you take your dog for a titre test once he has had his initial puppy vaccinations and six or 12-month booster.

The Diseases

Vaccinations protect your puppy and adult dog against some nasty diseases, so it's important to keep your English Springer Spaniel up to date with protection.

Canine Distemper (CDV) is a contagious disease that affects different parts of the body, including the gastrointestinal and respiratory tracts, spinal cord and brain.

Common symptoms include a high fever, eye inflammation, eye and/or nose discharge, struggling for breath, coughing, vomiting, diarrhoea, loss of appetite and lethargy, and hardening of nose and footpads. It can also result in bacterial infections and serious neurological problems.

Canine Parvovirus (CPV) is a highly contagious viral disease that causes acute gastrointestinal illness in puppies commonly aged six to 20 weeks old, although older dogs are sometimes also affected. Symptoms include lethargy, depression and loss or lack of appetite, followed by a sudden onset of high fever, vomiting, and diarrhoea. Sadly, it is often fatal.

Infectious Canine Hepatitis (ICH), also called Canine Adenovirus or CAV, is an acute liver infection. The virus is spread in the poop, urine, blood, saliva, and nasal discharge of infected dogs, and other dogs pick it up through their mouth or nose.

The virus then infects the liver and kidneys. Symptoms include fever, depression, loss of appetite, coughing and a tender abdomen. Dogs can recover from mild cases, but more serious ones can be fatal.

Rabies is a fatal virus that attacks the brain and spinal cord. All mammals, including dogs and humans, can catch rabies, which is most often contracted through a bite from an infected animal. Rabies usually comes from exposure to wild animals like foxes, bats and raccoons.

Leptospirosis (Lepto) is a bacterial disease that causes serious illness by damaging vital organs such as the liver and kidneys. Leptospirosis bacteria can spread in urine and can enter the body through the mouth, nose or open wounds.

Symptoms vary but include fever, jaundice (yellow gums and eyes), muscle pain and limping, weakness, reduced appetite, drinking more, vomiting, bloody diarrhoea, mouth ulcers and difficulty breathing.

An infected dog may quickly become restless and irritable, even showing aggression, or be excessively affectionate. One of the most well-known symptoms is foaming at the mouth, a sign that the disease is progressing.

Bordetella (Kennel Cough) - Dogs catch Kennel Cough when they breathe in bacteria or virus particles. The classic symptom is a persistent, forceful cough that often sounds like a goose honk (and different from a reverse sneeze).

Some dogs may show other symptoms, including sneezing, a runny nose or eye discharge, but appetite and energy levels usually remain the same. It is not often a serious condition and most dogs recover without treatment.

Lyme Disease gets into a dog's or human's bloodstream via a tick bite. Once there, the bacteria travel to different parts of the body and cause problems in organs or specific locations such as joints. These ticks are often founds in woods, tall grasses, thick brush and marshes – all places that English Springer Spaniels love.

Lyme Disease can usually be treated if caught early enough. It can be life-threatening or shortening if left untreated.

Giardia is an infection caused by a microscopic parasite that attaches itself to a dog's intestinal wall causing a sudden onset of foul-smelling diarrhoea. It may lead to weight loss, chronic intermittent diarrhoea, and fatty poop.

The disease is not usually life threatening unless the dog's immune system is immature or compromised. Treated dogs usually recover, although very old dogs and those with compromised immune systems have a higher risk for complications.

Titres (Titers in the USA)

Some breeders and owners feel strongly that constantly vaccinating our dogs is having a detrimental effect on our pets' health, especially as any vaccinations are now effective for several years.

Vets recommend boosters every three years for the core vaccines; however, one alternative is titres. The thinking behind them is to avoid a dog having to have unnecessary repeat vaccinations for certain diseases as he already has enough antibodies present. Known as a **VacciCheck** in the UK, they are still relatively uncommon here; they are more widespread in the USA.

Not everybody agrees with titres. One vet I spoke to said that the titre results were only good for the day on which the test was taken, and it is true that many boarding kennels do NOT accept titres.

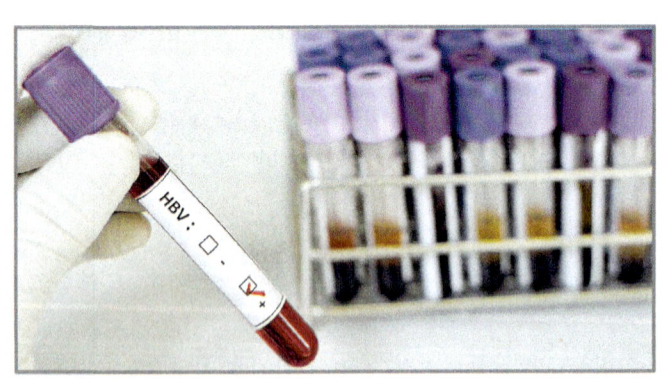

To *"titre"* is to take a blood sample from a dog (or cat) to determine whether he has enough antibodies to provide immunity against a particular disease, particularly Parvovirus, Distemper and Adenovirus (Canine Hepatitis).

If so, then a booster injection is not needed. Titering is NOT recommended for Leptospirosis, Bordetella or Lyme Disease, as these vaccines provide only short-term protection. Many US states also require proof of a Rabies vaccination.

The vet can test the blood at the clinic without sending off the sample, thereby keeping costs down for the owner. A titre for Parvovirus and Distemper currently costs around $100 in the US, sometimes more for Rabies, and a titre test in the UK costs as little as £40.

Titre levels are given as ratios and show how many times blood can be diluted before no antibodies are detected. So, if blood can be diluted 1,000 times and still show antibodies, the ratio would be 1:1000, which is a strong titre, while a titre of 1:2 would be "weak."

A **strong (high) titre** means that your dog has enough antibodies to fight off that specific disease and is immune from infection. A **weak titre** means that you and your vet should discuss revaccination - even then your dog might have some reserve forces known as *"memory cells"* that will provide antibodies when needed.

If you are going on holiday and taking your dog to kennels, check whether the kennel accepts titre records; many don't as yet.

In the UK, not many dog breeders use titres as yet, it is far more common in the US. But here's what some who do titre said: "I titre test periodically rather than do automatic boosters. They have all still had a full level of immunity on the tests - that's after their initial puppy vaccinations."

Another said: "When my puppies go to their new homes, I tell all my owners to follow their vet's advice about worming and vaccinating, as the last thing new owners require is to be at odds with their vets. All dogs must have their puppy vaccinations; it is now thought that the minimum duration of immunity is between seven and 15 years.

"However, a few owners do express concern about all the chemicals we are introducing into our puppies' lives and if they do, I explain how I try to give my dogs a chemical-free life, if possible, as adult dogs.

"Instead of giving my adult dogs their core vaccinations for Canine Distemper, Parvovirus and Adenovirus (Hepatitis) every three years, I just take my dogs down to the local vet and ask them to do something called a titre test, also known as a VacciCheck.

"They take a small amount of blood and check it for antibodies to the diseases. If they have antibodies to the diseases, there is no reason to give dogs a vaccination.

"However, you should note that there is a separate vaccination for Leptospirosis and Canine Parainfluenza, which is given annually. Leptospirosis is recommended by the BSAVA (British Small Animal Veterinary Association).

"Leptospirosis is more common in tropical areas of the world and not that common in England. In order to make a decision about whether to give this to your dog annually, you need to talk to your vet and do some research yourself so you can make an informed decision.

"We vaccinate our children up to about the age of 16. However, we don't vaccinate adults every one to three years, as it is deemed that the vaccinations they receive in childhood will cover them for a lifetime. This is what is being steadily proved for dogs and we are so lucky that we can titre test our dogs so we don't have to leave it to chance."

Another added: "I do not vaccinate my dogs beyond the age of four to five years, I now have them titre-tested. Every dog I have titre tested aged five to 10 years has been immune to the diseases vaccinated against when younger. I believe many vets over-vaccinate."

The (UK) Kennel Club now includes titre testing information in its Assured Breeder Pack, but has yet to include it under its general information on vaccines on its website. Google *"Pet vaccines: what owners need to know boughtbymany"* for more info.

Worming

All puppies need worming (technically, deworming). A good breeder will give the puppies their first dose of worming medication at around two weeks old, then probably again at five and eight weeks before they leave the litter – or even more often. Get the details and inform your vet exactly what treatment, if any, your pup has already had.

The main worms affecting puppies are roundworm and tapeworm. In certain areas of the US, the dreaded heartworm can also pose a risk. If you live in an affected area, discuss the right time to start heartworm medication when you visit your vet for puppy vaccinations – it's usually from a few months old.

The pill should be given every month when there is no heavy frost (frost kills mosquitos that carry the disease); giving it all year round gives the best protection. The heartworm pill is by prescription only and deworms the dog monthly for heartworm, round, hook, and whip worm.

Roundworm can be transmitted from a puppy to humans - often children – and can in severe cases cause blindness, or miscarriage in women, so it's important to keep up to date with worming.

Tip: Worms in puppies are quite common, usually picked up through their mother's milk. If you have children, get them into the habit of washing their hands after they have been in contact with the puppy – lack of hygiene is the reason why children are susceptible.

Most vets recommend worming a puppy once a month until he is six months old, and then around every two to three months. If your English Springer Spaniel is regularly out and about running through woods and fields, it is important to stick to a regular worming schedule, as he is more likely to pick up worms than one that spends more time indoors.

Fleas can pass on tapeworms to dogs, but a puppy would not normally be treated unless it is known for certain he has fleas - and then only with caution. You need to know the weight of your puppy and then speak to your vet about the safest treatment to get rid of the parasites.

NOTE: Buy age-appropriate worming treatments.

It is necessary for breeders to worm their puppies. However, there are ways to reduce worming treatments for adult dogs.

Following anecdotal reports of some dogs experiencing side effects with chemical wormers, more owners are looking to use natural wormers on their dogs. If you go down this route, check exactly which worms your chosen herbal preparation deals with – it may not be all of them.

A method of reducing worming medication by testing your dog's stools is becoming more popular. You send a small sample of your dog's poo(p) off in an envelope every two to three months. If the result is positive, your dog needs worming, but if negative, no treatment is necessary.

In the UK this is done by veterinary labs like Wormcount www.wormcount.com and similar options are available in the USA – there is even a *"fecal worm test"* available at just over $20 from Amazon.com.

With thanks to **English Springer Spaniel Health** for help with Vaccinations and Worming
www.englishspringerhealth.org.uk

6. Crate and Housetraining

Crates are becoming more popular year on year. Used correctly, they speed up housetraining (potty training), give you and your puppy short breaks from each other and keep him safe at night or when you are out.

Some owners also crate their adult Springers for short periods, although the breeders involved in this book only use crates for young dogs. Trainers, behaviourists and people who show, compete or train dogs all use crates.

Using A Crate

A crate should always be used in a humane manner. If you decide to use one, spend time getting your puppy or adult dog used to it, so he comes to regard the crate as his own safe haven and not a punishment cell or prison.

Crates may not be suitable for every dog – or owner. Dogs are social animals, they thrive on interaction. Being caged for long periods is a miserable existence for any dog, but particularly for a working breed like the English Springer Spaniel.

They are, however, very useful for puppies. We prefer a wire crate that allows air to pass through, although some breeders like the plastic ones.

A crate should NEVER be used as a means of confinement for a Springer while you are out of the house for six, eight or more hours every day.

1. Always remove your dog's collar before leaving him inside when you are not there. Sadly, dogs have been known to die after panicking when their collars or tags got caught.
2. If the door is closed, your dog must have access to water while inside during the day. Non-spill water bowls are available from pet shops and online, as are bowls to attach to the bars.

Crates are ideal for giving you or the puppy some down time. You cannot watch a puppy 24/7 and a crate is a safe place for him while you get on with doing other things. English Springer Spaniel puppies need LOTS OF SLEEP - but they don't know this, so a crate (or puppy pen) is an excellent place for resting without distractions.

Your puppy first has to get used to the crate so he looks forward to going in there - some breeders may have already started the process.

NOTE: An eight-week-old puppy should not be in a crate for longer than two hours at a time during the day.

Not every owner wishes to use a crate, but used correctly they:

- Are a useful housetraining tool

- 🐾 Create a canine den
- 🐾 Give you a break
- 🐾 Limit access to the rest of the house until potty trained
- 🐾 Are a safe place for the dog to nap or sleep at night
- 🐾 Provide a safe way to transport your dog in a car

Another very good reason to crate-train is that if your dog has to visit the vet or be confined for an illness, he will not have the added stress of getting used to a crate. Confining a Springer NOT used to a crate is very stressful for both dog and owner.

Which Crate and Where?

The crate should be large enough to allow your dog to stretch out flat on his side without being cramped, and he should be able to turn around easily and sit up without hitting his head on the top.

If the crate is too big for your pup, it can slow down housetraining. Some owners use a crate divider *(pictured, top right)* or block off a part of the crate while the pup is growing. A smaller area also helps him to feel more secure.

Tip: Partially covering the crate with an old blanket creates a den for your new puppy at night. Only cover on three sides - leave the front uncovered and a gap around the bottom on all sides for air to flow. You can also just cover half or part of the crate to make it cosier for the pup.

Place the crate in the kitchen or another room where there are people during the day, preferably one with a hard, easy-to-clean floor. Puppies are curious pack animals and like to see and smell what is going on. If you have children, strike the balance between putting the crate in a place where the pup won't feel isolated, yet allowing him some peace and quiet from the kids.

Avoid putting the crate in a closed utility room or garage away from everybody, or he will feel lonely and sad. If you are using a room off the kitchen, allow the pup free run of the room and use a pet gate or baby gate with narrowly-spaced bars so his head can't get stuck but he can still see what's going on.

If you've got the space, a playpen is great to use in addition – or as an alternative – to a crate.

The chosen location should be draught-free, not too hot and not in bright sunshine.

Opinions vary, but some owners put the crate right next to the bed for the first night or two – even raised up next to the bed - to help the puppy settle in quicker. A few have even been known to sleep downstairs on the sofa or an air mattress next to the crate for the first one or two nights!

Others believe in putting the crate in its permanent place from day one. Put the following items inside the crate during the day:

- 🐾 Bedding – Vet Bed *(pictured)* or other bedding your puppy won't chew in a few days
- 🐾 A blanket or item that has been rubbed with the mother's scent
- 🐾 A non-spill water bowl
- 🐾 A healthy chew to stop him gnawing the crate and bedding
- 🐾 Possibly a toy to keep him occupied

At night, remove the water and chew. Add an extra blanket if you think he might get cold overnight; he has been used to the warmth of his littermates and mother. Puppies are little chew machines so, at this stage, don't spend a lot of money on a fluffy floor covering for the crate, as it is likely to get destroyed.

The widely available and washable *"Vet Bed"* is a good choice for bedding. Made from double-strength polyester, they retain extra heat, allow air to flow through and are widely used in vets' clinics to make dogs feel warm and secure. They also have drainage properties, so your pup will stay dry if he has an accident.

Vet Beds are also a good option for older dogs, as the added heat is soothing for aging muscles and joints. You can buy "Vet Bedding" by the roll, which keeps costs down.

One breeder added: "Don't use beds with stuffing at this age, as once they learn to de-stuff a bed, it may become a lifelong habit and possibly graduate into de-stuffing furniture or pillows later!"

Tip: Consider putting a Snuggle Puppy in the crate with the new puppy. The Snuggle Puppy *(pictured)* is a safe soft toy with a heartbeat. (Remove it if your dog chews it and exposes the internal mechanism).

Whining

If your puppy is whining, whimpering or howling in the crate, make sure:

A. He doesn't need the toilet.
B. He is warm.
C. He is physically unharmed.

Then the reason is because he doesn't want to be alone. He has come from the warmth and security of his mother and litter, and the Brave New World can be a very daunting place for an eight-week-old puppy all alone in a new home.

He is not crying because he is in a cage. He would cry if he had the freedom of the room - he is crying because he is separated. Dogs are pack animals and being alone is not a natural state for them

However, with patience and the right training, he will get used to being alone and being in the crate. Some owners make the crate their dog's only bed, so he feels comfortable and safe in there, and many adult Springers love their crates as a place to rest.

Here are some other tips to help your puppy settle in his crate:

- Leave a ticking clock next to the crate, or
- Leave a radio on softly nearby
- Lightly spray DAP on a cloth or small towel and place in the crate

FACT: DAP, or Dog Appeasing Pheromone, is a synthetic form of the pheromone that nursing Springers (and other breeds) give off after giving birth and then again after weaning to reassure their puppies that everything is fine.

DAP has been found to help reduce fear in young puppies, as well as Separation Anxiety, phobias and aggression caused by anxiety in adult dogs. According to one French study: "DAP has no toxicities or side effects and is particularly beneficial for sick and geriatric dogs." Google *"Canadian Veterinary Journal Dog Appeasing Pheromone"* for more details of the study.

NOTE: There is also an ADAPTIL collar with slow-release DAP, which is designed to reduce fear in anxious adult dogs. It gets good reports from many, not all, owners.

Travel Crates

Special travel crates are useful for the car, or for taking your dog to the vet's, a show or on holiday. Choose one with holes or mesh in the side to allow free movement of air rather than a solid one, in which a dog can soon overheat.

Put the crate on the shady side of the interior and make sure it can't move around; put the seatbelt around it. If it's very sunny and the top of the crate is wire mesh, cover part of it so your dog has some shade and put the windows up and the air conditioning on.

Alternatively, you can buy a metal grille/dog guard to keep your dogs confined to the back of the car, **such as the one in this photo.**

Something similar or a sturdy **transit box, pictured,** is what most owners of working Springers use to transport their dogs.

One breeder adds: "Crate training applies to travel too. Often, people get frustrated if a dog has an accident in the car, but forget to let them out before they set off. I also use a Ventlock, **pictured,** on the car boot to keep it open slightly, allowing air to flow, if they have to be in there."

Dogs can also be safely transported using a seat belt harness – make sure it's the right size and fitted properly.

Allowing your dog to roam freely inside the car is against the law and not safe, particularly if you - like me – are a bit of a "lead foot" on the brake and accelerator!

And try to avoid letting your Springer ride with his head out of the window - even if he does look like Easy Rider! Wind pressure can cause ear infections or bits of dust, insects, etc. to fly into unprotected eyes. Your dog will also fly forward if you suddenly hit the brakes.

Tip Springers have thick coats. If it's a hot or even warm day, don't leave yours unattended in a vehicle, they can overheat alarmingly quickly.

Getting your Puppy Used to a Crate

Once you've got your crate, you'll need to learn how to use it properly so that it becomes a safe, comfortable den for your dog. Many breeders will have already started the process but, if not, here's a tried-and-tested method of getting your dog firstly to accept a crate, and then to actually want to spend time in there.

These are the first steps:

1. Drop a few puppy treats around and then inside the crate.
2. Put your pup's favourite toy in there.
3. Keep the door open.
4. Feed your puppy's meals inside the crate. Again, keep the door open.

> **Tip:** Place a chew or treat INSIDE the crate and close the door while your puppy is OUTSIDE the crate. He will be desperate to get in there! Open the door, let him in and praise him for going in. Fasten a long-lasting chew inside the crate and leave the door open. Let your puppy wander inside to spend some time eating the chew.

5. **After a while, close the crate door and feed him some treats through the mesh.** At first just do it for a few seconds at a time, then gradually increase the time. If you do it too fast, he may become distressed.
6. **Slowly build up the amount of time he's in the crate.** For the first few days, stay in the room, then gradually leave first one minute, then three, then 10, 30 and so on.

Photo: Stella's litter, bred by Lynne Lucas of Traxlerstarr Spaniels. Lynne trains her pups to use the crate as soon as they have left the whelping crate.

Next Steps

7. **Put your dog in his crate at regular intervals during the day - maximum two hours.**
8. **If your pup is not yet housetrained, make sure he has relieved himself BEFORE you put him in the crate.** Putting him in when he needs to eliminate will slow down training.
9. **Don't crate only when you are leaving the house.** Put him in the crate while you are home as well. Use it as a *"sleep zone"* or *"safe zone."* By using the crate both when you are home and while you are gone, your dog becomes comfortable there and not worried that you won't come back, or that you are leaving him alone. This helps to prevent Separation Anxiety.
10. **If you are leaving your dog unattended,** give him a chew and remove his collar, tags and anything else that could become caught in an opening or between the bars.
11. **Make it very clear to any children that the crate is NOT a den for them, but a** *"special room"* for the dog.
12. **Although the crate is your dog's haven and safe place, it must not be off-limits to humans.** You should be able to reach inside at any time.
13. **Try and wait until your dog is calm before putting him in the crate.** If he is behaving badly and you grab him and shove him in the crate straight away, he will associate the crate with punishment. Try not to use the crate if you can't calm him down, instead either leave the room or put the dog in another room until he calms down.

14. The crate should ALWAYS be associated with a positive experience in your dog's mind.

15. **Don't let your dog out of the crate when he is barking or whining**, or he'll think that this is the key to opening the door. Wait until he has stopped whining for at least 10 or 20 seconds before letting him out.

Reminder:

- During the day the crate door should not be closed until your pup is happy with being inside
- At night-time it is OK to close the door
- If you don't want to use a crate, use a pet gate, section off an area inside one room, or use a puppy pen to confine your pup at night

Housetraining

You have four major factors in your favour when it comes to toilet training an English Springer Spaniel:

1. They are an intelligent breed.
2. They are highly biddable (willing to accept instruction).
3. They love to please you.
4. They respond well to rewards - praise, treats, games or toys.

Puppies naturally want to keep their space clean; it's instinctive. From when he can first walk, a pup will move away from his mother and sleeping area to eliminate.

The aim of housetraining is to teach the puppy exactly WHERE this space starts and finishes.

When a puppy arrives at your home, he may think that a corner of the crate, the kitchen, your favourite rug or anywhere else in the house is an OK place for him to relieve himself.

Through training and vigilance, you will teach him that the house is part of his and your "space" and therefore it's not OK for him to pee or poop indoors.

Many good breeders will have already started the process, so when you pick up your puppy, all you have to do is carry on the good work!

FACT The speed and success of housetraining depends to some degree on the individual dog and how much effort the breeder has already put in. However, the single most important factor in success is undoubtedly the owner.

The more vigilant you are during the early days, the quicker your Springer will be housetrained. It's as simple as that.

How much time and effort are YOU prepared to put in at the beginning to speed up housetraining? Taking the advice in this chapter and being consistent with your routines and repetitions is the quickest way to get results. Clear your schedule for a week or so and make housetraining your No.1 priority – it'll be worth it.

I get complaints from some American readers when I write: "Book a week or two off work and housetrain your dog!" I know Americans get much shorter vacation time than most Europeans, but honestly, if you can take a few days off work to monitor housetraining at the beginning, it will speed the process up no end.

If you're starting from scratch, your new arrival thinks that the whole house is away from his sleeping quarters, and therefore a great place for a pee or a poop! And, if yours is a rescue Springer, he may well have picked up some bad habits before arriving at your home. In these cases, time, patience and vigilance are essential to teach your dog the new ways.

Springers, like all dogs, are creatures of routine - not only do they like the same things happening at the same times every day, but establishing a regular routine with your dog also helps to speed up obedience and toilet training.

Tip: To keep things simple in a pup's mind, have a designated area in your garden or yard that the pup can use as a toilet. Dogs are tactile creatures, so they pick a toilet area that feels good under their paws.

Dogs often like to go on grass - but this will do nothing to improve your lawn, so think carefully about what area to encourage your puppy to use.

Perhaps consider a small patch of crushed gravel in your garden – but don't let your puppy eat it - or a particular corner of the garden or yard away from any attractive or spiky plants.

Opinion is divided on puppy pads. Some breeders advise against using them as they can slow down potty training, and some say that newspapers can also encourage a pup to soil inside the house. Because dogs are tactile and puppy pads are soft and comfy, dogs like going on them! When you remove the pads, the puppy may be tempted to find a similar surface, like a carpet or rug.

A general rule of thumb is that puppies can last for one hour per month of age without urinating, sometimes longer. So:

- An eight-week pup can last for two hours
- A 12-week-old pup can last for three hours
- A 16-week pup can last for four hours
- A six-month-old can last for six hours

NOTE: This only applies when the puppy is calm and relaxed.

FACT: If a puppy is active or excited, he will urinate more often, and if he is excited to see you, he may urinate at will.

THE ENGLISH SPRINGER SPANIEL HANDBOOK Page **71**

To speed up the process even more, consider setting your alarm clock to get up in the night to let the pup out to relieve himself for the first week. Don't switch the lights on or make a fuss of the pup, just take him outside. You might hate it, but it can shorten the overall time spent housetraining.

....

Housetraining Tips

Follow these tips to speed up housetraining:

1. **Constant supervision is essential for the first week or two if you are to housetrain your puppy quickly. If nobody is there, he will learn to pee or poop inside the house.**

2. Take your pup outside at the following times:

    a) As soon as he wakes – every time
    b) Shortly after each feed
    c) After a drink
    d) When he gets excited
    e) After exercise or play
    f) Last thing at night
    g) Initially every hour or two - whether or not he looks like he wants to go

You may think that the above list is an exaggeration, but it isn't! Housetraining a pup is almost a full-time job in the beginning. If you are serious about toilet training your puppy quickly, then clear your diary for a week or two and keep your eyes firmly glued on your pup...learn to spot that expression or circling motion just before he makes a mess on your floor.

1. Take your pup to **the same place** every time, you may need to use a lead (leash) in the beginning - or tempt him there with a treat. Some say it is better to only pick him up and dump him there in an emergency, as it is better if he learns to take himself to the chosen toilet spot.

    Dogs naturally develop a preference for going in the same place or on the same surface. Take or lead him to the same patch every time so he learns this is his toilet area.

2. **No pressure – be patient. English Springer Spaniels do not perform well under pressure.** You must allow your distracted little darling time to wander around and have a good sniff before performing his duties – but do not leave him, stay around a short distance away. Unfortunately, puppies are not known for their powers of concentration, so it may take a while for him to select the perfect bathroom spot!

Photo: This little chap, bred by Lisa Cardy, of CallisWold Springers, is trying to decide if he really wants to go or not. Be patient - you can't rush the little darlings!

3. **Housetraining a Springer should ALWAYS be reward-based, never negative or aggressive.** Give praise and/or a treat IMMEDIATELY after he has performed his duties in the chosen spot. Persistence, praise and rewards are best for quick results.

4. **Share the responsibility.** It doesn't have to be the same person who takes the dog outside all the time. In fact, it's easier if there are a couple of you, as this is a very time-demanding business. Just make sure you stick to the same principles, command and patch of ground.

5. **Stick to the same routine.** Sticking to the same times for meals, exercise, playtime, sleeping and toilet breaks will help settle him into his new home and housetrain him quicker.

6. **Use the same word** or command when telling your puppy to go to the toilet – or while he is in the act. He will gradually associate this phrase or word with toileting.

7. **Use your voice ONLY if you catch him in the act indoors.** A short sharp sound is best - **ACK! EH!** It doesn't matter, as long as it is loud enough to make him stop.

    Then either pick him up or run enthusiastically towards your door, calling him to the chosen place and wait until he has finished what he started indoors. Only use the ACK! sound if you actually catch him MID-ACT.

8. **No punishment, no scolding, no smacking or rubbing his nose in it.** Your Springer will hate it. He will become either more stubborn or afraid to do the business in your presence, so may start going secretly behind the couch or under the bed.

    Accidents will happen. He is a baby with a tiny bladder and bowels and little self-control. Housetraining takes time - remain calm, ignore him (unless you catch him in the act) and clean up the mess.

FACT English Springer Spaniels have a highly developed sense of smell. If there's an "accident" indoors, use a special spray from your vet or a hot washing powder solution to completely eliminate the smell, which will discourage him from going there again.

9. **Look for the signs.** These may be:
    a. Whining
    b. Sniffing the floor in a determined manner
    c. Circling and looking for a place to go
    d. Walking uncomfortably - particularly at the rear end!

    Take him outside straight away, and try not to pick him up all the time. He has to learn to walk to the door himself when he needs to go outside.

10. **Use a crate at night-time.**

Springers love being with you and young puppies certainly won't pee or poop outside on their own when it's pouring down. One breeder advises new owners to invest in a good umbrella and be prepared for lots of early mornings in the first few weeks!

Troubleshooting

Don't let one or two little accidents derail your potty training - accidents WILL happen! Here is a list of some possible scenarios and action to take:

- **Puppy peed when your back was turned** - Don't let him out of his crate or living space unless you are prepared to watch his every move
- **Puppy peed or pooped in the crate** - Make sure the crate isn't too big; it should be just enough for him to stand up and turn around, or divided. Also, make sure he is not left in the crate for too long
- **Puppy pooped without warning** - Observe what he does immediately beforehand. That way, you'll be able to scoop him up and take him outside next time before an accident happens
- **Puppy pees on the same indoor spot daily** - Make sure you get rid of the smell completely and don't give your puppy too much indoor freedom too soon. Some breeders use *"tethering"* where the puppy is fastened to them on a lead indoors. That way they can watch the puppy like a hawk and monitor his behaviour. They only do this for a short time - a week or so - but it can speed up housetraining no end
- **Puppy not responding well** - Increase the value of your treats for housetraining and nothing else. Give a tiny piece of meat, chicken etc. ONLY when your English Springer Spaniel eliminates outdoors in the chosen spot.

Even after all your hard work, occasionally some dogs continue to eliminate indoors, often males, even though they understand housetraining perfectly well. This is called "marking" and they do it to leave a scent and establish your home as their territory. This can take time to cure - although neutering generally reduces the urge to mark indoors.

Apartment Living

English Springer Spaniels are not generally regarded as apartment dogs, but if you do live in an apartment, access to outdoors is often not so easy and you may wish to indoor housetrain.

Most dogs can be indoor housetrained fairly easily, especially if you start early. Stick to the same principles already outlined, the only difference is that you will be placing your Springer on puppy pads or newspaper instead of taking him outdoors.

Start by blocking off a section of the apartment for your pup. Use a baby gate or make your own barrier. You will be able to keep a better eye on him than if he has free run of the whole place, and it will be easier to monitor his "accidents."

Select a corner away from his eating and sleeping area that will become his permanent bathroom area – a carpeted area is to be avoided if at all possible.

At first, cover a larger area than is actually needed - about 3x3 or 4x4 feet - with puppy pads or newspapers and gradually reduce the area as training progresses. Take your puppy there as indicated in the **Housetraining Tips** section.

Praise him enthusiastically when he eliminates on the puppy pad or newspaper. If you catch him doing his business out of the toilet area, pick him up and take him back there. Correct with a firm voice - never a hand. With positive reinforcement and close monitoring, he will learn to walk to the toilet area on his own.

Owners attempting indoor housetraining should be aware that it does generally take longer than outdoor training. Some dogs will resist. Also, once a dog learns to go indoors, it can be difficult to train them to go outdoors on their walks. If you don't monitor your puppy carefully enough in the beginning, indoor housetraining will be difficult. The first week or two is crucial to your puppy learning what is expected of him.

Bell Training

Bell Training is a method that works well with some dogs. There are different types of bells, the simplest are inexpensive and widely available, consisting of a series of adjustable bells that hang on a nylon strap from the door handle.

Another option is a small metal bell attached to a metal hanger that fixes low down on the wall next to the door with two screws. As with all puppy training, do bell training in short bursts of five to 10 minutes or your easily-distracted little student will switch off!

1. Show your dog the bell, either on the floor, before it is fixed anywhere or by holding it up. Point to it and give the command *"Touch," "Ring,"* or whatever word you decide.

2. Every time he touches it with his nose, reward with praise.

3. When he rings the bell with his nose, give him a treat. You can rub on something tasty, like peanut butter, to make it more interesting.

4. Take the bell away between practice sessions.

5. Once he rings the bell every time you show it to him, move on to the next step.

6. Take the bell to the door you use for housetraining. Place a treat just outside the door while he is watching. Then close the door, point to the bell and give the command.

7. When he rings the bell, open the door and let him get the treat outside.

8. When he rings the bell as soon as you place a treat outside, fix the bell to the door or wall.

9. The next time you think he needs to relieve himself, walk to the door, point to the bell and give the command. Give him a treat or praise if he rings it, let him out immediately and reward him again with enthusiastic praise when he performs his duty.

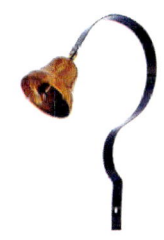

Tip In between training sessions, ring the bell yourself EVERY time you open the door to let him outside.

Some dogs can get carried away by their own success and ring the bell any time they want your attention, fancy a wander outdoors or see a passing squirrel!

Make sure that you ring the bell every time your puppy goes out through the door to relieve himself, but DON'T ring the bell if he is going out to play. And if he starts playing or dawdling around the garden or yard, bring him in!

Breeders on Crates and Housetraining

Lisa Cardy says: "My puppies are used to a crate when they go to their new homes as I put them in a crate to sleep at night. It's important that puppy is happy to be crated when the household is too busy to watch the pup or there are too many people around.

"Also, at night it is important for the safety of puppy while still in the chewing stage. I don't crate them once I can trust they won't chew the kitchen and are housetrained! Generally, they don't need a crate after eight or nine months, but some dogs like it as a bed.

"I recommend putting puppy in its own cage in a quiet place downstairs from night one. It will cry at first, but must get used to sleeping on its own - dogs need boundaries and to know their place in a household to feel secure.

"You might need to take the puppy out in the middle of the night, but if puppy is trained to use the crate, it should last from late evening, about 11pm, until 6am to 7am."

Photo of this CallisWold puppy courtesy of Lisa.

Lynne Lucas, who breeds field (working-type Springers): "I advise owners to crate my pups. They have been crated since birth, although never shut in unless I am cleaning; they regard it as their safe space.

"I advise families with children that a pup needs its rest and that having a crate gives pup their self-contained space. A tired pup is a grumpy and sometimes spiteful pup - no different to children!

"Start as you mean to go on; put the crate in a room where they cannot come to any harm. If you intend to crate your pup during the day, then they should not be shut in for any length of time. Gradually build it up, but never for more than two to three hours whilst you are out.

"Have a bedtime and stick to it - don't go to them at night, if they cry it won't last. As long as they can access paper for toileting, they will settle after a few nights - I do not advocate getting up in the night. Some owners have a larger crate and have one end for toileting and the other for sleeping if they are concerned about leaving the crate open.

"Put paper down, let pup out before bed and make sure that they toilet, and for the first few weeks let them out again early morning. I usually estimate about six weeks from arrival home to toilet train a pup both during the day and overnight. But a new owner must persevere in all weathers - don't just put pup outside and expect them to toilet on their own.

"Springers love company and in a cold wet garden in the middle of winter, they will not toilet at first on their own. I use the command 'Tinkles' and 'Go Poo' for my pups from when they first venture outside on the patio to toilet at about five weeks.

"A new owner must stay outside until they have been and then treat immediately with great exuberance. If you bring pup back in before they have been, they will without a doubt go on the floor; this is one of the hardest lessons to teach, but perseverance is the key.

"Some of my adult girls do still sleep in a very large crate together overnight, but the door is always open. This is their safe place and where they go if they want a little peace during the day. I don't have an age limit.

"Stella is the only one who doesn't sleep with the others as she can get very nervous of noise and has previously 'wrecked the joint!' so she is in the house at night, but will use the crate during the day. The crate is situated in a large walk-in cupboard at the side of the house and is heated in the winter."

Chris Brandon-Lodge added: "I use crates for puppies. They are helpful to give them a place of their own, but Springers should NEVER be left in there for long periods once adult."

Submissive Urination

This is an instinctual, physical response that can affect some young Spaniels. These dogs are often, but by no means always, naturally timid in nature. They may also be fearful of loud noises, new people and new situations.

Submissive urination typically happens when a dog feels excited, shy, anxious, or scared. Dogs are pack animals and young dogs may urinate when they meet other dogs to acknowledge dominance.

They may also display other submissive signs, such as flattening their ears back, tucking their tails under, cowering, avoiding eye contact, or even giving a *'submissive grin;'* pulling the lips right back (the lips are pulled further back here than when baring the teeth in an aggressive gesture).

Human contact submissive urination occurs when dogs are either so excited to see their owner or other people that they lose bladder control, or when they expect their submissive behaviour to stop perceived threats from humans. Well-meaning humans then make a fuss of the dog.

Unfortunately, the dog sees this as a reward for what they are doing – i.e. peeing as a greeting or to reduce a threat, and this reinforces the behaviour.

Submissive urination is NOT a housetraining issue, it is a reaction to a perceived situation. To stop it, you have to stop "rewarding" the dog for this behaviour.

Under no circumstances must you punish a Springer for doing it; it will only make your dog more anxious and the behaviour more entrenched.

With patience and tolerance from their owners, most puppies grow out of it. The best way of dealing with it is to ignore your dog when you arrive home – get your guests to do the same. Take off your coat, do a small job and only acknowledge the dog after a couple of minutes. You are trying to dial down the dog's emotions and keep arrivals low key

Tip: When you do greet him, let your dog approach you, not the other way round. Don't bend over him, this is a dominant gesture - get down to his level to pat and praise him. Avert your eyes; holding eye contact is seen as issuing a challenge by dogs.

If you have an anxious Springer, you need to put extra time and effort into socialisation, gradually helping your nervous little bundle to become more confident. **Again, always set your dog up to succeed; never overwhelm him or expose him to a frightening situation.**

Other reasons for peeing indoors when housetrained include a urinary tract infection, "marking," or an older dog losing continence or forgetting housetraining.

7. Feeding a Springer

Providing the right nutritional fuel helps keep your dog's biological machine in excellent working order. And while it is important for all breeds to have a healthy diet, it is especially important for English Springer Spaniels, because:

1. They are active, high-energy dogs that need the right fuel.
2. Good nutrition can have a beneficial effect on joints and other potential health issues.
3. They can become overweight if they get too many calories.
4. The right food can help reduce or eliminate food sensitivities and skin issues.

The topic of feeding can be a minefield; owners are bombarded with advertisements and numerous choices. There is not one food that gives every single dog the strongest bones, the most energy, the best coat, the easiest digestion, the least gas and the longest life.

The question is: *"Which food is best for MY Springer?"* Fortunately, most Springers do well on all types of diet and food only becomes an issue if:

- You are feeding too much, or
- Your dog has an upset stomach or itchy skin due to food

We don't recommend one brand or type of food over another, but we do have lots of tips to help you decide what's best for your Springer.

Feeding Puppies

Spaniel puppies should stay with the litter until at least eight weeks old to give the mother enough time to teach her offspring important rules about life.

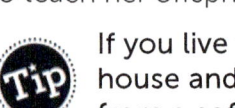

Tip: If you live far away from the breeder, fill a large container with water from the breeder's house and mix it with your own water back home. Different types of water, e.g. moving from a soft to a hard water area or vice versa, can upset a sensitive pup's stomach.

Initially, pups get all their nutrients from their mother's milk and then are gradually weaned (put on to a different food by the breeder) from three or four weeks of age. Unless the puppy has had an extremely varied diet at the breeder's, continue feeding the same puppy food and at the same times as the breeder when you bring your puppy home.

It is always a good idea to find out what the breeder feeds, as she knows what her bloodlines do well on.

If you decide to switch foods, do so gradually, as dogs' digestive systems cannot handle sudden changes of diet. (By the way, if you stick to the identical brand, you can change flavours in one go). These ratios are recommended by Doctors Foster & Smith Inc:

- Days 1-3 add 25% of the new food
- Days 4-6 add 50%

- Days 7-9 add 75%
- Day 10 feed 100% of the new food

If at any time your puppy starts being sick, has loose stools or is constipated, slow the rate at which you are switching the food. Puppies soon dehydrate, so seek veterinary advice if vomiting or loose or watery poop continues for more than a day.

Some breeders purposely feed their pups lots of different foods over the first few weeks of life to reduce the risk of them developing sensitive stomachs or becoming fussy eaters — although most Springers tend to be rather greedy!

As a general rule of thumb, feed Springer puppies:

- Four meals a day up to the age of 18 weeks
- Three meals a day at regular intervals from 18 weeks to 9 months
- Two meals a day from 9 to 18 months

You can then put your dog on one meal a day, although many vets now recommend feeding adult dogs two meals a day at the same times, one in the morning and one at tea time.

English Springer Spaniels are medium-sized dogs with relatively fast metabolisms, so twice a day suits them. It also reduces the risk of Bloat.

During the first six months, puppies grow quickly and it is important that they grow at **a controlled rate.**

NOTE: Giving your puppy more or less food will not affect his adult size, it will only affect his weight and rate of growth.

Regardless of what you may have read, do NOT let your puppy free feed - i.e. eat as much as he wants. It's very important during the first weeks and months that body weight is monitored.

FACT English Springer Spaniel puppies should look well-covered, not fat. Overfeeding leads to excess weight, which makes them vulnerable to health issues in later life.

There are three **Life Stages** to consider when feeding: **Puppy, Adult and Senior**, also called **Veteran.**

Some manufacturers also produce a **Junior** feed for adolescent dogs. If you decide on a commercially-prepared food, choose one approved either for **Puppies** or for **All Life Stages**.

An **Adult** feed won't have enough protein, and the balance of calcium and other nutrients will not be right for a pup. Puppy food is very high in calories and nutritional supplements. Look at switching to an **Adult** food when your pup is around 10 to 14 months old.

NOTE: Feeding elderly dogs is covered in **Chapter 17. Caring for Older Springers.**

Reading Dog Food Labels

A NASA scientist would have a hard job understanding some manufacturers' labels, so it's no easy task for us lowly dog owners. Here are some things to look out for on the manufacturers' labels:

- **The ingredients are listed by weight and the top one should always be the main content,** such as chicken or lamb. Don't pick one where grain is the first ingredient; it is a poor-quality feed. If your English Springer Spaniel has a food allergy or intolerance to wheat, check whether a food is gluten free; all wheat contains gluten

- **Chicken meal (dehydrated chicken) has more protein than fresh chicken, which is 80% water.** The same goes for beef, fish and lamb. So, if any of these "meals" are No. 1 on the ingredient list, the food should contain enough protein

> **Ingredients:**
> Deboned Chicken, Chicken Meal, Turkey Meal, Potatoes, Peas, Tomato Pomace, Dried Ground Potatoes, Ground Flaxseed, Chicken Fat (preserved with Mixed Tocopherols), Natural Chicken Flavor, Pea Fiber, Potassium Chloride, Spinach, Broccoli, Vitamin E Supplement, Carrots, Parsley, Apples, Blueberries, Kale, Sweet Potatoes, Taurine, L-Carnitine, Mixed Tocopherols added to preserve freshness, Zinc Proteinate, Glucosamine Hydrochloride, Chondroitin Sulfate, Zinc Sulfate, Calcium Carbonate, Niacin, Ferrous Sulfate. ✓

> **Ingredients:**
> Ground Yellow Corn, Chicken By-Product Meal, Corn Gluten Meal, Whole Wheat Flour, Animal Fat (preserved with Mixed-Tocopherols (form of Vitamin E), Rice Flour, Chicken, Soy Flour, Water, Propylene Glycol, Tricalcium Phosphate, Salt, Phosphoric Acid, Animal Digest, Calcium Phosphate, Potassium Chloride, Sorbic Acid (a Preservative), Dried Carrots, Dried Tomatoes, Avocado, Calcium Propionate (a Preservative), Choline Chloride, L-Lysine Monohydrochloride, Added Color (Yellow 5, Red, 40, Blue 2, Yellow 6), Vitamin E ✗

- Anything labelled *"human-grade"* is higher quality than normal dog food ingredients. E.g. human-grade chicken includes the breast, thighs and other parts of the chicken suitable for human consumption. Human-grade chicken complies with United States Department of Agriculture (USDA) welfare standards

- A certain amount of flavouring can make a food more appetising for your dog. **Choose a food with a specific flavouring,** like *"beef flavouring"* rather than a general *"meat flavouring,"* where the origins are not so clear

- **Find a food suitable for the breed and your dog's age and activity level.** Talk to your breeder or vet, or visit an online English Springer Spaniel forum to ask other owners' advice

- **Natural is best.** Food labelled *'natural'* means that the ingredients have not been chemically altered, according to the FDA in the USA. However, there are no such guidelines governing foods labelled *"holistic"* – so check ingredients and how they have been prepared

- In the USA, dog food that meets American Feed Control Officials' (AAFCO) minimum nutrition requirements has a label that states: *"[food name] is formulated to meet the nutritional levels established by the AAFCO Dog Food Nutrient Profiles for [life stage(s)]"*

Tip: If you live in the USA, we recommend looking for a food *"as fed"* to real pets in an AAFCO-defined feeding trial. The AAFCO label is the gold standard, and brands that do costly feeding trials indicate so on the package.

Dog food labelled *'supplemental'* isn't complete and balanced. Unless you have a specific, vet-approved need for it, it's not something you want to feed your dog long term. The **Guaranteed Analysis** listed on a sack or tin legally guarantees:

- Minimum percentages of crude protein and crude fat, and
- Maximum percentages of crude fibre and moisture

GUARANTEED ANALYSIS	
Crude protein (min.)	28.00 %
Crude fat (min.)	12.00 %
Crude fiber (max.)	4.50 %
Moisture (max.)	11.00 %
Docosahexaenoic acid (DHA) (min.)	0.05 %
Calcium (min.)	1.20 %
Phosphorus (min.)	1.00 %
Omega-6 fatty acids* (min.)	2.20 %
Omega-3 fatty acids* (min.)	0.30 %
Glucosamine* (min.)	500 mg/kg
Chondroitin sulfate* (min.)	500 mg/kg

* Not recognized as an essential nutrient by the AAFCO Dog Food Nutrient Profiles.

While it is a start, don't rely on it too much. One pet food manufacturer made a mock product with a guaranteed analysis of 10% protein, 6.5% fat, 2.4% fibre, and 68% moisture (similar to what's on some canned pet food labels) – the ingredients were old leather boots, used motor oil, crushed coal and water!

- **Protein** – found in meat and poultry, protein should be the first ingredient and is very important. It helps build muscle, repair tissue and contributes to healthy hair and skin. According to AAFCO, a growing puppy requires a diet with minimum 22% **protein,** while an adult requires 18% minimum

- **Fats** – these are a concentrated form of energy that give your dog more than twice the amount of energy that carbohydrates and proteins do. Common fats include chicken or pork fat, cottonseed oil, vegetable oil, soybean oil, fish oil, safflower oil, and many more. They are highly digestible and are the first nutrients to be used by the body as energy. AAFCO recommends minimum 8% fat for puppies and 5% for adults

- **Fibre** – found in vegetables and grains. It aids digestion and helps prevent anal glands from becoming impacted. The average dry dog food has 2.5%-4.5% crude fibre, but reduced calorie feeds may be as high as 9%-10%

- **Carbohydrates** typically make up anywhere from 30%-70% of a dry dog food. They come mainly from plants and grains, and provide energy in the form of sugars

- **Vitamins and Minerals** – have a similar effect on dogs as humans. Glucosamine and chondroitin are good for joints

- **Omegas 3 and 6** – fatty acids that help keep English Springer Spaniels' skin and coat healthy. Also good for inflammation control, arthritic pain, heart and kidneys

Well-formulated dog foods have the right balance of protein, fat, carbohydrates, vitamins, minerals and fatty acids. If you're still not sure what to choose for your English Springer Spaniel, check out these websites:

www.dogfoodadvisor.com run by Mike Sagman in the USA, and

www.allaboutdogfood.co.uk run by UK canine nutritionist David Jackson.

How Much Food?

Keeping your Springer at a healthy weight can be a challenge. You may have a highly-strung bundle of energy who is a fussy eater, making it hard to put the weight on. Or, more likely, a ravenous Springer who'd eat the entire contents of the kitchen given half a chance - or one in between.

Maintaining a healthy body weight is all about balancing calories taken in with calories burned. If a dog is exercised several times a day or taking part in a physical activity, he'll need more calories than a less active or older dog. There are many factors governing weight:

- Breed
- Gender
- Age
- Natural energy levels
- Temperament
- Metabolism
- Amount of daily exercise
- Health
- Environment
- Number of dogs in the house or kennel
- Quality of the food
- Whether your English Springer Spaniel is working, competing or simply a pet

Photo: Stella (Traxlerstarr Estella), aged six months, is full of beans – although not literally! Photo courtesy of Lynne Lucas, Traxlerstarr Spaniels, Surrey, England.

English Springer Spaniels are active dogs, but energy levels vary from one dog to the next. Dogs that have been spayed may be more likely to put on weight. Certain health conditions, e.g. underactive thyroid, diabetes, arthritis or heart disease, can lead to dogs putting on weight.

And just like us, a dog kept in a very cold environment will need more calories to keep warm than a dog in a warm climate, as extra calories are burned to keep warm.

FACT An English Springer Spaniel kept on his own is more likely to be overweight than one kept with other dogs, as he receives all of the food-based attention.

Manufacturers of cheap foods may recommend feeding more than necessary as a major ingredient is cereal, which doesn't add much in terms of nutrition, but increases the weight of the food – and possibly triggers allergies.

If you're having trouble getting your Springer to put on weight, speak to your vet or breeder. If you feed a complete feed, feed the amount for the **ideal adult weight**, not for the weight they are now. Type "**Belpatt English Springer Spaniel Weight**" into a search engine to get a rough idea of what your Springer should weigh as he or she grows. Bear in mind that puppies tend to grow in spurts, so anything 10% either side of the ideal weight is acceptable for young dogs.

Tip There is also an excellent leaflet that clearly explains each component of a dog's diet and how much to feed your dog based on weight and activity level. Search for *"National Academies Your Dog's Nutritional Needs"* online.

Feeding Options

We are what we eat. The right food is a very important part of a healthy lifestyle for dogs as well as humans. Here are the main options explained:

Dry dog food – or kibble, is a popular and relatively inexpensive way of providing a balanced diet. Millions of dogs thrive on kibble. It comes in a variety of flavours and with differing ingredients to suit the different stages of a dog's life. Quality has improved over the years, but cheap kibble is still false economy.

Canned food - dogs love the taste and it generally comes in a variety of flavours. Some owners feed kibble mixed with some canned food. These days there are hundreds of options, some are high quality made from natural, organic ingredients with herbs.

Read the label closely, the origins of cheap canned food can be somewhat dubious. Some dogs can suffer from stomach upsets with too much soft food. Avoid fillers and preservatives and brands with lots of grain, or recalls.

Semi-Moist - this food typically has a water content of around 60%-65%, compared to 10% in dry food, making it easier to digest. It also has more sugar and salt, so not suitable for all dogs.

Semi-moist treats are shaped like pork chops, bacon *(pictured)*, salamis, burgers, etc. They are the least nutritional of all dog foods, full of sugars, artificial flavourings and colourings, so avoid giving them regularly.

Home-Cooked - some owners want the ability to be in complete control of their dog's diet. Feeding a home-cooked diet can be time-consuming and expensive. The difficult thing (as with the raw diet) is sticking to it once you have started out with the best of intentions, but your dog will love it and he won't be eating preservatives or fillers. Some high-end dog food companies now provide boxes of freshly-prepared meals with natural ingredients.

Dehydrated - this dried food *(pictured)* is becoming increasingly popular. It looks similar to kibble, but is only minimally processed. It offers many of the benefits of raw feeding, including lots of nutrients, but with none of the mess or bacteria.

Gentle heating slowly cooks proteins and helps start the digestive process, making it easier on the digestive tract of older Spaniels, or those with sensitive stomachs. Owners just add water and let it stand for a minute or two to reconstitute the meal.

Freeze-Dried - this is usually raw, fresh food that has been freeze-dried by frozen food manufacturers. It's a more convenient, hygienic and less messy option than raw, and handy if you're going on a trip. It contains healthy enzymes but no preservatives, is highly palatable and keeps for six months to a year. It says *"freeze-dried"* on the packet, but the process bumps up the cost. A good option for owners who can afford it.

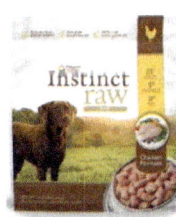

The Raw Diet

Opinions are divided on a raw diet. There is anecdotal evidence that some dogs thrive on it, particularly those with food intolerances or allergies, although scientific proof is lagging behind. Claims made by fans of the raw diet include:

- Reduced symptoms of - or less likelihood of - allergies, and less scratching
- Better skin and coats

- Easier weight management
- Improved digestion
- Less doggie odour and flatulence
- Higher energy levels
- Reduced risk of Bloat
- Helps fussy eaters
- Fresher breath and improved dental health
- Drier and less smelly stools, more like pellets
- Overall improvement in general health and less disease
- Most dogs love a raw diet

If your English Springer Spaniel is not doing well on a dry dog food or has skin issues, you might consider a raw diet. Some commercial dog foods contain artificial preservatives, grains and excessive protein and fillers – causing a reaction in some dogs. Dry, canned and other styles of processed food were mainly created as a means of convenience – for humans, not dogs!

Some nutritionists believe there are inherent beneficial enzymes, vitamins, minerals and other qualities in meats, fruits, vegetables and grains in their natural, uncooked state. However, critics of a raw diet say that the risks of nutritional imbalance, intestinal problems and food-borne illnesses caused by handling and feeding raw meat outweigh any benefits.

It is true that owners must pay strict attention to hygiene when preparing a raw diet and it may not be a suitable option if you have small children. The dog may also be more likely to ingest bacteria or parasites such as Salmonella, E. Coli and Ecchinococcus - although freeze-dried meals reduce the risk. If you do switch your dog over to raw feeding, do so over a period of at least a week.

FACT Raw is not for every dog; it can cause loose stools, upset stomach and even vomiting in some, and there are other dogs who simply don't like the taste.

There are two main types of raw diet, one involves feeding raw, meaty bones *(pictured above)* and the other is known as the BARF diet (Biologically Appropriate Raw Food or Bones And Raw Food), created by Dr Ian Billinghurst.

Raw Meaty Bones

- Raw meaty bones or carcasses form the bulk of the diet. **Cooked bones should NOT be fed, as they can splinter**
- Table scraps both cooked and raw, such as vegetables
- Australian veterinarian Dr Tom Lonsdale is a leading proponent of the raw meaty bones diet. He believes the following foods are suitable:
- Chicken and turkey carcasses, after the meat has been removed for human consumption
- Poultry by-products, e.g. heads, feet, necks and wings
- Whole fish and fish heads
- Sheep, calf, goat, and deer carcasses sawn into big pieces of meat and bone
- Pigs' trotters and heads, sheep heads, brisket, tail and rib bones
- A certain amount of offal can be included in the diet, e.g. liver, lungs, trachea, hearts, tripe

- Table scraps and some fruit and vegetable peelings, but should not make up more than one-third of the diet

Low-fat game animals, fish and poultry are the best source of food. If you feed meat from farm animals (cattle, sheep and pigs), avoid excessive fat and bones too large to be eaten. It depends on price and what's available locally - start with your local butcher or farm shop.

FACT Dogs are more likely to break their teeth eating large knuckle bones and bones sawn lengthwise than when eating meat and bone together.

You'll also need to think about WHERE and WHEN you are going to feed. A dog takes some time to eat a raw bone and will push it around the floor, so the kitchen may not be the most hygienic place. Outside is one option, but what do you do when it's raining? If you live in a hot climate, evening feeding may be best to avoid flies. Establishing the right quantity is based on your dog's activity levels, appetite and body condition. A very general guide of raw meaty bones for the average dog is:

15%-20% of body weight per week, or 2%-3% a day.

Dr Lonsdale says: "Wherever possible, feed the meat and bone ration in one large piece requiring much ripping, tearing and gnawing. This makes for contented pets with clean teeth." More information is available from www.rawmeatybones.com

NOTES: Pregnant or lactating females and growing puppies need more food. This diet may not be suitable for old dogs used to a processed diet or those with dental issues, or in households with children, due to the risk of bacterial infection from raw meat.

Monitor your dog while he eats, especially in the beginning. Don't feed bones with sharp points, and remove any bone before it becomes small enough to swallow.

Raw meaty bones should be kept separate from human food and any surface the uncooked meat or bones have touched should be thoroughly cleaned afterwards.

Tip Puppies can and do eat diets of raw meaty bones, but consult your breeder or vet before embarking on raw with a young dog.

The BARF diet - A variation of the raw meaty bones diet. A typical BARF diet is made up of 60%-75% of raw meaty bones - with about 50% meat, such as chicken neck, back and wings - and 25%-40% of fruit and vegetables, offal, meat, eggs or dairy foods. There is lots of information on the BARF diet online.

Springer Feeding Tips

1. If you choose a manufactured food, pick one where meat or poultry (or meat or poultry meal) is the <u>first</u> item listed. Many dogs do not do well on cheap cereals or sugar, so choose a high quality one.

2. If a Springer has sensitive skin, "hot spots" or allergies, a cheap food bulked up with grain will only make this worse. A dry food described as *"hypoallergenic"* on the sack means *"less likely to cause allergies."*

3. Consider feeding a probiotic - such as a spoonful of natural, live yoghurt - to each meal to help maintain healthy gut bacteria.

4. Feed your adults twice a day, rather than once. Smaller feeds are easier to digest, and reduce the risk of Bloat as well as gas.

5. Establish a feeding regime and stick to it. Dogs like routine. Stick to the same times, morning and tea-time. Feeding too late won't give your dog's body time to process the food before bed. Feeding at the same times also helps your dog establish a toilet regime.

6. Take away uneaten food between meals. Most Springers love their food, but any dog can become fussy if food is constantly available. Remove the bowl after half an hour – even if there is some left. A healthy, hungry dog will look forward to the next meal. If he's off his food for a couple of days or more, it could be a sign of illness.

7. Feeding time is a great training opportunity - particularly for the commands **SIT** and **STAY** and the release.

8. Use stainless steel or ceramic bowls. Plastic bowls don't last as long and can trigger an allergic reaction around the muzzle in some sensitive dogs. Consider using a **spaniel bowl, pictured.** This is an elevated bowl with a narrow top to keep your Springer's ears out of their food and water.

9. Use apple or carrot slices, or other healthy alternatives, as training treats for puppies.

10. If you feed dried animal product treats, check the country of origin. Some use toxic chemicals that can damage kidneys. Dried jerky-type treats can be very good for teeth, but read the labels carefully.

11. Don't feed too many tidbits or treats between meals as they throw a balanced diet out of the window and cause obesity. Feed leftovers in the bowl as part of a meal, rather than from the table, as this encourages attention-seeking behaviour, begging and drooling.

12. Don't feed cooked bones, as these can splinter and cause choking or intestinal problems. And avoid rawhide, as a dog can gulp it without chewing, causing an internal blockage.

13. Obesity leads to all sorts of health issues, such as joint problems, diabetes, high blood pressure and organ disease. Your Spaniel's tummy should be higher than his rib cage - if his belly is level or hangs down below it, reduce his food.

14. Check your dog's faeces (aka stools, poo or poop)! If the diet is suitable, the food should be easily digested and produce dark brown, firm stools. If your dog is producing light or sloppy poo or lots of gas, his diet may well need changing. Consult your vet or breeder for advice.

15. These are poisonous to dogs: grapes, raisins, chocolate, onions, Macadamia nuts, any fruits with seeds or stones, tomatoes, avocados, rhubarb, tea, coffee, alcohol and Xylitol artificial sweetener.

16. And finally, always make sure that your dog has access to clean, fresh water.

Change the water and clean the bowl every day or so – it gets slimy!

17. If your dog is not responding well to a particular family member, get him or her to give the feeds.

....

Food Allergies

Dog food allergies are a reaction to food that involves the body's immune system and affect about one in 10 dogs. They are the third most common canine allergy after atopy (inhaled or contact allergies) and flea bite allergies.

Food allergies affect males and females in equal measure as well as neutered and intact pets. They can start when your dog is five months or 12 years old - although the vast majority start when the dog is between two and six years old. It is not uncommon for dogs with food allergies to also have other types of allergies. Here are some common symptoms of problems with food:

- Itchy skin - your dog may lick or chew his paws or legs and rub his face with his paws or on the furniture, carpet, etc.
- Excessive scratching
- Recurring ear or skin infections that clear up with antibiotics but recur when the antibiotics run out
- Hair loss
- Hot patches of skin – *"hot spots"*
- Redness and inflammation on the chin and face
- Increased bowel movements (maybe twice as often as usual)

The problem with food allergies is that the symptoms are similar to symptoms of other issues, such as environmental or flea bite allergies, intestinal problems, mange and yeast or bacterial infections.

There's also a difference between dog food **allergies** and dog food **intolerance**:

ALLERGIES = SKIN PROBLEMS AND/OR ITCHING

INTOLERANCE = DIARRHOEA AND/OR VOMITING

Dog food intolerance can be compared to people who get an upset stomach from eating spicy curries. Symptoms can be cured by changing to a milder diet.

With dogs, certain ingredients are more likely to cause a reaction than others. Unfortunately, these are also the most common ingredients in dog foods! In order of the most common triggers in dogs in general, they are:

Beef - Dairy Products - Chicken - Wheat - Eggs - Corn - Soya (Soy in the US)

Veterinarian Dr Samantha Goldberg told us: "Many meats are triggers. However, cooked meats may trigger differently than raw due to protein denaturing at cooking. Not all diets are equal!

"Always aim for the highest quality diet you can afford with a high meat content. Also look at the process of production - some can appear good in theory, but if they have been processed within an inch of their life, they won't have many nutrients left. Grains per se are not all "bad," but finely-milled grains tend to produce glucose spikes when digested. Rolled or whole grains are digested more slowly.

"The balance of Omega 3 and 6 oils can also be very important for health. Omega 6 can be good for the skin and Omega 3 for joints, but too much or an imbalance is not good."

Tip: A dog is allergic or sensitive to an <u>ingredient</u>, not to a particular brand, so it's important to read the label. If your Springer reacts to beef, for example, he'll react to any food containing beef, regardless of how expensive it is or how well it has been prepared.

AVOID corn, corn meal, corn gluten meal, artificial preservatives (BHA, BHT, Propyl Gallate, Ethoxyquin, Sodium Nitrite/Nitrate and TBHQBHA), artificial colours, sugars and sweeteners, e.g. corn syrup, sucrose and ammoniated glycyrrhizin, powdered cellulose, propylene glycol.

Food Trials

The only way to completely cure a food allergy or intolerance is complete avoidance, which is not as easy as it sounds. First you have to determine your dog DOES have an allergy to food - and not pollen, grass, etc. - and then you have to discover WHICH food is causing the reaction.

A **food trial or exclusion diet** involves feeding one specific food for 12 weeks, something the dog has never eaten before.

Before you embark on one, know that they are a real pain-in-the-you-know-what! You have to be incredibly vigilant and determined, so only start one if you are prepared to see it through to the end or you are wasting your time.

The chosen food must be the **only thing** eaten during the trial. During the trial, your dog shouldn't roam freely, as you can't control what he is eating or drinking when out of sight.
Don't give:

- Treats
- Rawhide (not recommended anyway)
- Pigs' ears
- Cows' hooves
- Flavoured medications (including heartworm treatments) or supplements
- Flavoured toothpastes
- Flavoured plastic toys

A more practical, less scientific approach is to eliminate ingredients one at a time by switching diets over a period of a week or so.

If you switch to home-cooked or raw, you know exactly what your dog is eating; if you choose a commercial food, a hypoallergenic one is a good place to start.

They all have the word *"hypoallergenic"* in the name and do not include wheat protein or soya. They are often based around less common ingredients.

Grain Intolerance

Although beef is the food most likely to cause allergies in the general dog population, there is plenty of anecdotal evidence to suggest that GRAIN can also be a problem. *"Grain"* is wheat or any other cultivated cereal crop. Some dogs also react to starch, which is found in grains and potatoes, as well as bread, pasta, rice, etc.

Dogs don't process grains as well as humans. Foods high in grains and sugar can cause increases in unhealthy bacteria and yeast in the stomach, which crowds out the good bacteria and allows toxins to affect the immune system. They also cause lots of GAS!

The itchiness related to food allergies can then cause secondary bacterial and yeast infections, which may show as hot spots, ear or bladder infections, excessive shedding, reddish or dark brown tear stains. You may also notice a musty smell.

FACT ❯ Drugs like antihistamines and steroids will help temporarily, but they do not address the root cause.

Before you automatically switch to a grain-free diet, in a recent study by University of California, Davis, vets found a link between a form of heart disease called **taurine-deficient dilated cardiomyopathy** and some popular grain-free dog foods where legumes (e.g. beans, lentil, peas, soy) or potatoes were the main ingredients.

Lead author Joshua Stern said that while many owners may not want to see *"by products"* listed in their dog's food, they often contain organ meat like heart and kidney, which are good sources of taurine.

Some food allergy symptoms - particularly the scratching, licking, chewing and redness - can also be a sign of environmental allergies or flea bites. See **Chapter 13. Skin and Allergies** for more details.

★ If you've switched diet to little effect, it's time to see a vet. Many vets promote specific dog food brands, which may or may not be the best option for your English Springer Spaniel. Do your own research.

Bloat

Bloat occurs when there is too much gas in the stomach. It is known by several different names: **twisted stomach, gastric torsion** or **Gastric Dilatation-Volvulus (GDV)** and occurs mainly in larger breeds with deep chests, such as the Dobermann. Although it is not common in English Springer Spaniels, individual dogs have been known to get it.

Bloat is statistically more common in males than in females and in dogs over seven years old.

As the stomach swells with gas, it can rotate 90° to 360°. The twisting stomach traps air, food and water inside and the bloated organ stops blood flowing properly to veins in the abdomen, leading to low blood pressure, shock and even damage to internal organs.

The causes are not fully understood, but there are some well-known risk factors. One is the dog taking in a lot of air while eating - either because he is greedy and gulping the food too fast, or stressed, e.g. in kennels where there might be food competition.

A dog that is fed once a day and gorges himself could be at higher risk, another reason why most owners feed twice a day. Exercising straight after eating or after a big drink also increases the risk - like colic in horses. Another potential cause is diet. Fermentable foodstuffs that produce a lot of gas can cause problems for the stomach if the gas is not burped or passed into the intestines. Symptoms are:

- Swollen belly
- Standing uncomfortably or hunched
- Restlessness, pacing or looking for a place to hide
- Rapid panting or difficulty breathing
- Dry retching, or excessive saliva or foam
- White or colourless gums
- Excessive drinking
- Licking the air
- General weakness or collapse

Tips to Avoid Canine Bloat:

- Some owners buy a frame for food bowls so they are at chest height for the dog, other experts believe dogs should be fed from the floor – do whichever slows your Springer down
- Avoid dog food with high fats or those using citric acid as a preservative, also avoid tiny pieces of kibble
- If your Springer is a guzzler, invest in an anti-gulp bowl **(pictured above)**
- Feed twice a day rather than once
- Don't let your dog drink too much water just before, during or after eating
- Stress can possibly be a trigger, with nervous and aggressive dogs being more susceptible. Maintain a peaceful environment, particularly around mealtimes
- Avoid vigorous exercise before or after eating, allow one hour either side of mealtimes before strenuous exercise

FACT Bloat can kill a dog in less than one hour. If you suspect your English Springer Spaniel has it, get them into the car and off to the vet IMMEDIATELY. Bloat is one of the leading killers of dogs after cancer.

Overweight English Springer Spaniels

Some Springers are obsessive about food - which is great for training, but not so good for maintaining a healthy weight. According to VCA (Veterinary Centers of America):

"In North America, obesity is the most common preventable disease in dogs. Approximately 25-30% of the general canine population is obese, with 40-45% of dogs aged 5-11 years old weighing in higher than normal."

You may think you are being kind to your beloved Spaniel by giving him extra treats and scraps, but the reality is that you are shortening his life.

The extra weight puts huge strain on his organs, often resulting in a reduced lifespan. It is far easier to regulate your dog's weight and keep it at a healthy level than to slim down a pleading Springer once he becomes overweight. Overweight dogs are susceptible to:

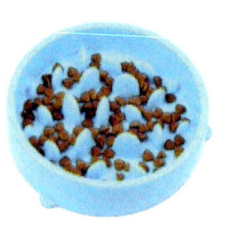

Joint disease – excessive body weight increases joint stress, which then tends to lead to a vicious circle of less exercise and weight gain, further reducing exercise.

Heart and lung problems – fatty deposits within the chest cavity and too much circulating fat contribute to cardio-respiratory and cardiovascular disease.

Diabetes – a major risk factor for overweight dogs.

Tumours – obesity increases the risk of mammary tumours in females. (Study: "Effects of Obesity and Obesity-Related Molecules on Canine Mammary Gland Tumors," by H-Y Lim et al).

Liver disease – fat degeneration can result in liver insufficiency.

Reduced lifespan - one of the most serious proven findings in obesity studies is that obesity in both humans and dogs reduces lifespan.

Most English Springer Spaniels are extremely loyal companions and very attached to their humans. They are a part of our family. However, beware of going too far.

FACT Studies show that dogs regarded as "family members" by the owner (anthropomorphosis) are at greater risk of becoming overweight. This is because attention given to the dog often results in food being given as well.

If you have to put your dog on a diet, be aware that a reduced amount of food will also mean reduced nutrients, so he may need a supplement during this time.

Don't despair if your English Springer Spaniel is overweight. Many problems associated with being overweight are reversible with weight loss.

Fussy Eaters

The English Springer Spaniel Health website says: "English Springer Spaniels are rarely fussy eaters and really do not mind being fed the same food each day. Don't fall into the trap of indulging your ESS by offering choice cuts, scraps at the table and special treats as an alternative to their diet.

"This may well cause the dog to turn its nose up at ordinary food, making it fussy because it has worked out that there is a possibility of something better on offer."

Should you find that your ESS is reluctant to eat what you are giving (or goes 'off' its food):

- Make sure that the diet you are offering is complete, balanced, digestible and with a high nutrient density
- Feed little and often, dividing the total daily intake into 3-4 meals
- Temperature can have a marked effect on palatability, and warming the food (in a microwave) can sometimes help considerably
- Include a little more fat in the diet (providing it does not upset the digestive process), as in addition to being a rich source of energy, it helps to increase the flavour of the food
- Always remove food that is not eaten after 30 minutes as fresh food is likely to prove more enticing
- Make sure there are no visible clinical signs of an underlying health problem (persistent diarrhoea, sickness, depression, temperature, excess drinking or urination)

"The amount you feed each mealtime is an individual calculation, but you should be guided by the manufacturer's instructions in relation to the age and activity levels of your ESS. You should aim for a dog to be well covered, but still retaining a shape (i.e. be able to feel its ribs and see its waistline).

"Please remember not to be over generous when feeding your ESS, as those appealing, pleading eyes might just tempt you to give more food than you should!"

Expert Opinion

No one diet is right for every dog. Here are views and advice from people with over 100 years of experience with Springers between them.

Chris Brandon-Lodge, Cottonstones English Springer Spaniels, Shropshire: "I feed my dogs mostly kibble and butcher's dog mince, which I cook.

"I've never had problems with fussy eaters, but that is because when you have several there is the competition factor. I know a couple who have one of my dogs and another Springer, and the second dog is never in a hurry to eat and will sometimes leave it to come back to later."

Pictured in the pink of condition are Chris's Millie (centre) and her two daughters, Teasel (left) and Tilly.

"It's difficult to overfeed a Spaniel puppy, but once they get towards a year it's very easy. They are essentially greedy dogs and there's nothing worse than seeing a fat Spaniel! So don't overdo it and be ready to reduce the food quantity if the weight is piling on - the hindquarters is where it shows."

Lynne Lucas, Traxlerstarr Spaniels, Surrey: "I feed all my girls raw. I feed raw chicken carcasses to them in the morning, apart from Calamity who now has to have Royal Canin AnAllergenic due to her allergies They have beef trachea, tripe sticks, lambs tails, marrow/beef rib or lamb ribs as treats sometimes.

"The evening meal is Natures Menu Freeflow chicken/beef/green tripe with blueberries, strawberries, mixed fresh veg, eggs, frozen sprats, lambs' hearts and other offal, salmon oil - not all each night. I mix and match with the mince, and vitamins and joint supplements each day. Calamity has the fruit and veg as well.

"I think that if you can feed raw, it is best. The girls have shiny coats and are full of life so I would never change. I wean my pups with a very high grade of wet and dry food from Scrumbles, this gives the owners the option of either carrying on with a very high grade of food or switching to raw.

"After being raw fed all her life, Calamity became intolerant to meat, eggs, fish and grain; in other words, everything she was fed. It took a while to pinpoint why she was poorly. She would go off her food, become very bloated and was in obvious pain in her stomach, but we could not work out why, I had a new vet who recommended a full allergy panel and she came back as intolerant to everything.

"She was switched to Royal Canin Anallergenic food along with raw veg and fruit and she is now back to her old self. Although when the others are having a lovely juicy bone, she has to make do with a carrot and cauliflower; she is not amused!

"My girls only become fussy when they are in season; they pick at their food and sometimes don't eat at all, I just leave it until they decide they are hungry. There are some Springers, I'm sure, that are fussy, but not many, as they love their food. If I had a fussy eater, I would not keep trying different foods as they will eat when they are hungry."

"If they decide to change the pup's food then do it gradually over about a week by adding new to existing at different percentages until the new food is the majority in the bowl. This helps the tummy issues which can happen with a straight changeover.

"Don't always go by the feeding advice on the food as each breed is different; if your pup is getting more exercise then it will need more food.

"I have not heard of any ESS with Bloat but you should never run your dog after a meal. I always make sure they have run beforehand and therefore they are hungry - it is very bad for any breed to run after a meal.

"I recommend that when my new owners take their pup home, they invest in an anti-gulp bowl to slow down their feeding as they can ingest too much air and this can cause stomach pains."

Lisa Cardy, CallisWold Springer Spaniels, North Yorkshire: "My dogs are fed on Skinners working food dry. I add wet food if I feel they need extra in the winter or need to put on some weight. I am not a fan of raw feeding as it makes it difficult if you need to kennel the dog for any reason and it's expensive and difficult to store.

"I haven't had a fussy eater, but it is similar to fussy children - if a dog is allowed to be a fussy eater, they will be! A dog won't starve themselves and sometimes they just aren't hungry - like people!

"I put food down and give them a reasonable amount of time to eat it but then pick it up if not eaten, I don't leave it down for them to graze. This would be my tip to new owners, and if you need to change food, do it gradually."

....

If your Springer is happy and healthy, has lots of energy and is interested in life, is not too fat and not too thin, doesn't scratch a lot and has dark brown, firm stools, then... CONGRATULATIONS, you've got it right!

8. Springer Traits

With an English Springer Spaniel you are getting a handsome, loveable and energetic companion who approaches life with optimism and bags of enthusiasm.

If you've decided to share your life with one, it helps to have an insight into what is going on in that active mind of his!

You have to learn what your Springer needs from you, and he has to learn what you expect from him, before the two of you can develop a beautiful relationship.

This chapter helps you to do just that - and to bring out the best in your Springer.

....

Just as with humans, a dog's personality is made up of a combination of temperament and character – or **Nature and Nurture.**

Temperament is the nature - or inherited characteristics - a dog is born with; it's the predisposition to act or react to the world around him. For example, the amount of natural working instinct your Springer has is dominated by genetics and varies from one dog to the next.

One bred from generations of flushing Spaniels will have lots of **drive**, whereas one bred from show Spaniels may be (but not always) content with not as much physical and mental exercise.

Good breeders not only produce puppies from physically healthy dams and sires, but they also consider temperament when choosing which dogs to breed.

Character is what develops through the dog's life and is formed by a combination of **temperament AND environment.**

How you treat your dog will have a huge effect on his personality and behaviour.

Start off on the right foot with your puppy by establishing the rules of the house and good routines, while making time to teach the all-important **Recall** while your dog is young and still wants to follow you.

Treat him well and make lots of time for socialisation, training and, as his body matures, exercise.

All dogs need different environments and experiences to keep them stimulated and well-balanced, and English Springer Spaniels enjoy activities that challenge their minds as well as their bodies.

Typical English Springer Spaniel

Every English Springer Spaniel is unique. While they share some characteristics, no two Springers are identical in looks or temperament. They all have their own special ways - it's part of their appeal.

However, to give you an idea of why yours acts like he does, here are some typical traits common within the breed:

- The English Springer Spaniel is considered a healthy and hardy dog
- Breeds from working backgrounds have greater physical and mental demands than other dogs, such as companion breeds, and Springers with a lot of natural drive are better suited to active households. They have been described as *"Cockers on steroids!"* and even if yours is a pet, he still has these instincts to some extent
- One thing that surprises many new owners is the amount of exercise some need; a couple of hours a day is not unusual, particularly for working-bred Springers. The good news is that they should be happy to chill out and snuggle up with their owners afterwards
- Springers are intelligent, busy dogs. They love to play both indoor and outdoor games and enjoy activities that challenge them - they can do well in Agility, Flyball and other competitions
- The Springer is usually happy to go for a walk whatever the weather
- They love playing in the snow and swimming - and usually swim well. They are generally hardy - active working dogs may be kept in outdoor kennels - and most cope well with cold conditions
- Springers have a very keen sense of smell and are happiest running off the lead (leash) with their noses to the ground. They are used as sniffer dogs by police and customs services
- With their trademark constantly wagging tail, they have a naturally upbeat temperament
- They are "biddable." Provided you put the time in, they are an easy breed to train - and can be trained to a high level in a number of different fields. Their intelligence and eagerness to please are powerful training aids
- The same goes for housetraining; a Springer can get the hang of it in a couple of weeks, provided you are vigilant in the beginning
- Some Springers can be quite sensitive and do not respond well to rough handling or heavy-handed training
- Treated well and properly socialised, a Springer generally gets on well with everybody and other dogs and often cats
- Having said that, some have a fairly strong sense of prey, so don't leave your pet rabbit lying around! And keep your dog on a lead around farm animals until he can be trusted not to chase them. You may never stop some Springers chasing rabbits, squirrels, birds, etc.
- They are usually good with children - provided they and the kids are well socialised and have been taught to show respect

- 🐾 Sometimes described as *"Velcro dogs,"* Springers are essentially pack animals. They may follow you from room to room - even the bathroom - and do not like being left alone for long. If you are away from the home a lot, consider another type of dog not so dependent on humans and activity for happiness. Springers can develop Separation Anxiety

- 🐾 They are fairly high maintenance when it comes to grooming, especially show-type Springers, which have longer, denser coats

- 🐾 Springers love mud, puddles and running through the undergrowth and so may not be the best choice for the extremely houseproud

- 🐾 An under-exercised, under-stimulated Springer will display poor behaviour, as any dog would

- 🐾 Springers are honest dogs, devoted to their owners and incredibly eager to please you; they will steal your heart. OK, that's not very scientific, but ask anyone who owns one!

Canine Emotions

As pet lovers, we are all too keen to ascribe human characteristics to our dogs; this is called **anthropomorphism** - "the attribution of human characteristics to anything other than a human being."

Most of us dog lovers are guilty of that, as we come to regard our pets as members of the family - and Springers certainly regard themselves as members of the family.

An example of anthropomorphism might be that the owner of a male dog might not want to have him neutered because he will "miss sex," as a human might if he or she were no longer able to have sex. This is simply not true.

A male dog's impulse to mate is entirely governed by his hormones, not emotions. If he gets the scent of a bitch in heat, his hormones (which are just chemicals) tell him he has to mate with her. He does not stop to consider how attractive she is or whether she is *"the one"* to produce his puppies.

No, his reaction is entirely physical, he just wants to head on over there and get on with it!

It's the same with females. When they are in heat, a chemical impulse is triggered in their brain making them want to mate - with any male, they aren't at all fussy. So, don't expect your little Princess to be all coy when she is in heat, she is not waiting for Prince Charming to come along - the tramp down the road or any other scruffy pooch will do! It is entirely physical, not emotional.

English Springer Spaniels are incredibly loyal and loving - and if yours doesn't make you smile from time to time, you must have had a humour by-pass. All of this adds up to one thing: a beloved family member that is all too easy to spoil.

> **Tip** Springers form deep bonds with their humans and respond well to positive motivation - praise, treats and toys. Teach yours to respect the authority figure, which is you. In the beginning, think of yourself as a kindly but firm teacher with a hyperactive and distracted young student!

In the household hierarchy, they should also see other household members as authority figures, which is why everyone sticking to the same rules is so important.

Learn to understand his mind, patiently train him to be comfortable with his place in the household, teach him some manners and household rules - like not jumping up, stealing things or barking to demand attention - and you will be rewarded with a companion who is second to none and fits in beautifully with your family and lifestyle.

Dr Stanley Coren is well known for his work on canine psychology and behaviour. He and other researchers believe that in many ways, a dog's emotional development is equivalent to that of a young child. He says: "Researchers have now come to believe that the mind of a dog is roughly equivalent to that of a human who is two to two-and-a-half years old. This conclusion holds for most mental abilities as well as emotions.

"Thus, we can look to human research to see what we might expect of our dogs. Just like a two-year-old child, our dogs clearly have emotions, but many fewer kinds of emotions than found in adult humans.

"At birth, a human infant only has an emotion that we might call excitement. This indicates how excited he is, ranging from very calm up to a state of frenzy. Within the first weeks of life the excitement state comes to take on a varying positive or a negative flavour, so we can now detect the general emotions of contentment and distress.

"In the next couple of months, disgust, fear and anger become detectable in the infant. Joy often does not appear until the infant is nearly six months of age and it is followed by the emergence of shyness or suspicion. True affection, the sort that it makes sense to use the label "love" for, does not fully emerge until nine or ten months of age."

So, our English Springers can truly love us – but we knew that already!

According to Dr Coren, dogs can't feel shame. So, if you are housetraining your puppy, don't expect him to feel ashamed if he makes a mess in the house, he can't; he simply isn't capable of feeling shame. But he will not like it when you ignore him when he's behaving badly, and will love it when you praise or reward him for relieving himself outdoors.

FACT He is simply responding to you with his simplified range of emotions.

English Springers can also be sensitive and show empathy - *"the ability to understand and share the feelings of another."* They can pick up on the mood and emotions of the owner. And is that not pride they display when dropping that pheasant or prize toy at your feet, or strutting their stuff in the show ring?

One emotion that all dogs can experience is jealousy. It may display itself by being overly-protective of humans, food or toys. An interesting article was published in the PLOS (Public Library of Science) Journal in 2014 following an experiment into whether dogs get jealous.

Building on research that shows that six-month old infants display jealousy, the scientists studied 36 dogs in their homes and videoed their actions when their owners showed affection to a realistic-looking stuffed canine *(pictured)*.

Over three-quarters of the dogs pushed or touched the owner when they interacted with the decoy. The envious mutts were more than three times as likely to do this for interactions with the stuffed dog, compared to when their owners gave their attention to other objects, including a book.

Around a third tried to get between the owner and the plush toy, while a quarter of the put-upon pooches snapped at the dummy dog!

Professor Christine Harris from University of California in San Diego said: "Our study suggests not only that dogs do engage in what appear to be jealous behaviours, but also that they were seeking to break up the connection between the owner and a seeming rival."

The researchers believe that the dogs thought that the stuffed dog was real. The authors cite the fact that 86% of the dogs sniffed the toy's rear end during and after the experiment!

Professor Harris said: "We can't really speak of the dogs' subjective experiences, of course, but it looks as though they were motivated to protect an important social relationship.

"Many people have assumed that jealousy is a social construction of human beings - or that it's an emotion specifically tied to sexual and romantic relationships.

"Our results challenge these ideas, showing that animals besides ourselves display strong distress whenever a rival usurps a loved one's affection."

Cause and Effect

When treated well, socialised and trained, English Springer Spaniels make wonderful canine companions. Once you've had one, no other dog seems quite the same. But sometimes, just like other breeds, they can develop behaviour problems.

Poor behaviour may result from a number of factors, including:

- Lack of socialisation
- Lack of training
- Poor breeding
- Boredom, due to lack of exercise or mental challenges
- Being left alone too long
- Being badly treated
- A change in living conditions
- Anxiety, insecurity or fear
- Being spoilt

Bad behaviour may show itself in different ways:

- Chewing or destructive behaviour
- Nipping, biting
- Excessive barking
- Stealing things
- Becoming overly protective of food, toys, a person, etc. (resource guarding)
- Aggression or excitability on the lead
- Jumping up

- Soiling or urinating inside the house
- Constantly demanding your attention
- Aggression towards people or other dogs - this is not common with Springers

FACT: Avoid poor behaviour by devoting lots of time early on to socialise and train your Springer, and to nip any potential problems in the bud.

If you are rehoming a rescue Springer, you'll need extra time and patience to help your new arrival unlearn any bad habits he may have picked up.

10 Ways to Avoid Unwanted Behaviour

Here are some tips to help you start out on the right foot:

1. **Buy from a good breeder**. They use their expertise to match suitable breeding pairs, taking into account factors such as good temperament, health and being *"fit for function."*

2. **Start socialisation right away**. Give a new puppy a couple of days to get used to his new surroundings and then start socialising him - even if this means carrying him places until the vaccination schedule is complete.

    Socialisation does not end at puppyhood. English Springers are social creatures that thrive on sniffing, hearing, seeing, and even licking. While the foundation for good behaviour is laid down during the first few months, good owners reinforce social skills and training throughout a dog's life.

    Springers love being the centre of attention - but they must learn when young that they are not also the centre of the universe. Socialisation helps them to learn their place in that universe and to become comfortable with it.

3. **Start training early** - you can't start too soon. Start teaching your puppy to learn his name as well as some simple commands a day or two after you bring him home.

4. **Basic training should cover several areas:** housetraining, chew prevention, puppy biting, simple commands like SIT, COME, STAY and familiarising him with collar and lead. Adopt a gentle but firm approach and keep training sessions short and FUN - start with five minutes a day and build up. No harsh treatment.

    Puppy classes or adult dog obedience classes are a great way to start; be sure to do your homework together afterwards. Spend a few minutes each day reinforcing what you have both learned in class - owners need training as well as dogs!

5. **The importance of teaching your Springer the Recall** cannot be over-emphasised. They have an inbuilt desire to run free and you have an inbuilt desire for them to come back to you; the Recall is essential!

6. **Reward your dog for good behaviour.** All behaviour training should be based on positive reinforcement. Springers respond very well to praise and rewards, and this trait speeds up the training process. The main aim of training is to build a good understanding between you and your dog.

7. **Ignore bad behaviour**, no matter how hard this may be. If, for example, your dog is chewing his way through your kitchen, shoes, or couch, jumping up or chasing the kids, remove him from the situation and then ignore him. For most dogs even negative attention is some attention.

Or if he is constantly demanding your attention, ignore him. Remove him or yourself from the room so he learns that you give attention when you want to give it, **not** when he demands it. If your pup is a chewer - and most are - make sure he has plenty of durable toys to keep him occupied.

8. **Take the time to learn what sort of temperament your dog has.** Is he by nature confident or anxious? What was he like as a tiny puppy, did he rush forward or hang back? Does he fight to get upright when on his back or is he happy to lie there? Is he a couch potato or a ball of energy?

   Your puppy's temperament will affect his behaviour and how he reacts to the world. A nervous Springer will certainly not respond well to a loud approach on your part, whereas an energetic, strong-willed one will require more patience and exercise, and a firm hand.

9. **Exercise and stimulation.** A lack of either is another reason for dogs behaving badly. Regular daily exercise, games and toys and organised activities are all ways of stopping your dog from becoming bored or frustrated.

   Pictured looking very alert is Lynne Lucas's Esther, aged four months.

10. **Learn to leave your dog.** Just as leaving your dog alone for too long can lead to problems, so can being with him 100% of the time. The dog becomes over-reliant on you and then gets stressed when you leave; this is called *Separation Anxiety*.

    When your dog first arrives at your house, start by leaving him for a few minutes every day and gradually build it up so that after a while you can leave him for up to four hours.

11. **Love your Springer - but don't spoil him,** however difficult that might be. You don't do your dog any favours by giving too many treats, constantly responding to his demands for attention or allowing him to behave as he wants.

Separation Anxiety

It's not just dogs that experience Separation Anxiety - people do too. About 7% of adults and 4% of children suffer from this disorder. Typical symptoms for humans are:

- Distress at being separated from a loved one
- Fear of being left alone

Our canine companions aren't much different. When a puppy leaves the litter, his owner becomes his new pack. It's estimated that as many as 10% to 15% of dogs suffer from Separation Anxiety, which is an exaggerated fear response caused by being apart from their owner.

Separation Anxiety affects millions of dogs and is on the increase. According to behaviourists, it is the most common form of stress for dogs.

FACT English Springer Spaniels CAN suffer from it, especially if they have not spent enough time away from their owners when young. Even if yours does not show signs, being over-reliant on you can lead to other insecurity issues, such as becoming:

- Anxious
- Over-protective
- Too territorial
- Too suspicious or aggressive with other people and/or dogs

Separation Anxiety can be equally distressing for the owner - I know because one of our dogs suffered from it. He howled whenever we left home without him. He'd also bark if one of us got out of the car - even if other people were still inside.

Fortunately, his problem was relatively mild. If we returned after only a short while, he was usually quiet. Although if we silently sneaked back and peeked in through the letterbox, he was never asleep. Instead he'd be waiting by the door looking and listening for our return.

Tell-Tale Signs

Does your English Springer Spaniel do any of the following?

- Follow you from room to room - even the bathroom - whenever you're home?
- Get anxious or stressed when you're getting ready to leave the house?
- Howl, bark or whine when you leave?
- Chew or destroy things he's not supposed to?
- Dig or scratch at the carpet, doors or windows trying to join you?
- Soil or urinate inside the house when left alone, even though he is housetrained
- Exhibit restlessness - such as licking his coat excessively, pacing or circling?
- Greet you ecstatically every time you come home - even if you've only been out to empty the bins?
- Wait by the window or door until you return?
- Dislike spending time alone in the garden or yard?
- Refuse to eat or drink if you leave him?
- Howl or whine when one family member leaves - even when others are still in the room or car?

Causes

English Springer Spaniels are pack animals and being alone is not a natural state for them. Puppies have to learn to get used to periods of isolation slowly and in a structured way before they can become comfortable with being alone.

A Springer puppy will emotionally latch on to his new owner, who has taken the place of his mother and siblings.

He will want to follow you everywhere initially and, although you want to shower him with love and attention, it's best to start leaving him, starting with a minute or two, right from the beginning.

In our case I was working from home when we got Max. With hindsight, I should have left him alone more often in those critical first few days, weeks then months.

Adopted dogs may be particularly susceptible to Separation Anxiety. They may have been abandoned once already and fear it happening again.

One or more of these causes can be a trigger:

- Getting used to people being around ALL of the time; not being left alone for short periods when young
- Being left for too long by owners who are out of the house for most of the day
- Anxiety or lack of confidence due to insufficient socialisation, training or both
- Boredom
- Being given TOO MUCH attention
- All of the dog's attention being focused on one person - usually because that person spends time with him, plays, feeds, trains and exercises him
- Making too much of a fuss when you leave and return to the house
- Mistreatment in the past, an insecure rescue dog may well feel anxious when left alone

FACT It may be very flattering that your Springer wants to be with you all the time, but Separation Anxiety is a form of panic that is distressing for your dog. Socialisation helps a dog to become more confident and self-reliant.

A different scenario is Separation Anxiety in elderly dogs. As dogs age, their senses, such as scent, hearing and sight, diminish. They often become "clingier" and more anxious when they are separated from their owners - or even out of view.

You may even find that your elderly Spaniel reverts to puppyhood and starts to follow you around the house again. In these cases, it is fine to spend more time with your old friend and gently help him through his final years.

So, what can you do if your dog is showing signs of Canine Separation Anxiety? Every dog is different, but here are tried and tested techniques that have worked for some dogs.

Tips to Combat Separation Anxiety

1. After the first couple of days at home, leave your new puppy or adult dog for short periods, starting with a minute, then two, then gradually increasing the minutes you are out of sight.
2. Use a crate. Crate training helps a dog to become self-reliant.

Photo: Stepping out very confidently is Diamond (Meadowdale Solitaire at Woodspa), owned by Lesley McCourt.

3. Consider making his night-time bed NOT in your bedroom to get him used to being out of your presence for several hours every night.
4. Introduce your Springer to other people, places and animals while young.
5. Get other members of your family to feed, walk and train the dog, so he doesn't become fixated on just one person.
6. Exercise your dog before you leave him alone. Take him for a walk, do an activity or play a game before leaving and, if you can, leave him with a view of the outside world, e.g. in a room with a patio door or low window.
7. **Keep arrivals and departures low key and don't make a big fuss.**
8. Leave him a **"security blanket,"** such as an old piece of clothing that still has your scent on it, a favourite toy, or leave a radio on softly in the room with the dog. Avoid a heavy rock station! If it will be dark when you return, leave a lamp on a timer.
9. Associate your departure with something good. Give him a rubber toy, like a Kong, filled with a tasty treat, or a frozen treat. This may take his mind off your departure. (Some dogs may refuse to touch the treat until you return home).
10. Structure and routine can help to reduce anxiety. Carry out regular activities, such as feeding and exercising, at the same time every day.

11. Dogs read body language very well and may start to fret when they think you are going to leave them. One technique is to mimic your departure routine when you have no intention of leaving. Put your coat on, grab your car keys, go out of the door and return a few seconds later. Do this randomly and regularly and it may help to reduce your dog's stress levels when you do it for real.

12. Quite often, WE are the reason our dog develops Separation Anxiety. We give the puppy too much attention and then spend all our time with him, causing him to become too reliant on us. However lovable your Springer is, **do not shower him with attention all the time,** particularly if he is showing early signs of anxiety when separating.

13. If you have to regularly leave the house for a few hours at a time, make an arrangement so the dog is not on his own all day. Consider dropping him off with a neighbour - or doggie day care if you can afford it.

14. Getting another dog to keep the first one company can help, but can you afford double the food and veterinary bills? We also don't recommend getting two Springers from the same litter as their strongest bond can be to each other, not you.

15. There are many natural calming remedies available for dogs in spray, tablet or liquid form, such as DAP (Dog Appeasing Pheromone), CBD oil or melatonin. Another option is to leave him with a Snuggle Puppy, which is warm and has a heartbeat.

Sit-Stay-Down

Another technique for helping to reduce Separation Anxiety is the *"sit-stay"* or *"down-stay"* exercises using positive reinforcement. The goal is to be able to move briefly out of your dog's sight while he is in the *"stay"* position.

Through this, he learns that he can remain calmly and happily in one place while you go about your normal daily life.

You have to progress slowly:

1. Get your dog to sit and stay and then walk away from him for five seconds.
2. Then 10, 20, a minute and so on.
3. Reward your dog every time he stays calm.
4. Then move out of sight or out of the room for a few seconds.
5. Return and give him a treat if he is calm.
6. Gradually lengthen the time you are out of sight.

If you're watching TV snuggled up with your dog and you get up for a snack, say *"Stay"* and leave the room. When you return, praise him quietly. It is a good idea to practise these techniques after exercise or when your dog is a little sleepy (but not exhausted), as he is likely to be more relaxed.

FACT ▸ Canine Separation Anxiety is not the result of disobedience or lack of training. It's a psychological condition; your dog feels anxious and insecure.

NEVER punish your dog for showing signs of Separation Anxiety - even if he has chewed your best shoes or dug a hole in your expensive rug. This will only make him more anxious.

NEVER leave your dog unattended in a crate for more than four hours maximum - or if he is frantic to get out, as it can cause physical or mental trauma. If you're thinking of leaving an animal in a crate all day while you are out of the house, consider a rabbit or a hamster - not an English Springer Spaniel!

Breeders on Springers

We asked three Kennel Club Assured Breeders to talk about the breed's traits, and any advice for new owners:

Chris Brandon-Lodge, Cottonstones English Springer Spaniels, who has been involved with Springers for 40 years: "I think the Springer's size and temperament and their generally happy attitude to life is very appealing. They usually get on well with children.

"My line is a specific and continuous line since our first bitch. It's a show-cross-working line, which we find produces a good-looking stamp of dog with an excellent sensible temperament. I can only speak for my own line, but they are very easy-going, sensible and obedient.

Photo: Enjoying a life on the ocean wave is Cottonstones Black Tulip, aged four, bred by Chris.

"Springers are highly intelligent, generally very easy to train, and obedient. They are mainly motivated by affinity with the owner, but they also seem to have an inbuilt desire to please.

"Always use a calm, gentle but firm voice when asking for cooperation, and a fierce tone when the dog has not done as asked or is disobedient.

"The tone of the human voice is vital, and when you say: **"No!"** you must sound assertive and mean it - it's no good saying: "Naughty dog" in a soppy voice!"

"Excessive barking is not common in my experience with Springers. As for watchdogs, they will give a warning bark and are protective, but that is not their prime role."

Lisa Cardy, "My dogs are working lines. They are great family dogs, very good-natured, clever, loyal and very attractive. They are intelligent and have innate desire to please their owner. They also like treats, so are generally easy to train.

"Springers can be protective of their families, but I wouldn't say they are guard dogs - most are too friendly! I have known a few who were possessive with food and toys but often this is down to training issues.

"Springers should be very friendly and calm when told to be. My Springer Poppy will go out running all over the place, but the minute I call her name she returns to my side and sits immediately looking up at me. This shows her desire to see what I want her to do next.

"I recommend puppies are crated for rest and break times - both for puppy and new owners during the day."

Photo of two of Lisa's puppies.

"Don't let puppy get overtired - this leads to bad behaviour, and rest is also vital for their development. They will chew and bite, as all puppies do, so be aware and distract with toys, etc.

"I haven't found Springers to be particularly barky. They generally are very good with children, and gentle. But, like all dogs, they should never be left on their own with small children."

Lynne Lucas, Traxlerstarr Spaniels, Surrey: "My girls are all related through three to four generations. I have heard many stories about having bitches together, but my girls all get on so well and have since day one; they love to run and play together.

"They all have their own personalities: Myrtle is very vocal (everyone knows when I am in the woods). Stella can be a little reactive with some dogs if the owner allows their dog to run at her, so I keep a close eye on her."

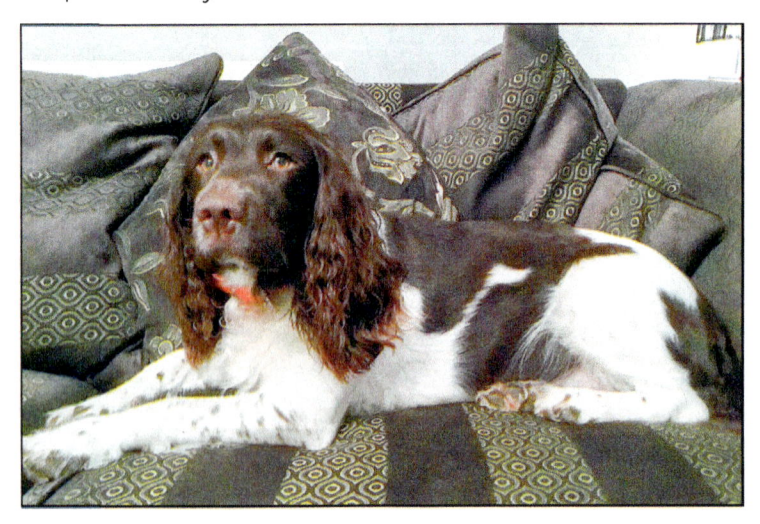

Photo: Stella chilling out at home on "the forbidden sofa!".

"Agatha prefers to stick to me like glue; Esther, the baby, is all over the place keeping up with the others, and grandma Calamity does her own thing - but they love to be out together.

"English Springer Spaniel pups are very nippy up to about five months, when they lose their baby needle-sharp teeth.

"Because of this, I made a decision to not home my pups with families who have children under six years old, as they find it very difficult to cope with it and it can lead to them becoming frightened of the puppy.

"I see via social media that some owners have a problem with their dogs barking when they are out of the house - never more so than in recent times when families have been together at home with their dog. Then life started to return to normal, the dog was suddenly left alone and they become anxious and vocalise.

"If any owner has this problem, I would recommend building up the time away from the house gently so that your pup does not think that they have been abandoned.

"Springers can have a tendency to bark at doorbell, visitors and unusual noises - and this should be discouraged, as it can prove antisocial. But a barking dog at certain times can be a deterrent, as for a good watchdog, they are very nosey so always on look-out.

"English Springer Spaniels are happy, loyal and energetic dogs that just love life and dirty puddles - the muddier the better!"

9. Basic Training

Training a young dog is not unlike bringing up a child. Put in lots of time early on to work towards a good mutual understanding and you'll be rewarded with a well-adjusted, sociable member of the family you can proudly take anywhere!

Although the English Springer Spaniel is an active breed, energy levels vary from one dog to the next. Dogs from working backgrounds tend to need more physical and mental stimulation than those from show lines. They will probably also have a stronger prey drive (instinct to chase after critters), so training should always be tailored to meet the needs of the individual dog.

A well-trained Springer doesn't magically appear overnight - it requires lots of time and patience on your part. They make super family dogs, but let yours behave exactly how he wants and you could finish up with an out-of-control adult who rules YOU!

A Head Start

You already have a head start over many other breeds. Firstly, Springer Spaniels are intelligent and pick things up easily. Secondly, they have been selectively bred to work alongside Man (and Woman) and to follow their commands — so you have a dog who is:

1. Receptive to training, and
2. Eager to please you

Focus is something to be aware of. On the one hand, Springers have an amazing ability to focus on one thing, such as a scent.

Try to call yours back when he is nose to the ground locked on to a scent and it's almost impossible unless you've spent plenty of time instilling the **Recall**.

This focus can, however, be channelled if you put in the time to make training fun and interesting.

On the other hand, when they are out and about, they are easily distracted from you by scents, other dogs, birds, people, anything moving, food scraps, new places to explore, etc.

The importance of teaching your Springer the Recall while still a pup cannot be over-emphasized.

Springers enjoy a challenge, games to keep them mentally occupied and playing with their owners or other dogs (provided they have been properly socialised). They also enjoy organised activities and competitions, which can help to keep them stimulated.

> **Tip:** Most Springer Spaniels are greedy and most are affectionate. Give yours a chance to shine; praise and reward him often until the particular training task becomes ingrained.

Shouting, scolding or physical punishment will have the opposite effect. Your Springer will switch off or otherwise respond poorly to rough or negative training methods.

The secret of good training can be summed up in four words:

- Consistency
- Reward
- Praise
- Patience

Tip: Police and service dogs are trained to a very high level with only a ball for reward. Don't always use treats with your Spaniel; praise or play time can be enough. Also, try getting your pup used to a small piece of carrot or apple as a healthy and slimming alternative to manufactured treats.

Here are some encouraging words and tips from two breeders, starting with Chris Brandon-Lodge, of Cottonstones English Springer Spaniels: "Springers are highly intelligent and generally very easy to train. They are mainly motivated by affinity with the owner; they seem to have an inbuilt desire to please.

"Always use a calm, gentle but firm voice when asking for cooperation and a fierce tone when the dog has not done as asked or is disobedient. The tone of the human voice is vital and when you say **"No,"** you must sound assertive and mean it."

Lynne Lucas, Traxlerstarr Spaniels: "English Springer Spaniels are one of the most intelligent breeds and are therefore first choice as sniffer dogs for the authorities. They are very keen to learn and have such a sense of achievement when they have learnt something new.

"They have a high reward drive, be it a ball, toy or just plain treats. They learn quickly and with constant use of new commands they will not forget. All my girls also know the clock - they know dinnertime to the minute and also bedtime at 8pm ON THE DOT!

"Always have treats in pockets to reward the slightest achievement - even at home - from the day they arrive. I always strongly advise my new owners that **Recall** is so important and must be achieved at home before venturing out.

"Also 'up the ante' with the treats as they get bored, I don't treat for long but use 'TOUCH' and when they return, I touch their snout so they know they have done well. Many owners use clicker training; I have never used that method, it's just personal preference.

"I always carry a whistle and train my pups to come to a short pip. It is better than shouting all the time, and I find they react better to it."

The Intelligence of Dogs

Psychologist and canine expert Dr Stanley Coren has written a book called *The Intelligence of Dogs* in which he ranks the breeds. He surveyed dog trainers to compile the list and used *Understanding of New Commands* and *Obeying First Command* as his standards of intelligence.

Photo: UK working Springer.

Dr Coren says there are three types of dog intelligence:

- Adaptive Intelligence (learning and problem-solving ability). Specific to the individual dog and is measured by canine IQ tests
- Instinctive Intelligence. Specific to the individual dog and is measured by canine IQ tests
- Working/Obedience Intelligence. This is breed-dependent

He divides dogs into six groups and the brainboxes of the canine world are the 10 breeds ranked in the 'Brightest Dogs' section of his list. It will come as no surprise to anyone who has ever been into the countryside and seen sheep being worked by a farmer and his right-hand man (his dog) to learn that the Border Collie is the most intelligent of all dogs.

No 2 is the Poodle, followed by the German Shepherd, Golden Retriever, Doberman Pinscher, Shetland Sheepdog, Papillon, Rottweiler and Australian Cattle Dog. All dogs in this class:

- Understand New Commands with Fewer than Five Repetitions
- Obey a First Command 95% of the Time or Better

The English Springer Spaniel is not far behind, ranked 13 out of 138 breeds. They are near the top of the second group, **Excellent Working Dogs**. They:

- Understand new commands with 5 to 15 repetitions
- Obey first command: 85% of the time or better

The full list can be seen on Wikipedia.

Five Golden Rules

1. Training must be reward-based, not punishment based.
2. Keep sessions short or your dog will get bored.
3. Never train when you are in a rush or a bad mood.
4. Training after exercise is fine, but never train when your dog is exhausted.
5. Keep sessions fun and finish on a high.

Tip: Establishing the natural order of things is not something forced on a dog through shouting or violence; it is brought about by mutual consent and good training.

Dogs are happiest and behave best when they are familiar and comfortable with their place in the household.

If you have adopted an older dog, you can still train him, but it will take a little longer to get rid of bad habits and instil good manners. Patience and persistence are the keys here.

Socialisation is a very important aspect of training. A good breeder will have already begun this process with the litter and then it's up to you to keep it going when puppy arrives home.

Young pups can absorb a great deal of information, but they are also vulnerable to bad experiences. They need exposing - in a positive manner - to different people, other animals and situations. If not, they can find them very frightening when they do finally encounter them later.

If they have a lot of good experiences with other people, places, noises, situations and animals before four or five months old, they are less likely to either be timid or nervous or try to establish dominance later.

Don't just leave your dog at home in the early days, take him out and about with you, get him used to new people, places and noises. Dogs that miss out on being socialised can pay the price later.

All pups are chewers. If you are not careful, some young pups and adolescents will chew through anything – wires, phone chargers, remote controls, bedding, rugs, etc. Young dogs are not infrequent visitors to veterinary clinics to have *"foreign objects"* removed from their stomachs.

Most English Springer Spaniel puppies, especially those with a lot of working instinct, can be "mouthy" and will nip and play-bite, this is normal. So, train your young pup to chew only the things you give – don't give him your old slippers, an old piece of carpet or anything that resembles something you DON'T want him to chew, he won't know the difference between the old and the new. Buy purpose-made long-lasting chew toys.

A puppy class is one of the best ways of getting a pup used to being socialised and trained. This should be backed up by short sessions of a few minutes of training a day back home. English Springer Spaniels are great family dogs for anyone prepared to put in a fair bit of time to train one.

Some dogs, even well-trained ones, try to push the boundaries when they reach adolescence – any time between six months and two years old. Owners can't understand why their young dogs suddenly start behaving badly and unlearning some of their training; some males may start to "mark" or urinate in the house, even when they are housetrained.

In all cases, go back to basics and put the time in – sadly, there is no quick fix. You need to be firm with a strong-willed or high energy dog, but all training should still be carried out using positive techniques.

Tip: If you do need some professional one-on-one help (for you and the dog), choose a Spaniel specialist and/or a trainer registered with the Association of Professional Dog Trainers (APDT) or other organisation using positive training methods. The old Alpha dominance theories have gone out the window.

Training Tips

1. **Start training and socialising straight away.** Like babies, puppies learn quickly and it's this learned behaviour that stays with them through adult life. Start with just a few minutes a day a couple of days after arriving home.

2. **Your voice is a very important training tool.** Your dog has to learn to understand your language and you have to understand him. Commands should be issued in a calm, authoritative voice - not shouted. Praise should be given in a happy, encouraging voice, accompanied by stroking or patting. If your dog has done something wrong, use a stern voice (not a hysterical shriek).

3. **Avoid giving your dog commands you know you can't enforce** or he learns that commands are optional. Give your dog only one command - twice maximum - then gently enforce it. Repeating commands will make him tune out; telling your dog to *"SIT, SIT, SIT, SIT!!!"* is

neither efficient nor effective. Say a single *"SIT,"* gently place him in the Sit position and praise him.

4. **Train gently and humanely.** Springer Spaniels can be sensitive and do not respond well to being shouted at or hit.

5. **Keep training sessions short and upbeat.** If obedience training is a bit of a bore, pep things up a bit by *"play training"* by using constructive, non-adversarial games.

6. **Do not try to dominate your dog.** Training should be mutual, i.e. your dog should do something because he WANTS to do it. Springers are not interested in dominating you, they want to please you.

7. **Begin training at home around the house and garden/yard.** How well your dog responds at home affects his behaviour away from the home. If he doesn't respond well at home, he certainly won't respond any better out and about where there are 101 distractions, e.g. interesting scents, food scraps, other dogs, people, small animals or birds.

8. **Mealtimes are a great time to start training.** Teach Sit and Stay at breakfast and dinner, rather than just putting the dish down and letting him dash over immediately.

9. **Use his name often and in a positive manner** so he gets used to the sound of it. He won't know what it means at first, but it won't take long before he realises you're talking to him.

10. <u>**DON'T use his name when reprimanding, warning or punishing.**</u> He should trust that when he hears his name, good things happen. He should always respond to his name with enthusiasm, never hesitancy or fear. Use words such as *"No!" "Ack!"* or *"Bad Boy/Girl"* in a stern (not shouted) voice instead.

    NOTE: Some parents prefer not to use *"No!"* with their dog, as they use it so often around the kids that it can confuse the pup! You can use *"Leave."*

11. **In the beginning, give your dog attention when YOU want to – not when he wants it.** When you are training, give your puppy lots of positive attention when he is good. But if he starts jumping up, nudging you constantly or barking to demand your attention, ignore him. Wait a while and pat him when you are ready and always AFTER he has stopped demanding your attention.

12. **You can give Spaniels TOO MUCH attention in the beginning.** This may create a rod for your own back when they grow into needy adults that are over-reliant on you. They may even develop Separation Anxiety, which is stressful for both dog AND owner.

13. **Don't give your dog lots of attention (even negative attention) when he misbehaves.** Springers love your attention and if yours gets lots when he's naughty, you are inadvertently reinforcing bad behaviour.

14. **Timing is critical.** When your puppy does something right, praise him immediately. If you wait a while, he will have no idea what he has done right. Similarly, when he does something wrong, correct him straight away.

15. **If he has an "accident" in the house, don't shout or rub his nose in it; it will have the opposite effect.** He may start hiding and peeing or pooping behind the couch or other inappropriate places. **If you catch him in the act**, use your *"No!"* or *"Ack!"* sound and immediately carry him out of the house. Then back to basics with housetraining. If you find something but don't catch him in the act, ignore it. If your pup is constantly relieving himself indoors, he either has a medical or behaviour issue or - more likely - you are not keeping a close enough eye on him!

16. **Start as you mean to go on.** In terms of training, treat your cute little pup as though he were fully-grown. Introduce the rules you want him to live by as an adult.

17. **Make sure that everybody in the household sticks to the same set of rules.** If the kids allow him on to the couch or bed and you forbid it, your Springer won't know what is allowed and what isn't.

Teaching Basic Commands

The Three Ds

The three Ds – **Distance, Duration** and **Distraction** – are the cornerstone of a good training technique.

Duration is the length of time your dog remains in the command.

Distance is how far you can walk away without your dog breaking the command.

Distraction is the number of external stimuli - such as noise, scents, people, other animals, etc. - your dog can tolerate before breaking the command.

Only increase one of the Three Ds at a time. For example, if your new pup has just learned to sit on command, gradually increase the time by a second or two as you go along. Moving away from the dog or letting the kids or the cat into the room would increase the Distance or Distraction level and make the command too difficult for your pup to hold.

If you are teaching the Stay, gradually increase EITHER the distance OR the time he's in the Stay position; don't increase both at once.

Tip: Start off by training your dog in your home before moving into the garden or yard where there are more distractions - even if it is quiet and you are alone, outdoor scents and sights will be a big distraction for a young dog. Once you have mastered the commands in a home environment, progress to the park or other safe open space.

Implement the Three Ds progressively and slowly, and don't expect too much too soon. Work within your dog's capabilities, move forward one tiny step at a time and set your Springer up to consistently SUCCEED, not fail.

Treats

Different treats have different values and using them at the right time will help you to get the best out of your Springer:

1. **High Value Food** is human food - usually animal-based - such as chicken, liver, cheese, sausage and ham. All should be cooked and cut into pea-sized treats – you're looking to reward your dog, not make him overweight, so make sure you don't give too many! Place the tiny treats

in a freezer bag in the freezer, which keeps them fresh, then you can grab a handful when you go out training. There's not much water content and they quickly thaw.

When training, we want our dog to want more High Value Food. He smells and tastes it on his tongue but it is gone in a flash, leaving him wanting more. *So, all treats should be only as large as a pea - even if you're training a Great Dane!*

2. **Medium Value Food** such as moist pet shop treats or a healthy alternative like sliced apple or carrot.

3. **Low Value Food** such as kibble. Use your dog's own food if you feed dry or buy a small bag if not.

IMPORTANT: Whenever you are asking your dog **to do something new,** make it worth his while. Offer a High Value treat. Once your dog understands what you are asking, you can move down to Medium Value treat.

When he does it every time use Low Value... reducing the frequency after a while and then only give it every other time... then only occasionally until you have slowly stopped giving any treat when asking for that task.

The aim at this point is to start getting you in control of your dog. After all, you will be a better team if your dog is a willing partner and does what you tell him to do. Being in control brings good things.

The Sit

Teaching the Sit command to your English Springer Spaniel is relatively easy. Teaching a young pup to sit still for any length of time is a bit more difficult. The clue is in the name - he will spring up at the slightest distraction! If your little protégé is very distracted or high energy, it may be easier to put him on a lead (leash) to hold his attention.

1. **Stand facing each other and hold a treat between your thumb and fingers or in your hand just an inch or so above his head** and let him sniff it. Don't let your fingers and the treat get much further away or you might have trouble getting him to move his body into a sitting position. In fact, if your dog jumps up when you try to guide him into the Sit, you're probably holding your hand too far away from his nose. If your dog backs up, you can practise with a wall behind him.

2. **As he reaches up to sniff it, move the treat upwards and back over the dog** towards his tail at the same time as saying *"Sit."* Most dogs will track the treat with their eyes and follow it with their noses, causing their noses to point straight up.

3. **As his head moves up toward the treat, his rear end should automatically go down towards the floor.** TaDa! (drum roll!).

4. **The second he sits, say *"Yes!"*** Give him the treat and tell your dog he's a good boy/girl.

Stroke and praise him for as long as he stays in the sitting position.

5. **If he jumps up on his back legs** and paws you while you are moving the treat, be patient and start all over again. At this stage, don't expect your bouncy little pupil to sit for more than a nanosecond!

NOTE: For positive reinforcement, use the words *Yes!, Good Boy!* or *Good Girl!*

Another method is to put one hand on his chest and with your other hand, gently push down on his rear end until he is sitting, while saying *"Sit."* Give him a treat and praise; he will eventually associate the position with the word "sit."

Once your dog catches on, leave the treat in your pocket (or have it in your other hand). Repeat, but this time your dog will just follow your empty hand. Say *"Sit"* and bring your empty hand in front of your dog's nose. Move your hand exactly as you did when you held the treat. When your dog sits, say *"Yes!"* and then give him a treat from your other hand or your pocket.

Gradually lessen the amount of movement with your hand. First, say *"Sit"* then hold your hand eight to 10 inches above your dog's face and wait a moment. Most likely, he will sit. If he doesn't, help him by moving your hand back over his head, like you did before, but make a smaller movement this time. Then try again. Your goal is to eventually just say *"Sit"* without having to move or extend your hand at all.

Once your dog reliably sits on cue, you can ask him to sit whenever you meet people (it may not work straight away, but it should help to calm him down a bit). The key is anticipation. Give your dog the cue before he gets too excited to hear you and before he starts jumping up on the person just arrived. Generously reward him the instant he sits.

The Stay

This is a very useful command, but it's not so easy to teach a lively and distracted young Springer pup - don't ask him to stay for more than a few seconds at the beginning.

Tip This requires concentration from your dog, so pick a time when he's relaxed and well-exercised, or just after a game or mealtimes - but not too exhausted to concentrate.

1. **Tell your dog to sit or lie down,** but instead of giving a treat as soon as he hits the floor, hold off for one second. Then say *"Yes!"* in an enthusiastic voice and give him a treat.

   If your dog bounces up again instantly, have two treats ready. Feed one right away, before he has time to move; then say *"Yes!"* and feed the second treat.

2. **You need a release word or phrase.** It might be *"Free!"* or *"Here!"* Once you've given the treat, immediately say the word and encourage your dog to get up.

   Repeat the exercise a few times, gradually waiting a tiny bit longer before releasing the treat. (You can delay the first treat for a moment if your dog bounces up).

3. **A common mistake is to hold the treat high and then give the reward slowly.** As your dog doesn't know the command yet, he sees the treat coming and gets up to meet the food.

Page **114** THE ENGLISH SPRINGER SPANIEL HANDBOOK

Instead, bring the treat toward your dog quickly - the best place to deliver it is right between his front paws. If you're working on a Sit-Stay, give the treat at chest height.

4. **When your dog can stay for several seconds, start to add a little distance.** At first, you'll walk backwards, because your dog is more likely to get up to follow you if you turn away from him. Take one single step away, then step back towards your dog and say *"Yes!"* and give the treat. Give him the signal to get up immediately, even if five seconds haven't passed.

5. **Remember DISTANCE, DURATION, DISTRACTION.** Work on one factor at a time. Whenever you make one factor more difficult, ease up on the others then build them back up. So, when you add distance, cut the duration of the stay.

6. Once he's mastered The Stay with you alone, **move the training on so that he learns to do the same with distractions.** Have someone walk into the room, or squeak a toy or bounce a ball once. A rock-solid stay is mostly a matter of working slowly and patiently to start with. Don't go too fast. If he does get up, take a breather and then give him a short refresher, starting at a point easier than whatever you were working on when he cracked.

> **Tip:** If you think he's tired or had enough, leave it for the day and come back later - just finish off on a positive note by giving one very easy command you know he will obey, followed by a reward.

Don't use the Stay command in situations where it is unpleasant for your dog. For instance, avoid telling him to stay as you close the door behind you on your way to work

Finally, don't use Stay to keep a dog in a scary situation.

Down

There are a number of different ways to teach this command, which here means for the dog to lie down.

NOTE: If you are teaching this command, then use the *"Off"* command to teach your dog not to jump up). This does not come naturally to a young pup, so it may take a little while to master.

Don't make it a battle of wills and, although you may gently push him down, don't physically force him down against his will. This will be interpreted as you putting pressure on him and it won't get the reaction you were hoping for.

1. Give the Sit command.

2. **When your dog sits, don't give him the treat immediately**, but keep it in your closed hand. Slowly move your hand straight down toward the floor, between his front legs. As your English Springer Spaniel's nose follows the treat, just like a magnet, his head will bend all the way down to the floor.

3. When the treat is on the floor between your dog's paws, start to move it away from him, like you're drawing a line along the floor. (The entire luring motion forms an L-shape).

4. At the same time say *"Down"* in a firm manner.

5. To continue to follow the treat, your dog will probably ease himself into the Down position. The instant his elbows touch the floor, say *"Yes!"* and immediately let him eat the treat. If your dog doesn't automatically stand up after eating the treat, just move a step or two away to encourage him to move out of the Down position.

Repeat the sequence above several times. Aim for two short sessions of five minutes per day.

If your dog's back end pops up, quickly snatch the treat away. Then immediately say *"Sit"* and try again. It may help to let him nibble on the treat as you move it toward the floor. If you've tried to lure your dog into a Down, but he still seems confused or reluctant, try this trick:

1. Sit down on the floor with your legs straight out in front of you. Your dog should be at your side. Keeping your legs together and your feet on the floor, bend your knees to make a 'tent' shape.

2. Hold a treat right in front of your dog's nose. As he licks and sniffs the treat, slowly move it down to the floor and then underneath your legs. Continue to lure him until he has to crouch down to keep following the treat.

3. The instant his belly touches the floor, say *"Yes!"* and let him eat the treat. If your dog seems nervous about following the treat under your legs, make a trail of treats for him to eat along the way.

Some dogs find it easier to follow a treat into the Down from a standing position.

- Hold the treat right in front of your dog's nose, and then slowly move it straight down to the floor, right between his front paws. His nose will follow the treat

- If you let him lick the treat as you continue to hold it still on the floor, your dog will probably plop into the Down position

- The moment he does, say *"Yes!"* and let him eat the treat (some dogs are reluctant to lie on a cold, hard surface. It may be easier to teach yours to lie down on a carpet). The next step is to introduce a hand signal. You'll still reward him with treats, though, so keep them nearby or hidden behind your back.

1. Start with your dog in a Sit.

2. Say *"Down."*

3. **Without** a treat in your fingers, use the same hand motion you did before. As soon as your dog's elbows touch the floor, say *"Yes!"* and immediately get a treat to give him.

Tip: Important: Even though you're not using a treat to lure your dog into position, you must still give a reward when he lies down. You want him to learn that he doesn't have to see a treat to get one.

4. Clap your hands or take a few steps away to encourage him to stand up. Then repeat the sequence from the beginning several times for a week or two. When your dog readily lies down as soon as you say the cue and use your new hand signal, you're ready for the next step.

   To stop bending all the way down to the floor every time, you can gradually shrink the signal to a smaller movement. To make sure your dog continues to understand what you want him to do, progress slowly.

5. Repeat the hand signal, but instead of moving your hand all the way to the floor, move it ALMOST all the way down. Stop when it's an inch or two above the floor. Practise the Down

Page **116** THE ENGLISH SPRINGER SPANIEL HANDBOOK

for a day or two, using this slightly smaller hand signal. Then you can make your movement an inch or two smaller, stopping your hand three or four inches above the floor.

6. After practising for another couple of days, shrink the signal again. As you continue to gradually stop your hand signal farther and farther from the floor, you'll bend over less and less.

   Eventually, you won't have to bend over at all. You'll be able to stand up straight, say *"Down,"* and then just point to the floor.

Your next job is harder: practise your dog's new skill in different situations and locations. Start with calm places, like different rooms in your house or your garden/yard when there's no one around.

Then increase the distractions; so, do some sessions at home when family members are moving around, on walks and then at friends' houses, too.

The Recall

This basic command is the most important of all - and definitely one of the hardest with a lively and distracted English Springer.

It will require lots and lots of repetition and patience on your part, but you are limiting both your lives if you can't let your Spaniel do what he was born to do; run free.

A dog who obeys the Recall enjoys freedoms that other dogs cannot. Springers love to run free, but don't allow yours off-lead beyond fenced areas until he has learned some Recall. If yours has strong hunting instincts, you will have your work cut out, but the reward is a dog you can take anywhere.

Here are two suggestions:

1. Train your Springer to respond to a whistle, **see Chapter 10.**

2. If you're worried the Recall isn't fully instilled yet, consider fitting a GPS collar, **pictured**. This will let you know, via your phone, where your dog is at all times.

Tip: Whether you have a puppy or an older dog, the first step is always to establish that coming to you is the BEST thing he can do.

Any time your dog comes to you - whether you've called him or not - acknowledge that you appreciate it with praise, affection, play or treats. This consistent reinforcement ensures that your dog will continue to "check in" with you frequently.

1. Start off a short distance away from your dog.

2. Say your dog's name followed by the command *"Come!"* in an enthusiastic voice. You'll usually be more successful if you walk or run away from him while you call. Dogs find it hard to resist chasing after a running person, especially their owner.

3. He should run towards you!
4. A young dog will often start running towards you but then get distracted and head off in another direction. Pre-empt this situation by praising your puppy and cheering him on when he starts to come to you and **before** he has a chance to get distracted.

    Your praise will keep him focused so that he'll be more likely to come all the way to you. If he stops or turns away, you can give him feedback by saying *"Oh-oh!"* or *"Hey!"* in a different tone of voice (displeased or unpleasantly surprised). When he looks at you again, smile, call him and praise him as he approaches you.

5. When your puppy comes to you, give him the treat BEFORE he sits down or he may think that the treat was earned for sitting, not coming to you.
6. Another method is to use two people. You hold the treats and let your dog sniff them while the accomplice holds on to the dog. When you are about 10 or 15 yards away, get your helper to let the dog go, and once he is running towards you, say *"COME!"* loudly and enthusiastically.

    When he reaches you, stop, bend down and make a fuss of him before giving a treat. Do this several times. The next step is to give the Come command just BEFORE you get your helper to release the dog, and by doing this repetitively, the dog begins to associate the command with the action.

NOTE: "Come" or a similar word is better than "Here" if you intend using the "Heel" command, as "Here" and "Heel" sound very similar.

Progress your dog's training in baby steps. If he's learned to come when called in your kitchen, you can't expect him to do it straight away at the park, in the woods or on the beach when surrounded by distractions. When you first use the Recall outdoors, make sure there's no one around to distract your dog.

Breeder Lynne Lucas strongly recommends practising and practising the Recall in the home and then the garden or yard before venturing out into public spaces.

She has this advice: "Start by calling one command and then your dog's name, firstly indoors from one room to another and reward them for coming to you. Then venture further afield into the garden and repeat, etc. so that they can go off-lead when you venture out for the first time.

"Never let them move more than 10 feet away. Call them back repeatedly and reward. Yes, it can be boring, but you will reap the rewards of a pleasant walk with an obedient dog in the future."

Tip: Try and do all the initial Recall training within a safe, fenced area. If you're having problems with his attention span, consider using a long training lead so he can't run off.

Only when your dog has mastered the Recall in a number of locations and in the face of various distractions can you expect him to come to you regularly.

Collar and Lead (Leash) Training

You have to train your dog to get used to a collar and lead, then teach him to walk nicely beside you. This can be challenging with young Springers, who don't necessarily want to walk at the same pace as you - some puppies might even slump to the ground and refuse to move in the beginning!

All dogs will pull on a lead initially. It's not because they want to show you who's boss, it's simply that they are excited to be out and are forging ahead.

You will need a small collar to start off with. Some puppies don't mind collars, some will try to scratch or remove them, while others will lie on the floor.

You need to be patient and calm and proceed at a pace comfortable to him; don't fight your dog and don't force the collar on.

1. Start your puppy off with a lightweight collar and give praise or a treat once the collar is on, not after you have taken it off. Gradually increase the length of time you leave the collar on.

Tip: If you leave your dog in a crate or leave him alone in the house, take OFF the collar and tags. They may get caught, causing panic or injury.

2. Put the collar on when there are other things that will occupy him, like when he is going outside to be with you, when you are interacting with him, at mealtimes or when you are doing some basic training. Don't put it on too tight, you want him to forget it's there; **you should be able to get two fingers underneath.**

   Some pups may react as if you've hung a two ton weight around their necks, while others will be more compliant. If yours scratches the collar, get his attention by encouraging him to follow you or play with a toy to forget the irritation.

3. Once your puppy is happy wearing the collar, introduce the lead. Many owners prefer an extending or retractable lead, but consider a fixed-length one to start training him to walk close to you. Again, begin in the house or garden, don't try to go out and about straight away.

Tip: Think of the lead as a safety device to stop him running off, not something to drag him around with. You want a Springer that doesn't pull, so don't start by pulling him around.

4. Attach the lead and give him a treat while you put it on. Use the treats (instead of pulling on the lead) to lure him beside you, so that he gets used to walking with the collar and lead on.

   You can also make good use of toys to do exactly the same thing - especially if your dog has a favourite. Walk around the house with the lead on and lure him forwards with the toy.

   It might feel a bit odd but it's a good way for your pup to develop a positive relationship with the collar and lead with the minimum of fuss. Act as though it's the most natural thing in the world for you to walk around the house with your dog on a lead - and just hope the neighbours aren't watching! Some dogs react the moment you attach the lead and they feel some tension on it - a bit like when a horse is being broken for the first time.

Drop the lead and allow him to run around the house or yard, dragging it behind, but be careful he doesn't get tangled and hurt himself.

Try to make him forget about it by playing or starting a short fun training routine with treats. While he is concentrating on the new task, occasionally pick up the lead and call him to you. Do it gently and in an encouraging tone.

5. **Don't yank on the lead.** If it gets tight, just lure him back beside you with a treat or a toy. Remember to keep the hand holding the treat or toy down, so your dog doesn't get the habit of jumping up. If you feel he is getting stressed, try putting treats along the route you'll be taking to turn this into a rewarding game: good times are ahead... so he learns to focus on what's ahead of him with curiosity, not fear.

6. **Avoid taking your pup out on to the streets too soon.** Do some collar and lead training around the home first, or he will find everything too distracting.

One UK breeder said: "Springers have an innate desire to please their owner and like treats, so training should be easy.

However, one common problem with Springers is pulling on the lead. I recommend a slip lead rather than a collar and when training to walk on the lead, keep the dog by your side with a treat in your hand.

"The dog will stay focused on your hand rather than try to pull ahead. Another tip is to walk forward and when they pull turn around in a circle to distract them. Then continue walking. Keep turning around until they learn to stop pulling."

This method is described by dog trainer Victoria Stillwell as the "Reverse Direction Technique." When your dog pulls, say "Let's Go!" in an encouraging manner, then turn away from him and walk off in the other direction, without jerking on the lead. When he is following you and the lead is slack, turn back and continue on your original way.

It may take a few repetitions, but your words and body language will make it clear that pulling will not get your dog anywhere, whereas walking calmly by your side - or even slightly in front of you - on a loose lead will get him where he wants to go.

There is an excellent video (in front of her beautiful house!) which shows Victoria demonstrating this technique and highlights just how easy it is with a dog that's keen to please. It only lasts three minutes: https://positively.com/dog-behavior/basic-cues/loose-leash-walking

One US breeder added: "I agree with starting collar and leash training in the house and yard, but I don't try to lead the puppy. I follow puppy and let him lead me at first. Then I start stopping and calling them to me for a treat.

"As the puppy becomes more comfortable coming to me standing still, I then start backing up as the puppy comes to me, so they learn to keep coming to me even with tension on the leash. This is the first step in teaching them to follow me. I am starting to "lead" them."

Some dogs are perfectly happy to walk alongside you off-lead but behave differently when they have one on. Others may become more excitable or aggressive on a lead once they gain their confidence when their *Fight-or-Flight* instinct kicks in.

> **Tip:** Take collar and lead training slowly. Let him gain confidence in you, the lead and himself. Some dogs sit and decide not to move! If this happens, walk a few steps away, go down on one knee and encourage him to come to you, then walk off again.

Harnesses and Collars

Opinions on harnesses very, but it's fair to say that it is generally moving in the direction of harnesses being a good thing – provided you choose the right one that's a good fit.

Vet Vicky Payne, breeder of Quincegrove Working Springer Spaniels, East Sussex, said: "I used to be anti-harness, but now all my pups start on one.

"There is increasing evidence that pulling on a collar or slip lead causes damage to the windpipe, raises ocular pressure (on the eye), and may even damage the thyroid, so I want a pup to be happy about loose lead walking before I use a collar or slip.

"The type of harness is important, as some are designed to restrict the front legs or tighten when the dog pulls.

"Personally, I use Perfect Fit because it can be adjusted as the dog grows and will fit all shapes and sizes of Springer *(pictured here on a Cocker Spaniel),* but there are other good makes, like Ruffwear," *(pictured below).*

In the past a harness was more likely to be seen as an addition to, or replacement for, a collar for dogs that were pulling or tugging on the lead.

Today, there are lots of different types and, if you choose the right one, a harness is considered a positive way of training and enjoying a walk with your dog.

Lesley Field, UK English Springer Spaniel Breed Clubs' Joint Breed Health Co-ordinator, said: "Some suit big dogs, others small breeds, and some types will fit your Springer better than others. It's important to choose the right type and size, so that the harness does not stop your dog from moving freely.

"Make sure you know the reason for choosing to use one. For example, what kind of exercise do you have in mind? This could be anything from a daily walk in the park or hiking in the mountains or forests. Or it might be because training your dog to walk with a collar and lead isn't going as well as it might, as he is pulling, jerking or straining - which is both a risk to him as well as you.

"There are also other types of walking aids on the market, but please do your research as, unfortunately, some of these are not always suitable."

There are several different options when it comes to harnesses:

- ❧ **Back-clip -** this is generally the easiest for most dogs to get used to and useful for dogs with delicate throats that are

THE ENGLISH SPRINGER SPANIEL HANDBOOK Page **121**

easily irritated by collars. This type is for calm dogs or ones that have already been trained not to pull on the lead

- **Comfort wrap or step-in harness** - lay the harness on the ground, have your dog step in, pull the harness up and around his shoulders and then clip him in; simple!
- **Soft or vest harness** - typically made of mesh and comes in a range of colours and patterns. Some slip over the head and some can be stepped into
- **Front-clip or training harness** - this has a lead attachment in front of the harness at the centre of your dog's chest. Dog trainers often choose this type as it helps to discourage your dog from pulling on the lead by turning him around
- **No-pull harness** - similar to a training harness, designed to help discourage your dog from pulling. The lead attachment ring is at the centre of the dog's chest and the harness tightens pressure if the dog pulls, encouraging him to stay closer to you. Some styles also tighten around the dog's legs
- **Auto or car harness** - these are designed for car travel and have an attachment that hooks into a seat belt

When choosing a harness, decide what its primary purpose will be – is it instead of or in addition to a collar? Do you need one that will help to train your dog, or will a back-clip harness do the job?

You want to make sure that it is a snug fit for your dog, and if it's a front clip, that it hangs high on your dog's chest. If it dangles too low, it can't help control forward momentum.

Make sure the harness isn't too tight or too difficult to get on. It shouldn't rub under your dog's armpits or anywhere else. If possible, take your dog to try on a few options before buying one for the first time.

If you've never used a harness before, it's easy to get tangled up while your pup is bouncing around, excited at the prospect of a walk. It's a good idea to have a few "dry runs" without the dog.

Lay the harness on the floor and familiarise yourself with it. Learn which bits the legs go through, which parts fit where and how it clicks together once the dog is in.

Dealing with Common Problems

Puppy Biting and Chewing

All puppies spend a great deal of time chewing, playing, and investigating objects; it's natural for them to explore the world with their mouths and needle-sharp teeth. When puppies play with people, they often bite, chew, nip and mouth people's hands, limbs and clothing.

Play biting is normal for puppies; they do it all the time with their littermates. They also bite moving targets with their sharp teeth; it's a great game.

FACT Most dogs originally bred to work, like the English Springer Spaniel, are mouthy as pups.

But when they arrive in your home, they have to be taught that human skin is sensitive and body parts are not suitable biting material.

FACT Biting is not acceptable - not even from a puppy - and can be a real problem initially, especially if you have children. When your puppy bites you or the kids, he is playing and investigating; he is NOT being aggressive. But a lively young pup can easily get carried away with energy and excitement.

Puppy biting should be dealt with from the get-go. Every time you have a play session, have a soft toy nearby and when he starts to chew your hand or feet, clench your fingers (or toes!) to make it more difficult, and distract him with a soft toy in your other hand.

Keep the game interesting by moving the toy around or rolling it around in front of him. (He may be too young to fetch it back if you throw it). He may continue to chew you, but will eventually realise that the toy is far more interesting and livelier than your boring hand.

If he becomes over-excited and too aggressive with the toy, if he growls a lot, stop playing and walk away. When you walk away, don't say anything or make eye or physical contact with your puppy.

Simply ignore him, this is usually extremely effective.

If your pup is more persistent and tries to bite your legs as you walk away, thinking this is another fantastic game, stand still and ignore him. If he still persists, say *"NO!"* in a very stern voice, then praise him when he lets go.

If you have to physically remove him from your trouser leg or shoe, leave him alone in the room for a while and ignore all demands for your attention.

Tip Try not to put your pup in a crate at the moment when he is being naughty or he will associate the crate with punishment. Remove yourself or the pup from the room instead - or put him in a pen. Wait until he has stopped being naughty before you put him in his crate - or put him in BEFORE his excitable behaviour escalates into naughtiness.

Although you might find it quite cute and funny if your puppy bites your fingers or toes, it should be discouraged at all costs. You don't want biting and nipping to get out of hand - as an adolescent or adult dog he could inadvertently cause real injury, especially to children.

- Puppies growl and bite more when they are excited. Don't allow things to escalate, so remove pup from the situation **before** he gets too excited by putting him in a crate or pen
- Don't put your hand or finger into your pup's mouth to nibble on; this promotes puppy biting
- Limit your children's play time with pup - and always supervise the sessions in the beginning. Teach them to gently play with and stroke your puppy, not to wind him up

- Don't let the kids (or adults) run around the house with the puppy chasing - this is an open invitation to nip at the ankles
- If your puppy does bite, remove him from the situation and people - never smack him

Tip: English Springer Spaniels are very affectionate and another tried and tested method is to make a sharp cry of "OUCH!" when your pup bites your hand - even when it doesn't hurt.

This has worked very well for us. Most pups will jump back in amazement, surprised to have hurt you. Divert your attention from your puppy to your hand. He will probably try to get your attention or lick you as a way of saying sorry.

Praise him for stopping biting and continue with the game. If he bites you again, repeat the process. A sensitive dog should stop biting you.

You may also think about keeping special toys you use to play with your puppy separate from other toys he chews alone.

That way he can associate certain toys with having fun with you and may work harder to please you.

Springer Spaniels are playful and you can use this to your advantage by teaching your dog how to play nicely with you and the toy, and then by using play time as a reward for good behaviour.

As well as biting, puppies also chew, it is a normal part of the teething process. Some adolescent and adult dogs chew because they are bored - usually due to lack of exercise and/or mental stimulation. If puppy chewing is a problem, it is because your pup is chewing something you don't want him to.

So, the trick is to keep him, his mouth and sharp little teeth occupied with something he CAN chew on, such as a durable toy - see **Chapter 5. Bringing Puppy Home** for more information.

You might also consider freezing peanut butter and/or a liquid inside a Kong toy. Put the Kong into a mug, plug the small end with peanut butter and fill it with gravy before putting it into the freezer. (Check it doesn't contain the sweetener xylitol, which is harmful to dogs). Don't leave the Kong and the Springer on your precious Oriental rug! This will keep your pup occupied for quite a long time.

It is also worth giving the dog a frozen Kong or Lickimat when you leave the house if he suffers from Separation Anxiety. There are lots of doggie recipes for Kongs and other treats online.

Excessive Barking

English Springer Spaniels are not a breed known for being nuisance barkers, but any dog can bark too much; here are some of the most common reasons:

- His needs are not being met, resulting in him becoming noisy and/or naughty
- He has Separation Anxiety

- He has become too demanding of your attention
- He has a high prey drive (hunting instinct), when he may bark at every passing cat or fluttering leaf
- He is anxious and the bark is a warning to whatever is frightening him
- He has become too possessive of you/his food/his toys

You DO want your English Springer Spaniel to bark to alert you to strangers approaching your home before you hear anything - even if he immediately becomes their new best friend, especially if they have food!

The trick is to get him to bark at the right times and then to stop, as unwanted barking will drive you and your neighbours nuts.

Dogs, especially young ones, sometimes behave in ways you might not want them to until they learn that this type of unwanted behaviour doesn't earn any rewards.

The problem can also develop during adolescence when a dog becomes more confident.

They become overly-fond of the sound of their own voices until they learn that when they stop their demanding barking, good things happen, such as treats, praise, a game.

Also, puppies teethe until about seven or eight months of age, so make sure yours has hardy chews, and perhaps a bone with supervision, to keep him occupied and gnawing.

Tip: NEVER give a puppy or adult dog a reward when he is barking (unless you gave the Bark command) - always wait until he stops or he'll think the reward is for barking.

Barking can be a way of letting off steam or attracting attention. Ask yourself:

- Is my Springer getting enough exercise and mental stimulation or is he bored? Springers are lively dogs with active minds, and all this energy this needs channelling.
- Am I giving him enough time?
- Does he have Separation Anxiety?
- Is he lonely, bored, attention-seeking, possessive or over-protective?

Sometimes it is the English Springer Spaniel's alert system going into overdrive. Is he barking at people he can see through the window or coming to the door? You want an alert bark, but not a constant bark.

When commanding your dog to stop, tone of voice is very important. Do not use a high-pitched or semi-hysterical STOP!! or NO!! Use low, firm commands.

One method is to set up a situation where you know he is going to bark, such as somebody arriving at your house, and put him on a lead beforehand. When he has barked several times, give a short, sharp tug on the lead and the **"Quiet"** command - spoken, not shouted. Reward him when he **stops** barking, not before.

If he's barking to get your attention, ignore him. If that doesn't work, leave the room and don't allow him to follow, so you deprive him of your attention.

Do this as well if his barking and attention-seeking turns to nipping. Tell him to **"Stop"** in a firm voice, or use the **"ACK!"** sound, remove your hand or leg and, if necessary, leave the room.

FACT > As humans, we use our voice in many different ways: to express happiness or anger, to scold, to shout a warning, and so on. Dogs are the same; different barks and whines give out different messages.

LISTEN to your dog and try and get an understanding of English Springer Spaniel language. Learn to recognise the difference between an alert bark, an excited bark, a demanding bark, a fearful, high-pitched bark, an aggressive bark or a plain *"I'm barking 'coz I can bark"* bark!

Some Springers are quite talkative! As well as barking, they can howl, sing, whine, squeak, snuffle, grumble and so on. Some owners carry on entire conversations with their Springers! These sounds are nothing to worry about; they're just another of the Springer's endearing qualities.

Speak and Shush!

The Speak and Shush technique teaches your dog or puppy to bark and be quiet on command. When your dog barks at an arrival at your house, gently praise him after the first few barks. If he persists, tell him **"Quiet."**

Get a friend to stand outside your front door and say **"Speak"** or **"Alert."** This is the cue for your accomplice to knock on the door or ring the bell - don't worry if you both feel like idiots, it will be worth the embarrassment!

When your dog barks, say **"Speak"** and praise him profusely. After a few good barks, say **"Shush"** or **"Quiet"** and then dangle a tasty treat in front of his nose.

If he is food-motivated, he will stop barking as soon as he sniffs the treat, because it is **physically impossible for a dog to sniff and woof at the same time.**

Praise your dog again as he sniffs quietly and give him the treat. Repeat this routine a few times a day and your Springer will quickly learn to bark whenever the doorbell rings and you ask him to **"Speak."**

Eventually your dog will bark AFTER your request but BEFORE the doorbell rings, meaning he has learned to bark on command.

Even better, he will learn to anticipate the likelihood of getting a treat following your **"Shush"** request and will also be quiet on command.

With Speak and Shush training, progressively increase the length of required shush time before offering a treat - at first just a couple of seconds, then three, five, 10, 20, and so on.

Page **126** THE ENGLISH SPRINGER SPANIEL HANDBOOK

By alternating instructions to speak and shush, the dog is praised and rewarded for barking on request and also for stopping barking on request.

If you have an English Springer Spaniel who is silent when somebody approaches the house, you can use the following method to get him to bark on the command of **"Speak."**

This is also a useful command if you walk your dog alone, especially at night; your dog's barking will help to keep you safe:

1. Have some treats at the ready, waiting for that rare bark.
2. Wait until he barks - for whatever reason - then say **"Speak"** or whatever word you want to use.
3. Praise him and give a treat. At this stage, he won't know why he is receiving the treat.
4. Keep praising him every time he barks and give a treat.
5. After you've done this for several days, hold a treat in your hand in front of his face and say **"Speak."**
6. Your dog will probably still not know what to do, but will eventually get so frustrated at not getting the treat that he will bark.
7. At which point, praise him and give the treat.

We trained a quiet dog to do this in a week and then, like clockwork, he barked enthusiastically every time anybody came to the door or whenever we gave him the "Speak" command, knowing he would get a treat for stopping.

10. Gundog Training

English Springer Spaniels are popular family pets, but that's only half the story. They are also excellent working dogs.

The breed is the gundog of choice for many gamekeepers and sportsmen. The tallest of all land Spaniels, the English Springer is hardy, compact and strong, taller and faster than a Cocker, with a renowned sense of smell.

Originally developed to flush game, these days they also retrieve. They have a full-on, enthusiastic approach to life, and are biddable and happy to work in all kinds of weather over any terrain.

These dogs are known for their versatility. They can be trained for rough and walked-up shooting and are well-suited to beating or picking up at driven shoots. They can also work as a peg dog or in wildfowling. If you're a sportsman or woman with just one dog, the English Springer Spaniel is the one for you.

Starting Out

If you're planning to train a gundog yourself then you need patience, understanding and plenty of time. The reward will be a dog that makes you proud when out in the field.

The first thing you must do when you bring your new puppy home is to establish a strong bond; this is key to a good working relationship later on. You two are going to be partners and the youngster needs to be able to trust you completely.

You'll bring your puppy home at about eight weeks old. A puppy from gundog stock will have good natural ability and you can start working on his retrieving skills straight away.

Start by holding on to your puppy and rolling a ball in front of him (a ball leaves a scent trail, encouraging the puppy to use his nose as well as his eyes). The puppy will see the ball (the "retrieve") and get excited about picking it up. Let him go and he will retrieve it.

Give him lots of praise when he picks it up and speak in positive tones, encouraging him to bring the ball back to you. Don't be in a rush to take the ball off the pup, but when you do, praise him again.

Remember **Distance-Duration-Distraction**. So start out just throwing or rolling the ball a few feet in your garden where there's no distractions, and only repeat the exercise once or twice. When he starts to get the hang of it, you can increase one of the Ds. But **don't rush** - we can't stress this enough with gundogs.

For the next three months your main focus should be the bond between the two of you. This period is very important and your young Springer should want to be with you. Work on developing a positive relationship that is strong enough to withstand any setbacks in training; he must never be frightened of you.

At around four to six months you can move things on a little with the Retrieve. Walk with the dog running in front of you and, when he is not looking, drop the ball in some grass. Encourage him back to that place and he should find the ball and bring it back to you.

When he can do this, you may want to cover the ball with some vegetation, so he has to use his nose as well as his eyes. As you slowly progress, you may hide several balls for your dog to find. Retrieving should not be endless throw and fetch. Rather, you should develop your Springer's skills of finding, retrieving and delivering.

The aim of this exercise is to condition the puppy to believe that if he stays close to you, he will find exciting things; in this case a ball, later a pheasant or rabbit.

This is where the trust is so important. A young dog given the opportunity to retrieve will usually present you with the prize with great pride. He has returned to you because he is doing what he was bred to do - and you are the reason he's doing it.

NOTE: Different gundog breeds respond differently to training. While you would gradually throw retrieves further and further away in thicker and thicker cover for a Labrador, to avoid ending up with a cover-shy retriever, this technique is not recommended for a Springer.

Don't throw a retrieve further than 10 yards away initially. You don't want to instil in the dog's mind that he's going to find everything 30 or more yards away. You can do this quite easily by allowing the Springer to race about before dropping the tennis ball or small dummy into cover relatively close to you.

Tip: If your Springer lives in your home, rather than an outdoor kennel, the golden rule is that whenever the pup picks <u>anything</u> up inside the house, he must be encouraged to bring it back.

The youngster must be praised for his actions, before the item is taken away and placed out of his reach. Don't scold a puppy for picking up things indoors and then be puzzled why the dog is reluctant to retrieve a ball or dummy when he's outside!

If your puppy is reluctant to retrieve a certain item, such as a tennis ball, find something he does like to pick up. This could be a small fluffy toy or a dummy covered in rabbit skin.

Formal gundog training should not start until six to nine months old. If you start your dog younger than that, you may have to re-do the lessons later on.

Before then your puppy will need to be well-socialised with other dogs, animals and people. He also needs an introduction to basic commands, particularly the Recall, as well as Sit and Stay. Some trainers teach their dogs to walk on a lead, others wait until the dog is six months old - but by that time, the bond between you should be established and the dog should want to be at your side.

Unlike with a pet, don't spend too much time rigidly enforcing the obedience commands – more haste, less speed. Think of the early lessons as groundwork.

Create a solid foundation before you do anything and gundog training will proceed much more smoothly. A Springer with a free spirit, working on his own initiative, will make a better gundog.

Some dogs are more strong-willed than others and take longer to learn, but that is often because they have been overloaded with information. Make instructions clear and simple so they are easily understood.

If a dog doesn't follow your instructions, he just hasn't learned what you want him to do.

Some puppies are hyperactive and full of will. These often turn into the most exciting working partners as adults, but it's essential that their first few months – before any formal gundog training starts – allows the all-important owner/puppy bond to develop steadily.

The assumption by many owners is to give the boisterous puppy lots to do, in the hope that the activity and "training" will calm him down. However, in a very young dog it can have the opposite effect and the puppy boils over. Go gently.

Then, when you start gundog training, give your puppy time to take in the new information. Once he seems to be getting it right, allow him a chance to perfect that skill before rushing ahead to the next stage.

Focus on guiding the puppy gently into doing the right thing and steering him away from the wrong things. At all times use positive methods – reward your dog with lots of praise and rubs or pats - TREAT DON'T BEAT! And don't ask him to do too much. As with normal obedience training, set your puppy up to SUCCEED, not fail.

It's a good idea to allow your pup to burn off some steam before any gundog lesson - you want him to be receptive, not exhausted, so he will take in the lesson more easily.

The Next Steps

Dr Vicky Payne, veterinary surgeon and breeder of Quincegrove Working English Springer Spaniels, believes it is safest to start exercising your puppy on a harness and lead. The harness should not restrict the shoulders. Puppies' necks are sensitive and puppies do have a tendency to jump and pull in early training, so a collar or slip lead may cause discomfort and damage.

First, get your puppy into the harness - you may use a treat to lure him to put his head through the harness. Let your puppy have a play in the harness before attaching the lead, then allow the youngster to run about dragging the lead behind him.

Gradually pick the lead up, but if your puppy starts to get stressed, allow it to drop and just encourage the puppy to come back, lavishing him with praise as he does so. Do this for just a few minutes a session.

Very slowly build it up over subsequent days to the point where the puppy is happy to walk on a lead. Don't stress or frighten the pup.

Once your puppy is walking nicely on a harness and lead, switch to a flat collar and lead, before eventually introducing the gundog slip lead. If you are concerned about the lead becoming too tight if your puppy pulls, there are slip leads available with a double stop, **pictured,** so the neck loop can never become too tight.

Puppies should not be over-exercised. Don't overdo any of this play training with a gundog puppy before he's one year old. You could spoil the youngster's joints and once any damage is done, it can't be rectified. If the puppy lives indoors and you have children, he may be getting far more exercise than you think. This also applies if you have an older dog and the puppy tries to keep up with it all day.

Expert Advice

Vicky Payne has been breeding and shooting with English Springer Spaniels for 18 years. Here she shares her techniques for starting gundog training with a young dog:

"The early stages of your Springer Spaniel's training have all been about building a bond and developing the natural desire to hunt and retrieve.

"From around six months old, I start to make the training a little more gundog work-focused. I don't instil steadiness until my pups are very keen to retrieve anything from anywhere, and I use this time to get them retrieving from light cover, across tracks and small ditches, and even over small obstacles like branches. All this helps them to become confident adult dogs.

"Early cues will all come from your voice and body language, but formal gundog work requires handlers to be quiet, and to give most of their cues with a whistle. Don't introduce the whistle until your puppy is proficient at sitting and recalling to verbal cues.

"To introduce the whistle, give your whistle (usually a single *'peep'* for Sit, and a repeated short *'pip'* for Recall), then immediately say your cue word. Your puppy should sit or recall, then reward him as usual.

"After a few sessions, try the whistle on its own; most puppies anticipate and will be sitting or running back to you before you need to use your voice! Keep sessions short with just five or six practices each time, but you can train several times a day.

"Spaniels also need to learn to stop when there's movement and to the sounds of a shot, as well as staying still until sent for a retrieve. Shot should be introduced carefully to avoid making the puppy gun-shy. I like to have a friend let off a starting pistol some distance away while my puppy and I have a game.

"Over several sessions the starting pistol can be fired closer to the puppy - as long as he doesn't show any signs of nervousness. Later in training, the shot is introduced as a new cue - just like the whistle.

"So the training sequence is **shot - say Sit - puppy sits - puppy gets a reward.** Over several sessions the vocal back-up is dropped and the puppy sits to shot alone.

"To develop your puppy's obedience to staying still when dummies are thrown, start by asking your puppy to sit, then quietly drop a dummy behind you. If he stays in a Sit, give him a tasty treat. If he moves, pick up the dummy and try again. Some trainers use **place boards** (small raised platforms which the dog sits on) for this exercise.

"Next, throw the dummy out to the side of you, again positioning yourself so you can prevent the puppy getting the dummy if he can't resist temptation. Over several weeks you should be able to start by your puppy's side and throw a dummy forward. Now you can add in a retrieve as a reward by releasing him to fetch the dummies about half of the time.

"Steadiness to the flush is trained in a similar way, but with the puppy moving. Start with your puppy on the lead walking to heel, say Sit, and then throw the dummy gently to one side so you can step in front if your puppy tries to grab it. Reward with a treat if they stay in the Sit.

"This is another exercise to do in short sessions every few days until your pup starts to anticipate the game; now you can throw the dummy without saying anything and your puppy should sit automatically!

"This new game can then be made more difficult by throwing the dummy in front of you, and later dropping the dummy while the puppy is hunting, to simulate a real flush.

"Sometimes reward with a retrieve, but sometimes pick the dummy yourself and reward with a chest rub (Springers love a chest rub) or a treat."

Photo: Vicky on a shoot in Sussex with Mars (Quincegrove Life On Mars).

Vicky continues: "Over your dog's first 18 months you will build a repertoire of retrieves, starting with **'seen'** retrieves where the dog sees the dummy fall, then **'memories,'** (where he sees it fall then is moved away or where he doesn't see it fall, but where he has previously retrieved from), right out to the hard **'blind'** retrieves where your dog trusts you to point him in the right direction.

"A good trainer or gundog club can help you train these retrieves, as well as offering opportunities to hunt in a variety of terrain.

"At around 18 months it will be time to introduce your pup to game if you plan to take him beating, picking up, or trialling. Professional assistance is vital at this stage to help you manage the excitement that working with live game scent brings.

"Expect your well-trained Springer to forget a few of his lessons, and have a plan ready to set him up for success."

Vicky's Facebook page, with some interesting videos of training working Springers is at: www.facebook.com/quincegrovehealthtestedworkingspringers and her website is at:

http://workingspringerspaniels.uk

Professional Help

Professional gundog trainer and Kennel Club Assured Breeder Stewart North has been breeding and training gundogs for 20 years. He has produced 15 Field Trial Winners and has over 100 Working Test Awards to his credit.

Stewart said: "I have this basic advice for anyone thinking of training a working gundog: Most puppy buyers choose a pup based on price, location, sex and colour without considering temperament, health and exercise. Very few buyers research the breeder and their dogs before viewing puppies.

"Acting on impulse is one sure way of making the wrong decision! Asking to see the dam, SIRE and previous progeny will give you a much better indication of what your future pup will turn out to be."

Vicky adds: "Although working-type Springers are generally healthy, breeders should be able to show you copies of the sire's and dam's health test results. These should include eye testing, DNA test results, and hip and elbow grades, if these have been done."

See **Chapter 12. Springer Health** for the relevant certificates.

Stewart continues: "If you want a good hunting working gundog, then the best advice I can give is not to start too early with obedience training.

"A puppy needs to be well-socialised with people and other dogs, too much leash work, sit/stay and steadiness work can decrease the drive and confidence of a young dog.

"Allow the pup to grow up without too much discipline, concentrate on play-retrieve and recall-reward, then at about nine months of age the proper training can start.

"Visit a local trainer or experienced gundog handler to get a feel for the environment, teaching methods and - most importantly - the bond between dog and handler."

If you're starting out with your first gundog, it's a good idea to get some professional help - at least at the beginning. Here's some advice on what to look for:

1. You should be made to feel welcome. The trainer should be an experienced gundog handler with evidence of success in competition, or perhaps a field trial judge.
2. The fee should reflect the level of facilities and numbers in the class. One-to-one lessons cost more, but with the right trainer it may well be worth it.
3. The trainer should have a positive attitude towards English Springer Spaniels. It will soon be obvious if they do not like or understand the breed.
4. Vaccinations, regular worming and flea treatment should always be insisted upon before joining a class. Similarly, bitches in season should be excluded.
5. Training methods should be positive and reward-based. There should be no harsh handling or electric collars evident.
6. The trainer should be respected by all present — an attentive, interested and happy class will be evidence of that.
7. Expect to make progress slowly. It is up to you to make sure you practise between lessons in your own time.
8. The facilities and equipment available for the class should help learning. A safe environment is essential, with access to suitable equipment and water.

9. Access to a well-stocked rabbit pen would be a plus. If the trainer does not have their own, expect them to help you access one when the time is right.

10. As the training reaches its final stages, you should be offered the opportunity to have your gundog introduced to the real thing, and even shot over on a training day.

11. Patience and a common-sense approach will ensure that in the end you have a well-trained canine companion for the future.

12. To find out more about training near you, contact the Kennel Club in the UK or ESSFTA in the US.

If you don't have a personal recommendation of a good instructor, **The Gundog Club** is a good place to start looking for one in the UK. Their instructors offer help and support to gundog owners who want to train their dogs for fieldwork, or who simply want a better-behaved dog. A list of Accredited Trainers in England and Wales is at: https://thegundogclub.co.uk/instructors

ESSFTA (The English Springer Spaniel Field Trial Association) has information about hunting and field trialling with English Springers in the US on its website at: https://essfta.org

FAQs

Q: I've had my 10-week-old puppy a week and he is learning really quickly, but I can't stop him biting me. Today he drew blood. Should he go back to the breeder?

A: Almost all puppies mouth, but some may bite too hard and need to learn "bite inhibition." Dogs need to understand that we humans are delicate, and their teeth should never touch us.

To teach him bite inhibition, keep lots of soft toys to hand, and put one in his mouth whenever he opens it to get hold of you. Do not play roughly with him, because it gives the wrong message about how to interact. Puppies do have a need to bite and chew, so make sure he has plenty of safe items to gnaw upon. **Never smack a biting puppy, he needs to see your hands as the source of good things.**

Q: We have a five-month-old puppy that is starting to habitually bark for attention. We don't want this to become a habit and have a noisy gundog, do you have any advice on how to prevent it?

A: A dog will usually bark for one of the following reasons: as a warning, when it is excited, as a form of attention-seeking, in response to anxiety and boredom, or finally as a social behaviour in response to other dogs. The puppy must learn when it is appropriate to bark and when it needs to be quiet.

Give your puppy adequate interactive exercise so he has less pent-up energy. Avoid over-exercising a young dog; the aim is to simply burn off excess energy, not exhaust the puppy.

Avoid leaving him alone for long periods of time. Train the puppy to be left for increasingly longer amounts of time, initially for very brief periods. Don't increase the length of time you leave the puppy until he has learned to settle quietly for shorter periods.

Never comfort or feed the puppy when it is barking for attention — this is rewarding unwanted behaviour. Don't shout at him to stop barking, as this may cause him to bark even more.

Try getting his attention with a clap or use the whistle. As soon as the puppy is quiet, redirect its attention to something productive and rewarding (like a toy) and after getting his attention, practise simple commands, such as "Sit" or "Down," in order to shift its focus.

Q: Last year I bought a Springer puppy and planned to train him. He settled in at home very well with my seven-year-old gundog Alfie. Now the young Spaniel is 11 months old I have started to do some training with him, but he does not seem to concentrate on me, looking around instead for Alfie. What should I do?

A: Your young gundog has bonded with Alfie more than he has bonded with you, the trainer. He spends most of his day around Alfie so doesn't need you to make any decisions for him. He will look to Alfie and then will follow by example.

Split the two gundogs up and kennel them separately for a while. Train the young Spaniel pup alone. Don't even take them out in the car together. You need your youngster to be focused on you at all times when training starts properly and you should also start to spend more time with your young dog to form more of a solid one-to-one relationship.

He was looking for reassurance from Alfie, and this now has to come from you, the trainer. Once he starts to understand he can rely on you his concentration will get better and his training more responsive.

Q: I am training two six-month-old puppies but they don't always do as I ask. Can I allow them to go for a run to burn off energy before a training session?

A: Training begins long before a lead is placed around a puppy's neck. From the time the puppy comes into its new home, it can be taught simple things, as it is important to build a strong bond with the puppy before its serious training begins.

For example, sitting for food can be started early, simply sitting is not enough. The puppy must learn to feast its eyes on you before it is allowed to eat. Formal obedience training can begin between six and 12 months, but this depends on the individual puppy's physical and mental development.

German English Springer Spaniel Heather (Okka vom Belauer), owned by Svenja Arendt, pictured after searching a muddy pond for wounded ducks that might have been missed in the dark on the previous day's shoot.

Q: I am getting a fully-trained gundog next month. How long do I need to settle her in before taking her out working with me? How long will it take my new gundog to bond with me?

A: A Spaniel should be fully trained at around two-and-a-half to three years old and will have gained a strong bond with its owner during that time. To gain the dog's trust, you need to take things slowly.

Start by walking the dog on the lead at least two or three times a day and continue this regime for at least two-and-a-half weeks.

When she's not on the lead you should continually call the dog and encourage her to come to you. In this way she will get used to your voice and tone of command.

Don't take the dog out working until she has bonded with you. Be patient. Bitches sometimes take longer than dogs to bond fully. Take time to gain the dog's trust. It will be strange enough for the dog in this new environment, without being asked to work for someone she does not know.

....

Learning the Language

If you're relatively new to the gundog world, there's a whole new language you need to learn! Here's a list of gundog terminology you're likely to come across:

Action and style - the way a dog works when hunting or retrieving, particularly used with Spaniels.

Back wind - wind directly coming from behind the handler.

Blind retrieve - a dummy/bird which has either fallen or been placed out of sight of the dog.

Cheek wind - wind direction from left or right of the handler.

Cold game - previously shot game such as pheasant, duck, partridge etc., which is cold stored or frozen and can be used for "out of season" retrieving practice.

Cover - natural or planted vegetation which serves as both protection and concealment for game.

Creep/creeping - used to describe a gundog that slowly moves forward when told to sit.

D/DC - docked and dew clawed.

Dead - a verbal command given to a dog to release a retrieve.

Decoy/distraction - when retrieving, any object that may distract a dog away from what it has been sent to retrieve.

Drive - the speed and style of a gundog, especially when entering thick cover such as bramble.

Dummy - made from various materials and comes in numerous shapes, the standard object for teaching retrieving, *pictured.*

Eye wipe - when one dog fails to find a retrieve and then another dog is successful. In the case of a field trial it is found by one of the judges.

Fetch - the verbal command used to send a dog out on a seen retrieve. Commonly used for marked retrieves.

Field Trial - a competitive event where gundogs compete against one another on live game. There are field trials for retrievers, spaniels, pointers and setters.

Flush - the act of finding and flushing (making it fly or run) game that is hiding in cover for the Gun to shoot.

FTAW - Field Trial Award Winner. A dog that has won an award at a field trial, for example Certificate of Merit (COM) or higher, but not actually won the trial itself.

FTCh - Field Trial Champion. A dog that has won at least three days' worth of field trial open stakes.

FTW - Field Trial Winner. A dog that has been placed first in a field trial.

Game sense - a dog's ability to use its natural senses and ability to find dead or injured game.

Get in - a spoken command given to a gundog normally meaning to "get in" water or cover.

Get on - like the command "Back," tells your dog to proceed in a straight line until finding a dummy/bird, or can be used to start a Spaniel hunting.

Get out - a verbal command given when using hand signals to send the dog either the left or right.

Give - a verbal command to get a gundog to release the retrieved item.

Go back - used to send your dog in a straight line until finding a dummy/bird. Often associated with blind retrieves rather than marked retrieves.

Gun sense - a dog's ability to have awareness of the swing of a gun and to follow the general direction of the shot.

Gun shy - a dog that fears loud noises, in particular the sound of gunfire.

Hard mouth - a dog that regularly damages game when retrieving. Considered a major fault.

Hi lost – a verbal command given to a gundog meaning to hunt in a particular area when out on a retrieve.

Hup - a verbal command to "Sit," most often heard in the Spaniel world.

Line (taking a line) - the route a dog takes to the game or dummy going out and on return to the handler.

Marked retrieve - a retrieve that has actually been seen by the gundog.

Memory retrieve - a retrieve that has been placed in view of the dog, but time and distance have elapsed before the dog is actually sent for the retrieve.

Over - a command instructing the dog to jump, or get over, any obstacle such as a stretch of water, a fence, ditch or fallen tree.

Pace - the speed at which the dog hunts.

Peg dog - a dog that sits next to a peg and its handler, the Gun, during a drive and may retrieve shot game on command at the end of the drive.

Pegging - catching live uninjured or unshot game.

Pick-up dog/Picker-up - a handler and dog(s) who stand well behind the gun line and systematically retrieve the dead and injured game.

Pottering - refers to a dog that hunts without pace or style, or one that lingers on an old scent, leaves it, and then comes back to it.

Pricked - game that has been shot and potentially injured, but not killed.

Quartering/quarter - the methodical side-to-side hunting pattern that a flushing or pointing dog is trained to follow to cover the ground efficiently and thoroughly.

Run - in a field trial or working test, this describes the activities that occur while a competitor is under the control of the judge.

Runner - a shot and injured bird or ground game that leaves a scent trail along the ground and requires picking up immediately by a dog so it can be humanely despatched.

Running in - when a dog leaves a handler without being sent to retrieve a dummy/bird.

Slip lead - a lead used by gundog handlers. A slip lead is a combination of both a dog lead and a dog collar, normally made of hemp or nylon.

Soft mouth - a dog that will pick up and hold game softly but firmly on the retrieve.

Steadiness - a required skill of any gundog, it should sit still when a bird, ground game or even a dummy is flushed or thrown, or when a gun is fired.

Style - the tail and body action of a dog when hunting for dummies or game.

There - a verbal command given to a gundog to hunt in a particular area when out on a retrieve.

Tongue/squeaking - when a dog makes an excited noise such as barking, whining or squeaking while working. This can often occur on the dog's way out to a retrieve and is considered a fault.

Working test - a competitive event normally held in the spring or summer using canvas dummies rather than live game.

With thanks to Dr Vicky Payne, MRCVS, David Tomlinson, Ellena Swift, Neil McIntosh, Tony Buckwell and Stewart North.

11. Exercise and Socialisation

There's no getting away from the fact that the English Springer Spaniel is an active breed in body and mind - and BOTH need lots of exercise. The Kennel Club recommends more than two hours of physical exercise per day for an adult Springer.

The Importance of Exercise

One thing all dogs have in common – including every Springer ever born - is the need for daily exercise. It helps to keep your dog happy, healthy and free from disease.

Just as with humans, exercise:

- Strengthens respiratory and circulatory systems
- Helps get oxygen to tissue cells
- Helps to keep Springers mentally stimulated and socialised
- Keeps muscles toned and joints flexible
- Wards off obesity
- Aids digestion
- Releases endorphins which trigger positive feelings

The amount of exercise an individual dog needs varies according to temperament, natural energy levels, your living conditions, whether he is kept with other dogs and, importantly, what he gets used to.

FACT The other factor – and it can be a significant one - is whether your English Springer is bred from show, working or dual bloodlines.

There are, of course, individual variations, but working-type dogs generally have a higher *"drive"* than those bred from show lines.

It makes sense. English Springer Spaniels were not bred as companion dogs; they were developed to do a job alongside humans in the field. Springers and other gundogs are bred to be out all day in all weathers. They have to be alert to commands and ready and willing to run endless miles to flush and retrieve game. They also have to work under their own initiative when out of sight of their master or mistress.

All of this adds up to a hardy dog that is constantly on the alert, eager to please and ready to go all day long.

That's not to say Springers don't love snuggling up with you; they certainly do - they just need their exercise as well.

Show-type and dual-purpose Springers have had some of this drive tempered to make them calmer and more suitable for the show ring or family home.

Types of Exercise

When we talk about "exercising" a dog, most people think this means going out for a walk two or three times a day - and it does for many owners. However, there are other forms of exercise that all help to keep your Springer happy and socialised.

Mental exercise is extremely important. Springers love a challenge or a game, which can be just as important as a walk. They will fetch a ball or toy for hours on end; some become almost obsessive.

Regular short training sessions, retrieving, hiding objects and rewarding your dog with praise when he finds them, playing with other dogs, providing interactive toys that make your dog use his brain to get the treat, or maybe even setting up a mini agility course in your yard or garden, all help to keep your Springer stimulated.

Playing in a fenced area with toys or balls is also a great way to exercise (for both of you!). However, a garden or yard should not be seen as a replacement for daily exercise away from the home, where your dog can experience new places, scents, people and dogs. Your dog will enjoy going for walks on the lead, but all Springers have an inbuilt desire to run free.

Teach your Springer the Recall while he's still young and find a safe area where he can regularly run free and let off steam.

NOTE: Playing Frisbee isn't recommended for growing Springers, as high-impact jumping can lead to joint issues later in life.

Owning more than one dog - or having friends with dogs - is another way for well-socialised Springers to get lots of exercise. A couple of dogs running around together get far more exercise than one dog on his own.

A Springer is a great choice for active families. Once trained, they also make excellent sporting companions. If you intend to jog, cycle or ride with your Springer alongside, gradually build up the distance and speed, and don't push your dog too far. These incredibly loyal and enthusiastic dogs will run until they drop to keep up with you.

But you can hike all day with a fit adult Springer and you won't tire him out!

WARNING: Springers like to go out and play whatever the weather! They are best suited to outdoorsy people. If you're a bit of a couch potato and not too keen on bad weather, a different breed would be a better choice.

Most enjoy swimming, which is a great form of exercise - for older dogs too, as it does not place any stress on joints. Many veterinary practices now use water tanks for remedial therapy as well as canine recreation. Springers will dash in and out of the water all day long if you'll let them, but remember that swimming is a lot more strenuous for a dog than walking or running.

Don't repeatedly throw that stick or ball into the water; overstretching him could place a strain on his heart; all dogs should exercise within their limits – on both land and water. We also advise gently drying your Springer's ears after swimming to reduce the risk of ear infections.

Springers have no road sense! You must make sure it's safe, away from traffic and other hazards, before letting yours off the lead - and only after he has learned the Recall - or stay in a safe area away from traffic.

And never underestimate a Springer's prey instinct! They love to chase. Keep them on a lead near livestock and wild animals if you are in the countryside, unless you have trained yours not to chase.

Tip: Springers have an amazing sense of smell - and when their noses kick in, their ears tend to switch off! The Recall is the most important thing you can teach your dog, so spend as long as it takes to teach your dog to come back to you.

If you are worried about losing your dog before he has fully learned the Recall, or are nervous about him being out of sight, consider fitting a GPS collar when you let yours run free, see **Chapter 9. Basic Training.**

Springers love a challenge and the list of potential activities you can take part in is as long as your arm, including: Canine Good Citizen, Agility, Field Trials, Shooting/Hunting, Showing, Flyball, Rally Obedience, Tracking, Nose Work, Barn Hunt, even Dock Diving, which is now taking place in the UK as well as the US.

An under-exercised or bored Springer will find something to occupy him - and it could well involve destructive behaviour. Leaving the dog in a crate too often is NOT the solution, as an over-crated Springer is likely to develop anxiety or behaviour issues. The answer is more exercise and mental stimulation and possibly training sessions.

Mental Stimulation

Springers are engaged, busy dogs with active minds, and they can become easily bored. They are playful and love a game or challenge. If their "drive" is not channelled in a positive manner, it can turn to naughtiness, destructive or attention-seeking behaviour, or depression.

If you return home to find your favourite cushions shredded or the contents of the kitchen bin strewn around the floor, ask yourself:

"Is he getting enough exercise/mental stimulation?" and "Am I leaving him alone for too long?"

Have toys and chews, and factor in regular play time with your Springer – even gentle play time for old dogs.

Tip: A washable *Snuffle Mat, pictured,* is an interesting toy as it can help to satisfy a Springer's hunting instinct and reduce boredom. Hide a treat, toy or food in there and let your Springer work out how to get it.

NOTE: Always use under supervision.

FACT Sticks can easily splinter in a dog's mouth or stomach (and can even pierce its mouth or throat, causing serious injury), and jumping up for Frisbees can cause back damage. Balls should be at least tennis ball size so as not to choke your dog.

A Springer at the heart of the family getting regular exercise and mental challenges is a happy dog and a loyal companion second to none.

If you haven't the time or energy levels to devote a couple of hours a day to a Springer, consider getting a smaller breed from a non-working background with a lower drive.

NOTE: Both dognapping and dog attacks are on the increase - even in dog parks and public parks. Keep a close eye on your dog and, if you are at all worried, avoid popular dog walking areas and find other places where your dog can exercise safely. The UK police are advising owners not to walk their dogs at the same time and places each day, but to vary their routine.

....

Routine

Establish an exercise regime early in your dog's life. If possible, get your dog used to walks at similar times every day and gradually build that up as the puppy reaches adulthood. Start out with a regime you know you can continue with, as your dog will come to expect it and will not be happy if the walks suddenly stop.

Tip: If you haven't enough time to give your Springer the exercise he needs, consider employing a daily dog walker, if you can afford it, or take him to doggie day care once or twice a week. As well as the exercise, he will love the interaction with other dogs.

Springers are enthusiastic, curious dogs that love investigating new scents and places, which is why you need to plug every little gap in and under your fence – they will be off given half a chance!

Most Springers love snow. Be aware that snow and ice can clump on paws, ears, legs and tummy. Salt or de-icing products on roads and pathways contain chemicals that can be poisonous to dogs and cause irritation – particularly if he tries to lick it off.

If your dog gets iced up, bathe paws and other affected areas in lukewarm - NOT HOT - water.

Photo: Della (Cottonstones Ribble), bred by Chris Brandon-Lodge, may have got slightly carried away playing in the snow while on holiday in Switzerland with her owners!

Older dogs still need exercise to keep their body, joints and systems functioning properly. They need a less strenuous regime – they are usually happier with shorter walks, but still enough to keep them physically and mentally active.

Again, every dog is different; some are willing and able to keep on running to the end of their lives, others slow right down.

If your old or sick dog is struggling, he will show you he's not up to it by stopping and looking at you or sitting/lying down and refusing to move. If he's healthy and does this, he is just being lazy!

Regular exercise can add months or even years to a dog's life.

Exercising Puppies

There are strict guidelines for puppies. It's important not to over-exercise young pups as, until a puppy's growth plates close, they're soft and vulnerable to injury.

Too much impact can cause permanent damage. So, playing Fetch or Frisbee for hours on end with your young Springer is definitely not a good plan, nor is allowing a pup to freely run up and down stairs in your home. You'll end up with a damaged dog later in life and a pile of vet's bills.

Just like babies, puppies have different temperaments and energy levels; some need more exercise than others. Start slowly and build it up. The worst combination is over-exercise and overweight.

Don't take your pup out of your fenced garden or yard until the all-clear after the vaccinations - unless you carry him around to start the socialisation process. Begin with daily short walks (literally just a few minutes) on the lead. Get your young dog used to being outside the home environment and experiencing new situations as soon as possible. The general guideline for exercise is:

Five minutes of on-lead exercise every day per month of age

So, a total of 15 minutes per day when three months (13 weeks) old

30 minutes per day when six months (26 weeks) old, etc.

This applies until around one year to 18 months old, when much of their growing has taken place. Slowly increase the time as he gets used to being exercised and this will gradually build up muscles and stamina.

Tip: It is OK for your young pup to have free run of your garden or yard, provided it has a soft surface such as grass.

This does not count in the five minutes per month rule, but the time should still be controlled. Puppies shouldn't be running around for hours, even if it is on grass or a soft surface.

If the yard is stone or concrete, limit the time your dog runs around on it, as the hard surface will impact joints.

It is also fine for your pup to run freely around the house to burn off energy - although not up and down stairs or jumping on and off furniture.

A pup will take things at his own pace and stop to sniff or rest. If you have other dogs, restrict the time your pup is allowed to play with them, as he won't know when he's had enough.

One breeder added: "For the first 18 months whilst the puppy's bones are soft and developing, it's best not to over-exert and put strain on the joints.

"Daily gentle walking is great, just not constant fast and hard running/chasing in the puppy stage, as too much is a big strain."

And when your little pup has grown into a beautiful adult Springer with a skeleton capable of carrying him through a long and healthy life, it will have been worth all the effort.

A long, healthy life is best started slowly

Exercise Recap

- A Springer needs mental as well as physical exercise
- Aim for a couple of hours a day
- Don't over-exercise puppies - and avoid stairs and high impact activities
- Triple check the fencing around your garden or yard to prevent The Great Escape
- Aim for at least two good walks away from the house every day with an adult Springer
- Vary your exercise route – it will be more interesting for both of you
- Do not throw a ball or toy repeatedly if your dog shows signs of over-exertion. Springers have no sense of their own limitations. Stop the activity after a while - no matter how much he begs you to throw it again
- The same goes for swimming, cycling, jogging or any organised activity; ensure any exercise is within your dog's capabilities – look out for heavy panting
- Don't strenuously exercise your dog straight after or within an hour of a meal as this can cause Bloat. Canine Bloat is extremely serious, if not fatal. See **Chapter 7. Feeding a Springer** for details
- Springers love games, challenges and interaction with their owners
- Some dogs, particularly adolescent ones, may try to push the boundaries when out walking on the lead. If yours stops dead and stares at you or tries to pull you in another direction, ignore him

    Do not return his stare, just continue along the way you want to go, not his way

- In hot weather, exercise your dog early morning or in the evening, particularly if yours has a dense coat
- Exercise old dogs more gently - especially in cold weather when it is harder to get their bodies moving. Have a cool-down period after exercise to reduce stiffness and soreness; it helps to remove lactic acids - our 13-year-old loved a body rub
- Make sure your dog has constant access to fresh water. Dogs can only sweat a tiny amount through the pads of their paws, they need to drink water to cool down

Tip: Your Springer will get used to your regime. If you over-stimulate and constantly exercise him as a puppy, he will think this is the norm.

This may not be such an attractive prospect when your fully-grown dog constantly needs and demands your attention a year or two later, or your work patterns change and you have less time to exercise him. The key is to start a routine that you can stick to.

Admittedly, when it is raining or freezing cold, the last thing you may want to do is to venture outdoors with your dog. But make the effort; the lows are more than compensated for by the highs.

Springers love their outdoor walks, but don't let yours dictate if he doesn't want to go out, it will only make him lazier, fatter and less sociable with others.

Exercise helps you bond with your dog, keep fit, see different places and meet new companions - both canine and human. In short, it enhances both your lives.

Socialisation

Your adult dog's character will depend largely on two things: inherited temperament and environment, or **NATURE AND NURTURE**. And one absolutely essential aspect of nurture for all dogs is socialisation.

FACT › Scientists now realise the importance that socialisation plays in a dog's life. There is a fairly small window regarded as the optimum time for socialisation - and this is up to the age of four to five months.

Socialisation means *"learning to be part of society,"* or *"integration."* This means helping dogs become comfortable within a human society by getting them used to different people, environments, traffic, sights, noises, smells, animals, other dogs, etc.

It actually begins from the moment the puppy is born, and the importance of picking a good breeder cannot be over-emphasised.

Not only will he or she breed for good temperament and health, but the dam (puppy's mother) will be well-balanced, friendly and unstressed, and the pup will learn a lot in this positive environment.

Learning When Young Is Easiest

Most young animals, including dogs, are naturally able to get used to their everyday environment until they reach a certain age. When they reach this age, they become much more suspicious of things they haven't yet experienced. This is why it often takes longer to train an older dog.

When you think about it, humans are not so different. Babies and children have a tremendous capacity to learn, we call this early period our *"formative years."*

As we age, we can still learn, but not at the speed we absorbed things when very young. Also, as we get older, we are often less receptive to new ideas or new ways of doing things.

This age-specific natural development allows a puppy to get comfortable with the normal sights, sounds, people and animals that will be a part of his life. It ensures that he doesn't spend his life jumping in fright, barking or growling at every blowing leaf.

The suspicion that dogs develop later also ensures that they react with a healthy dose of caution to new things that could really be dangerous - Mother Nature is clever!

It is essential that your dog's introductions to new things are all **positive**. Negative experiences lead to a dog becoming fearful and untrusting.

Your dog may already have a wonderful temperament, but he still needs socialising to avoid him thinking that the world is tiny and it revolves around him. Springers can be very demanding – don't let yours become an attention-seeker.

FACT Good socialisation gives confidence and helps puppies – whether bold or timid – to learn their place in society. The ultimate goal is to have a happy, well-adjusted Springer you can take anywhere.

Ever seen a therapy or sniffer dog in action and noticed how incredibly well-adjusted to life they are? This is no coincidence.

These dogs, *pictured*, have been extensively socialised and are ready and able to deal in a confident manner with whatever situation they encounter. They are relaxed and comfortable in their own skin - just like you want your dog to be.

Tip Spend as much time as you can socialising your dog when young. It's just as important as training. Start as soon as you bring your puppy home. Regular socialisation should continue until your dog is around 18 months of age.

After that, don't just forget about it; socialisation isn't only for puppies, it should continue throughout life. As with any skill, if it is not practised, your dog will become less proficient at interacting with other people, animals, noises and new situations.

Developing the Well-Rounded Adult

Dogs that have not been properly integrated are more likely to react with fear or aggression to unfamiliar people, animals and experiences.

Springers who are relaxed around strangers, dogs, cats and other animals, honking horns, cyclists, joggers, veterinary examinations, traffic, crowds and noise are easier to live with than dogs who find these situations challenging or frightening.

And if you are planning on taking part in field, trails, shooting, or canine competitions, get your Springer socialised and used to the buzz of these events early on.

FACT Well-socialised dogs live more relaxed, peaceful and happy lives than dogs that are constantly stressed by their environment.

Socialisation isn't an *"all or nothing"* project. You can socialise a puppy a bit, a lot, or a whole lot. The wider the range of new experiences you expose him to (positively) when young, the better.

Socialisation should never be forced, but approached systematically and in a manner that builds confidence and curious interaction.

If your pup finds a new experience frightening, take a step back, introduce him to the scary situation much more gradually, and make a big effort to do something he loves during the situation or right afterwards.

For example, if your puppy seems to be frightened by noise and vehicles at a busy road, a good method would be to go to a quiet road, sit with the dog away from - but within sight of - the traffic. Every time he looks towards the traffic say *"YES!"* and reward him with a treat.

If he is still stressed, you need to move further away. When your dog takes the food in a calm manner, he is becoming more relaxed and getting used to traffic sounds, so you can edge a bit nearer - but still just for short periods until he becomes totally relaxed. Keep each session short and **POSITIVE**. (See <u>Chapter 10. Gundog Training</u> for getting your Springer used to the sound of gunshot).

Meeting Other Dogs

When you take your gorgeous and vulnerable little pup out with other dogs for the first few times, you are bound to be a bit apprehensive. To begin with, introduce your puppy to just one other dog – one that you know to be friendly, rather than taking him straight to the park where there are lots of dogs of all sizes racing around, which might frighten the life out of your timid little darling.

On the other hand, your pup might be full of confidence right from the off, but you still need to approach things slowly. If your puppy is too cocksure, he may get a warning nip from an older dog, which could make him more anxious when approaching new dogs in the future.

Tip **Always make initial introductions <u>on neutral ground,</u> so as not to trigger territorial behaviour. You want your Springer to approach other dogs with friendliness, not fear.**

From the first meeting, help both dogs experience good things when they're in each other's presence. Let them sniff each other briefly, which is normal canine greeting behaviour.

As they do, talk to them in a happy, friendly tone of voice; never use a threatening tone.

Don't allow them to sniff each other for too long as this may escalate to an aggressive response. After a short time, get the attention of both dogs and give each a treat in return for obeying a simple command, e.g. *"Sit"* or *"Stay."* Continue with the *"happy talk,"* and rewards.

Learn to spot the difference between normal rough and tumble play and interaction that may develop into fear or aggression.

Here are some signs of fear to look out for when your dog interacts with other canines:

- Running away or freezing on the spot
- Licking the lips or lips pulled back
- Trembling or panting, which can be a sign of stress or pain

- Frantic/nervous behaviour, e.g. excessive sniffing, drinking or playing frenetically with a toy
- A lowered body stance or crouching
- Lying on his back with paws in the air – this is submissive, as is submissive urination
- Lowering of the head or turning the head away, when you may see the whites of the eyes as the dog tries to keep eyes on the perceived threat
- Growling and/or hair raised on his back (raised hackles)
- Tail lifted in the air or ears high on the head

Some of these responses are normal. A pup may well crouch on the ground or roll on to his back to show other dogs he's not a threat. If the situation looks like escalating, calmly distract the dogs or remove your puppy – don't shout or shriek. **Dogs will pick up on your fear.**

Another sign to look out for is *eyeballing.* In the canine world, staring a dog in the eyes is a challenge and may cause an aggressive response.

NOTE: Whereas we might look someone in the eye when we are first introduced, it is normal for dogs to sniff thescent glands in another dog's bottom!

Tip: Your puppy has to learn to interact with other dogs. Don't be too quick to pick him up; he will sense your anxiety, lose confidence and become less independent. The same is true when walking on a lead – don't be nervous every time you see another dog – your Springer will pick up on it and may react.

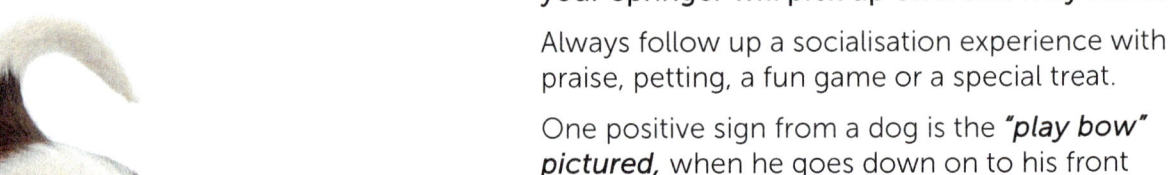

Always follow up a socialisation experience with praise, petting, a fun game or a special treat.

One positive sign from a dog is the *"play bow" pictured,* when he goes down on to his front elbows but keeps his backside up in the air.

This is a sign that he's feeling friendly towards the other dog and wants to play. Relaxed ear and body position and wagging tail are other positive signs.

Although Springers are not normally aggressive dogs, aggression is often grounded in fear, and a dog that mixes easily is less likely to be combative. Similarly, without frequent and new experiences, some Springers can become timid and anxious.

Take your new dog everywhere you can. You want him to feel relaxed and calm in any situation, even noisy and crowded ones. Take treats with you and praise him when he reacts calmly to new situations.

Once settled into your home, introduce him to your friends and teach him not to jump up. If you have young children, it is not only the dog that needs socialising! Youngsters also need training on how to act around dogs, so both parties learn to respect the other.

An excellent way of getting your new puppy to meet other dogs in a safe environment is at a puppy class. We highly recommend this for all puppies. Ask around locally if any classes are being run; some vets and dog trainers run classes for very junior pups who have had all their vaccinations. These help pups get used to other dogs of a similar age.

What the Breeders Say

Lynne Lucas: "I run the girls for about an hour a day. As they run with each other, they never stop, so I find that is sufficient for mine. All the families I place my pups with have an active lifestyle and have thoroughly researched the breed, so they are well aware when they contact me.

"Socialising your pup is very important so that they learn social skills from other pups or dogs. But I would class **training** as the most important thing your pup will have in their early months and years; training should never stop.

"I still continue to train my girls when out on a walk, i.e. Recall and Touch training - even Calamity who is now nine years old. Just remember that a bored Springer can be a destructive Springer."

Lisa Cardy: "Socialisation and training are vital for a puppy. A dog not well-trained is a problem taking on walks or going out anywhere, and not a pleasure to own."

Chris Brandon-Lodge: "My Spaniels have a long walk around the fields with me - only about 40 minutes, but they are outside with me a lot of the time and constantly on the go. A lot of my puppies have owners who are keen walkers and, once adult, a Springer will cope with most walks a human can do. Socialisation is vital."

THE ENGLISH SPRINGER SPANIEL HANDBOOK Page **149**

12. English Springer Spaniel Health

The English Springer Spaniel is regarded as a healthy, energetic breed with a lifespan of 11 to 14 years — maybe more if you're very lucky.

Health should always be a major consideration when choosing and raising a dog. Firstly, select a puppy from a breeder who produces Springers sound in both body and temperament — and this involves health screening. Secondly, play your role in helping to keep your dog healthy throughout his or her life.

NOTE: This chapter is intended to be used as an encyclopaedia to help you to identify potential health issues and act promptly in the best interests of your dog. Please don't read it thinking your ESS will get lots of these ailments — he or she WON'T!

....

It is becoming increasingly evident that genetics can have a huge influence on a person's health and even life expectancy, with lots of time and money currently being devoted to genetic research.

A human is more likely to suffer from a hereditary illness if the gene or genes for that disorder is passed on from parents or grandparents. That person is said to have a **"predisposition"** to the ailment if the gene is in the family's bloodline. Well, the same is true of dogs.

There is not a single breed without the potential for some genetic weakness. For example, many Cavalier King Charles Spaniels have heart problems and 25% of all West Highland White Terriers have a hereditary itchy skin disease.

Buying a puppy from non-tested parents means you have no idea if that puppy is going to be affected by certain hereditary diseases.

The 2015 UK scientific study **The Challenges of Pedigree Dog Health: Approaches to Combating Inherited Disease** states: *"The development of (such) pedigree dog breeds can be both a blessing and a curse: desirable features are rigidly retained, but sometimes, undesirable disease-causing genes can be inadvertently fixed within the breed."*

(To read the full study, type the title into Google and click on Table 1 at the bottom to view individual breed statistics).

In other words, bad genes can be inherited along with good ones. However, health testing is only PART of the story. Breeding two closely-related dogs can also increase the risk of health issues. You can check the COI (Coefficient of Inbreeding) on the Kennel Club website by typing the registered name of your puppy into their COI calculator at:
www.thekennelclub.org.uk/search/inbreeding-co-efficient

The breed average for English Springers is 10.7%. Anything around this or lower is acceptable. There's an excellent guide to COI at: www.dogbreedhealth.com/a-beginners-guide-to-coi

The good news is that once you have got your puppy there is plenty you can do to help your English Springer Spaniel live a long and healthy life.

....

Health Certificates for Puppy Buyers

Anyone thinking of getting an English Springer Spaniel puppy today can reduce the chance of their dog having a genetic disease by choosing a puppy from healthy bloodlines.

If you're actively searching for a puppy, you might be considering a breeder based on the look or colour of her dogs or their success in the field or show ring, but consider the health of the puppy's parents and ancestors as well. Could they have passed on unhealthy genes along with the good genes for all those features you are attracted to?

The way to reduce the hereditary diseases that can be screened for is for breeders to carry out DNA testing and NOT to mate two dogs with the faulty gene. Carriers carry the faulty gene(s) but do not show signs of the disease. The reason breeders don't remove all Carriers from their breeding stock is that the gene pool would become too small (resulting in a high COI), which also causes inbred health issues. As long as a Carrier is bred to a dog with a Clear result, no puppies will be affected by the disease.

Many inherited diseases are *"Autosomal Recessive,"* below are all possible outcomes – these are average results over thousands of litters. They are the same averages for all autosomal recessive genetic diseases.

PARENT CLEAR + PARENT CLEAR = pups clear

PARENT CLEAR + PARENT CARRIER = 50% will be carriers, 50% will be clear

PARENT CLEAR + PARENT AFFECTED = 100% will be carriers

PARENT CARRIER + PARENT CLEAR = 50% will be carriers, 50% will be clear

PARENT CARRIER + PARENT CARRIER = 25% clear, 25% affected and 50% carriers

PARENT CARRIER + PARENT AFFECTED = 50% affected and 50% carriers

PARENT AFFECTED + PARENT CLEAR = 100% will be carriers

PARENT AFFECTED + PARENT CARRIER = 50% affected and 50% carriers

PARENT AFFECTED + PARENT AFFECTED = 100% affected

Tip: Check what DNA tests the parents have had and ask to see original certificates where relevant - a good breeder will be happy to provide them. These are the main tests for hereditary illnesses:

UK:

All Kennel Club Assured Breeders **must** use the following (or equivalent) schemes. All other breeders are strongly advised to also use these:

- Eye testing PLA for primary glaucoma - the test is called a *gonioscopy*
- **Fucosidosis** or **Fuco** – a disease of the nervous system
- **PRA (cord1)** – an eye disease
- Eye screening scheme

The following tests are recommended:

- Hip Dysplasia

- PFK – a hereditary enzyme deficiency

Although it may look complicated, it's not. Breeders can pay for a combination DNA test, which checks for Fuco, PRA, PFK and a disease called AMS (Acral Mutilation Syndrome) all at the same time. AMS is a rare genetic disorder which causes Spaniels and a few other breeds to lose sensation in their paws and bite and mutilate them.

More detailed information for the UK can be found on the UK English Springer Spaniel Breed Clubs' Health website at: www.englishspringerhealth.org.uk

USA:

There are a number of recommended tests. The following tests are requirements for Canine Health Information Center (CHIC) certification. OFA (The Orthopedic Foundation for Animals) says: "For potential puppy buyers, CHIC certification is a good indicator the breeder responsibly factors good health into their selection criteria.

"The breed-specific list below represents the basic health screening recommendations. It is not all-encompassing. There may be other health screening tests appropriate for this breed. And, there may be other health concerns for which there is no commonly accepted screening protocol available."

- **Hip Dysplasia** - OFA or PennHIP Evaluation (at a minimum age of 24 months)
- **Elbow Dysplasia**
- **Eye Examination** - by a boarded ACVO Ophthalmologist
- **Progressive Retinal Atrophy (PRA)**
- **AKC DNA Profile** & DNA deposited with ESSFTA or OFA/CHIC

The following are optional but recommended:

- Fucosidosis
- PFK
- Degenerative Myelopathy
- Autoimmune Thyroiditis
- Cardiac Evaluation

In-depth information for the US can be found on The English Springer Spaniel Field Trial Association's website at https://essfta.org/english-springers/health-genetics-and-research-faq

Tip: A pedigree certificate from the Kennel Club or AKC does NOT mean that that puppy or its parents have been health screened. A pedigree certificate simply guarantees that the puppy's parents can be traced back several generations and that the ancestors were registered as purebred English Springer Spaniels.

As well as asking to see health certificates, prospective buyers should always find out exactly what contract the breeder is offering with the puppy. Good breeders offer a Puppy Contract.

FACT: If a puppy is sold as "Vet Checked," it does not mean that the parents have been health screened. It means that a veterinarian has given the puppy a brief physical and visual examination, worming and vaccinations are up to date, and the pup appears to be in good health on the day of the examination.

If you have already got your dog, don't worry! There is plenty of advice in this book on how to take excellent care of your Springer. Taking extra care with a puppy, feeding a quality food, monitoring your dog's weight, regular grooming and check-overs, plenty of exercise and socialisation will all help to keep him in tiptop condition.

Good owners can certainly help to extend the life of their dog.

English Springer Spaniel Insurance

Insurance is another point to consider for a new puppy or adult dog. Puppies from reputable breeders in the UK come with four weeks' or 30 days' insurance that can be extended before it expires.

USA breeders may or may not provide insurance, if not, ask if they can recommend a plan. If you are getting an older Springer, get insurance BEFORE any health issues develop, or you may find any pre-existing conditions are excluded.

If you can afford it, take out life cover. This may be more expensive, but will cover your dog throughout his or her lifetime - including for chronic (recurring and/or long term) ailments, such as joint, heart or eye problems, ear infections, epilepsy and cancer.

Insuring a healthy puppy or adult dog is the only sure-fire way to ensure vets' bills are covered before anything unforeseen happens - and you'd be a rare owner if you didn't use your policy at least once during your dog's lifetime.

Costs in the UK range from around £15 a month for Accident Only to around £30-£50 per month for Lifetime Cover, depending on where you live, how much excess you are willing to pay and the total in pounds covered per year.

The average cost of dog insurance in the US is around $50 per month. This varies a lot, depending on location, the excess, and total coverage per year in dollars. With advances in veterinary science, there is so much more vets can do to help an ailing dog - but at a price. Surgical procedures can rack up bills of thousands of pounds or dollars. Below are Trupanion real examples of insurance claims:

> Hip Dysplasia $7,815, Diabetes $10,496, Ingestion of foreign body $2,964, Bloat (GDV) $5,439, Cruciate ligament tear $5,439, Cancer $5,351 ($1.3 = approx. £1 at time of writing)

Of course, if you make a claim your monthly premium will increase. But if you have a decent insurance policy BEFORE a recurring health problem starts, your dog should be covered if the ailment returns. You have to decide whether insurance is worth the money. On the plus side:

1. Peace of mind financially if your beloved Spaniel falls ill, and
2. You know exactly how much hard cash to part with each month, so no nasty surprises.

Three Health Tips

1. **Buy a well-bred puppy** - Good Springer Spaniel breeders select their stock based on:

- General health and the health tests of the parents
- Conformation (physical structure)
- Temperament

Believe it or not, committed breeders are not in it for the money, often incurring high bills for health screening, stud fees, veterinary costs, specialised food, etc. Their main concern is to produce healthy, handsome puppies with good temperaments that are *"fit for function"* – whether from working or show lines.

2. Get pet insurance as soon as you get your dog - Don't wait until he has a health issue and needs to see a vet as most insurers exclude all pre-existing conditions on their policies. Check the small print to make sure all conditions are covered and that if the issue recurs, it will continue to be covered year after year. When working out costs of a dog, factor in annual or monthly pet insurance fees and trips to a vet for check-ups, vaccinations, etc.

3. Find a good vet - Ask around, rather than just going to the first one you find. A vet that knows your dog from his or her puppy vaccinations and then right through their life is more likely to understand your dog and diagnose quickly and correctly when something is wrong. If you visit a big veterinary practice, ask for the vet by name when you make an appointment.

We all want our dogs to be healthy - so how can you tell if yours is? Well, here are some positive things to look for in a healthy English Springer Spaniel:

Health Indicators

1. **Eyes** – The US Breed Standard states: "The eyes, more than any other feature, are the essence of the Springer's appeal." The eyes should be clear with a very alert, intelligent, expression and no sign of tears. The iris should match the coat colour. Watery eyes could be a sign of entropion (ingrowing eyelashes), while a droopy lower lid could be ectropion.

   Paleness around the eyeball (conjunctiva) could also be a sign of something amiss. A cloudy eye could be a sign of cataracts. Sometimes the dog's third eyelid (nictating membrane) is visible at the inside corner - this is normal. There should be no thick, green or yellow discharge from the eyes.

2. **Movement** – The Springer is a very active breed and healthy dogs move at all speeds freely and without pain. Look out for warning signs of stiffness when getting up from lying, limping, a reluctance to move, jump in the car or go up steps.

3. **Nose** – A dog's nose is an indicator of health. English Springer Spaniel noses are normally liver or black and, regardless of colour, they should be free from clear, watery secretions. Any yellow, green or foul-smelling discharge is not normal - in younger dogs this can be a sign of canine distemper. New-born Springer pups often have a *butterfly nose*, partly pink and partly black. This usually darkens within the first few weeks or months.

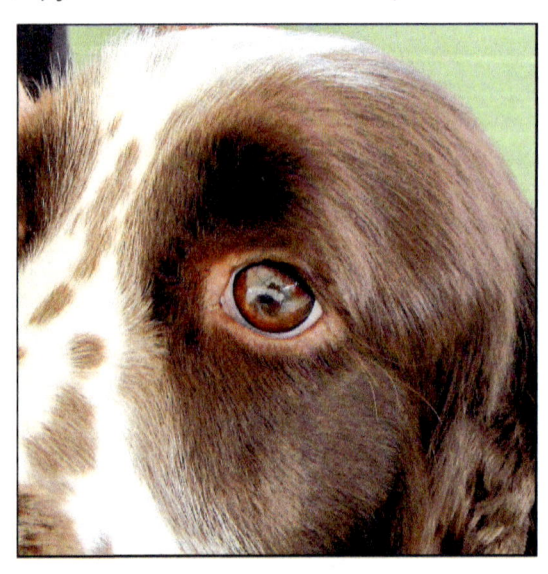

4. **Ears** - If you are choosing a puppy, gently clap your hands behind the pup - not so loud as to frighten him - to see if he reacts. If not, this may be a sign of deafness. The Springer's hairy, floppy ears means they can be susceptible to infections. Make sure the ears look clean and smell nice.

5. **Mouth** - Springer gums are usually pink. Paleness or whiteness can be a sign of anaemia, Bloat or lack of oxygen due to heart or breathing problems. Blue gums or tongue are a sign that your dog is not breathing properly. Red, inflamed gums can be a sign of gingivitis or other dental disease.

    Young dogs have sparkling white teeth, whereas older dogs have darker teeth, but they should not have any hard white, yellow, green or brown bits. Your dog's breath should not smell unpleasant.

6. **Energy** - English Springer Spaniels are very energetic, alert dogs. Yours should have good amounts of energy with fluid movements. Lack of energy or lethargy could be a sign of an underlying problem.

Photo of a very fit Elsie courtesy of Lynne Lucas, Traxlerstarr Spaniels, Surrey, England.

7. **Coat and Skin** - These are easy-to-monitor indicators of a healthy dog. A healthy English Springer Spaniel coat is clean, thick and soft to the touch - not harsh - with feathering. Springers love charging at full pelt through the undergrowth, mud, puddles, etc. but the coat should not be allowed to get matted.

    Any dandruff, bald spots, a dull, lifeless, discoloured or oily coat, or one that loses excessive hair, can all be signs that something is amiss. Skin should be smooth without redness or rashes. If a dog is scratching, licking or biting a lot, he may have a condition that needs addressing.

    Open sores, scales, scabs, red patches or growths can be a sign of a skin issue or allergy. Signs of fleas, ticks and other external parasites should be treated immediately; check for small black or dark red specks, which may be fleas or flea poo, on the coat or bedding.

8. **Weight** - Your English Springer Spaniel's stomach should be above the bottom of his rib cage when standing, and you should be able to feel his ribs beneath his coat without too much effort and see a visible waistline. If the stomach is level or hangs below, your dog is overweight - or may have a pot belly, which can also be a symptom of other conditions.

9. **Temperature** - The normal temperature of a dog is 101°F to 102.5°F. (A human's is 98.6°F). Excited or exercising dogs may run a slightly higher temperature. Anything above 103°F or below 100°F should be checked out. The exceptions are female dogs about to give birth that will often have a temperature of 99°F. If you take your dog's temperature, make sure he is relaxed and *always* use a purpose-made canine thermometer.

10. **Stools** - Poo, poop, business, faeces - call it what you will - it's the stuff that comes out of the less appealing end of your English Springer Spaniel on a daily basis! It should be mostly firm and brown, not runny, with no signs of blood or worms. Watery stools or a dog not eliminating regularly are both signs of an upset stomach or other ailments. If it continues for a couple of days, consult your vet.

    If puppies have diarrhoea, they need checking out much sooner as they can quickly dehydrate.

11. **Smell** - Springers love running free outdoors and can have a doggie smell. But if yours has a musty, 'off' or generally unpleasant smell, it could be a sign of a yeast infection. There can be a number of causes; the ears may require attention or it could be a food allergy or anal sac issue - usually accompanied by *'scooting'* (dragging the rear end across the floor). Whatever the cause, you need to get to the root of the problem quickly before it develops into something more serious.

12. **Attitude** - A generally positive attitude is a sign of good health. English Springer Spaniels are alert, engaged and involved, so symptoms of illness may include one or all of the following: a general lack of interest in his surroundings, tail not wagging, lethargy, not eating food and sleeping a lot (more than normal). The important thing is to look out for any behaviour that is out of the ordinary for YOUR English Springer Spaniel.

There are many different symptoms that can indicate your canine companion isn't feeling great. If you don't yet know your dog, his habits, temperament and behaviour patterns, then spend some time getting acquainted with them.

What are his normal character and temperament? Lively or calm, playful or serious, a joker or an introvert, bold or nervous, happy to be left alone or loves to be with people?

How often does he empty his bowels, does he ever vomit? (Dogs will often eat grass to make themselves sick, this is perfectly normal and a natural way of cleansing the digestive system).

Tip You may not think your English Springer Spaniel can talk, but he most certainly can!

If you really know your dog, his character and habits, then he CAN tell you when he's not well. He does this by changing his patterns. Some symptoms are physical, some emotional and others are behavioural.

It's important to be able to recognise these changes, as early treatment can be the key to keeping a simple problem from snowballing into something more serious.

If you think your dog is unwell, it is useful to keep an accurate and detailed account of his symptoms to give to the vet, perhaps even take a video of him on your mobile phone. This will help the vet to correctly diagnose and effectively treat your dog.

Three Vital Signs of Illness

1. **Temperature** - A new-born puppy has a temperature of 94-97°F (34.4-36.1°C). This reaches the normal adult body temperature of around 101°F (38.3°C) at four weeks old. A vet takes a dog's temperature reading via the rectum.

   If you do this, only do it with a special rectal thermometer, like this electronic one *pictured*, which can also be used in the mouth. Infrared forehead thermometers are also widely available.

   NOTE: Exercise or excitement can cause temperature to rise by 2°F to 3°F (1-1.5°C) when your dog is actually in good health, so wait until he is relaxed before taking his temperature. If it is above or below the norms and the dog seems under par, give your vet a call.

2. **Respiratory Rate** - Another symptom of illness is a change in breathing patterns. This varies a lot depending on the size and weight of the dog. An adult dog will have a respiratory rate of 15-25 breaths per minute when resting. You can easily check this by counting your dog's breaths for a minute with a stopwatch handy. Don't do this if he is panting; it doesn't count.

3. **Behaviour Changes** - Classic symptoms of illness are any inexplicable behaviour changes. If there has NOT been a change in the household atmosphere, such as another new pet, a new baby, moving home, the absence of a family member or the loss of another dog, then the following symptoms may well be a sign that all is not well:

   - Depression or lethargy
   - Anxiety and/or shivering, which can be a sign of pain
   - Falling or stumbling
   - Loss of appetite
   - Restlessness, not settling, walking in circles, etc.
   - Being more vocal - grunting, whining or whimpering
   - Aggression
   - Tiredness - sleeping more than normal or not wanting to exercise
   - Abnormal posture

If any of them appear for the first time or worse than usual, you need to keep him under close watch for a few hours or even days. Quite often he will return to normal of his own accord. Like humans, dogs have off-days too.

If he is showing any of the above symptoms, then don't over-exercise him, and avoid stressful situations and hot or cold places. Make sure he has access to clean water. Keep a record and it may be useful to take a fresh stool sample to your vet.

If your dog does need professional medical attention, most vets will want to know:

WHEN the symptoms first appeared in your dog

WHETHER they are getting better or worse, and

HOW FREQUENT the symptoms are - intermittent, continuous or increasing?

Joints

Hip Dysplasia

Hip Dysplasia, or *Canine Hip Dysplasia (CHD),* is the most common inherited orthopaedic problem in dogs of all breeds.

The hips are the uppermost joints on the rear legs of a dog, either side of the tail, and *"Dysplasia"* means *"abnormal development."* Dogs with this condition develop painful degenerative arthritis of the hip joints.

The hip is a ball and socket joint. Hip dysplasia is caused when the head of the femur, or thigh bone, fits loosely into a shallow and poorly developed socket in the pelvis. The joint carrying the weight of the dog becomes loose and unstable, muscle growth slows and degenerative joint disease often follows.

Symptoms often start to show at five to 18 months of age. Occasionally, an affected dog will have no symptoms at all, while others may experience anything from mild discomfort to extreme pain.

Diagnosis is made by X-ray, and an early diagnosis gives a vet the best chance to tackle HD, minimising the chance of arthritis. Symptoms are:

- Hind leg lameness, particularly after exercise
- Difficulty or stiffness when getting up, climbing stairs or walking uphill
- A reluctance to jump, exercise or climb stairs
- A "bunny hop" gait or waddling gait
- A painful reaction to stretching the hind legs, resulting in a short stride
- Side-to-side swaying of the croup (area above the tail)
- Wastage of the thigh muscles

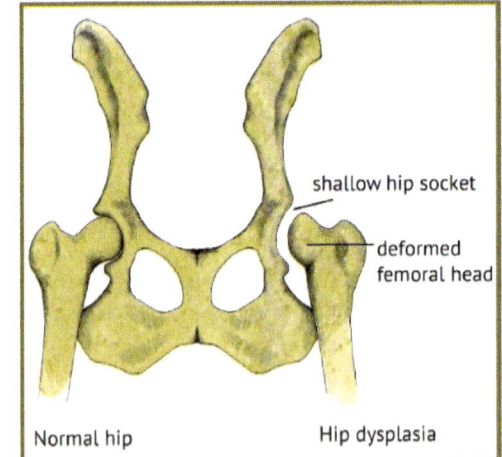

FACT While a predisposition to hip dysplasia is often inherited, other factors can trigger or worsen it, including:

- Too much exercise and high impact exercise, especially while the dog is still growing
- Obesity
- Extended periods without exercise
- Age

Prevention and Treatment

There is a system called *hip scoring,* run by the BVA and Kennel Club in the UK and PennHIP or OFA in the USA. A UK dogs' hips are X-rayed at a minimum age of 12 months; in the US, dogs must be 24 months old before they can receive their final hip certification.

In the UK, the X-rays are submitted to a specialist panel at the BVA who assess nine features of each hip, giving each feature a score. **The lower the score, the better the hips,** so the range can be from **0** NO DYSPLASIA to **106** BADLY DYSPLASTIC (53 in each hip). A hip certificate shows the individual score for each hip.

It is far better if the dog has evenly matched hips, rather than a low score for one and a high score for the other. Listed here are the American ratings, with the UK ratings in brackets:

- **Excellent** (0-4, with neither hip higher than 3)
- **Good** (5-10, with neither hip higher than 6)
- **Fair** (11-18)
- **Borderline** (19-25)
- **Mild** (26-35)
- **Moderate** (36-50)
- **Severe** (51-106)

This section of a UK BVA certificate, pictured, shows a hip score of 10, which is good. The median average (middle ranking) hip score for UK Springers is 9.

There is no 100% guarantee that a puppy from low scoring parents will not develop hip dysplasia, as the condition is caused by a combination of genes, rather than just one. However, the chances are significantly reduced with good hip scores.

In the USA, OFA (Orthopedic Federation for Animals) looked at over 18,000 hip scores from English Springer Spaniels and found that one in eight had some form of dysplasia. This ranks the Springer in the middle, 93rd out of 195 breeds involved.

Treatment is geared towards preventing the hip joint getting worse. If the dysplasia is not severe it is often dealt with by restricting exercise, **keeping body weight down** and managing pain with analgesics and anti-inflammatory drugs. Glucosamine, chondroitin and/or a daily supplement such as Yumove, which contains glucosamine, vitamins C and E, hyaluronic acid and green-lipped mussels, are also often recommended by vets.

Cortisone can be injected directly into the affected hip to provide almost immediate relief for a tender, swollen joint. Very severe cases may require surgery, which may involve replacing part or all of the damaged hip.

If you are buying a puppy, ask if the parents have been hip scored and, if so, to see the certificates.

Elbow Dysplasia

The elbow is at the top of a dog's front leg, near the body, and bends backwards. Like Hip Dysplasia, Elbow Dysplasia is a painful inherited disease that occurs when cells, tissue or bone don't develop correctly. This causes the elbow to form abnormally then to degenerate (arthritis).

Although not a major problem with UK Springers, recent OFA studies involving over 4,000 Springers in America found that 15% had elbow abnormalities.

A test called ***elbow scoring*** is compulsory in the USA for the CHIC certificate for breeding dogs, and there is the BVA (British Veterinary Association)/KC Elbow Dysplasia Scheme in the UK. Results are graded 0-3, with 0 being the best score.

Symptoms begin during puppyhood, typically at four to 10 months of age, although not all young dogs show signs. Look out for:

- Stiffness followed by temporary or permanent lameness aggravated by exercise
- Pain when extending or flexing the elbow
- Holding the affected leg away from the body

- 🐾 Groaning when getting up
- 🐾 Swelling around the joint
- 🐾 In advanced cases: grating of bone and joint when moving

Diagnosis is made by a veterinary examination and X-rays, requiring the dog to be anaesthetised. Treatment depends on age and severity, and may involve Non-steroidal Anti-inflammatory Drugs (NSAIDs) or injections.

Thanks to advances in veterinary medicine, surgery is now an option for many dogs who are severely affected. According to Embrace Pet Insurance, it costs $1,500-$4,000, (£1,100-£3,000) and results in partial or full improvement in the vast majority of cases.

Treatment is similar to that for Hip Dysplasia. Keeping your dog's weight in check and feeding the right diet are important, and the supplements mentioned earlier can also help to relieve pain and stiffness.

IOHC/HIF

This condition with the complicated name of Incomplete Ossification of the Humeral Condyle (IOHC) or Humeral Intracondylar Fissure (HIF) is not widespread, but is known to affect English Springer Spaniels as well as other (mainly Spaniel) breeds. Basically, it means that the elbow joint has a weakness that can cause it to fracture. It can also result in lameness without a fracture.

Surgery is needed either to repair fractures or prevent them from happening, and the aftercare is just as important as the surgery itself - difficult for owners as well as lively Springers. Strict rest (for the dog, not the owner!) is necessary for at least six weeks.

Typically this means a Springer being confined to a crate or small room and prevented from running, jumping, including on and off furniture, and going up or down stairs. Short walks out to the garden on a lead are allowed for toileting only.

Not a lot is known about the genetic causes of IOHC/HIF and there is currently a major surgical research study being undertaken at The Ralph Veterinary Referral Centre in Buckinghamshire, England.

Eyes

Primary Glaucoma

Glaucoma is a painful condition that puts pressure on the eye, and if it becomes chronic or continues without treatment, it will eventually cause permanent damage to the optic nerve, resulting in blindness.

A normal eye contains a fluid called aqueous humour to maintain its shape, and the body is constantly adding and removing fluid from inside of the eye to maintain the pressure inside the eye at the proper level.

Glaucoma occurs when the pressure inside the eyeball becomes higher than normal. Just as high blood pressure can damage the heart, excessive pressure inside the eye can damage the eye's internal structures. Unless Glaucoma is treated quickly, temporary loss of vision or even total blindness can result.

The cornea and lens inside the eye are living tissues, but they have no blood vessels to supply the oxygen and nutrition they need; these are delivered through the aqueous humour. In Glaucoma, the increased pressure is most frequently caused by this fluid not being able to properly drain away from the eye.

Our photo shows an eye with acute Glaucoma.

Fluid is constantly being produced and if an equal amount does not leave the inner eye, then the pressure starts to rise, similar to a water balloon. As more water is added the balloon stretches more and more.

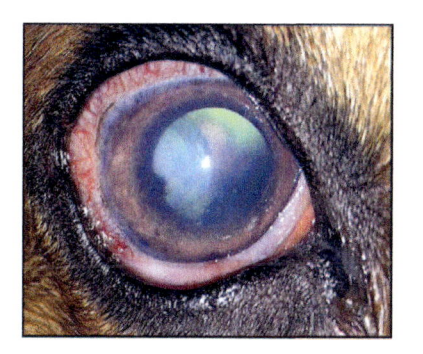

The balloon will eventually burst, but the eye is stronger so this does not happen. Instead the eye's internal structures are damaged irreparably.

Secondary Glaucoma is caused by another problem such as a wound to the eye, cataracts or cancer. Primary Glaucoma is normally inherited and this is the type of Glaucoma that breeding Springer and Cocker Spaniels should be tested for.

The test, called a **gonioscopy,** is compulsory for Assured Breeders in the UK. The KC/BVA recommend that this be done every three years.

Symptoms

The disease itself does not normally develop until a Spaniel is at least two or three years old, and more usually in middle age.

With Primary Glaucoma, both eyes are rarely affected equally or at the same time, it usually starts in one eye several months or even years before it affects the second one. Glaucoma is a serious disease and it's important for an owner to be able to immediately recognise initial symptoms. If treatment is not started within a few days - or even hours in some cases - of the pressure increasing, the dog will probably lose sight in that eye.

Here are the early signs:

- Pain
- A dilated pupil or one pupil looks bigger than the other
- Rapid blinking
- Red eyeballs
- Cloudiness in the cornea at the front of the eye
- The whites of an eye look bloodshot
- One eye looks larger or sticks out further than the other one
- Loss of appetite, which may be due to headaches
- Change in attitude, less willing to play, etc.

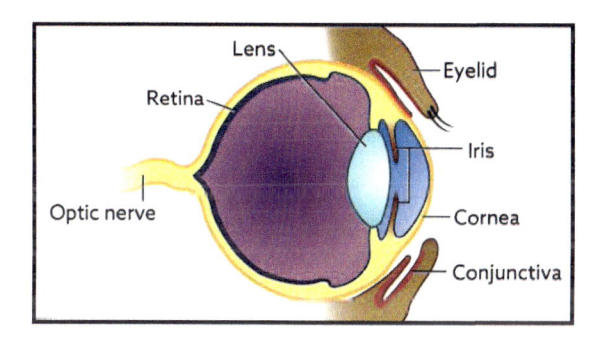

Most dogs will not display all of these signs at first, perhaps just one or two. A dog rubbing his eye with his paw, against the furniture or carpet or your leg is a common - and often unnoticed - early sign. Some dogs will also seem to flutter the eyelids or squint with one eye.

The pupil of the affected eye will usually dilate in the early stages of Glaucoma. It may still react to all bright light, but it will do so very slowly. If the pupil in one eye is larger than in the other, something is definitely wrong.

If you suspect your dog has Glaucoma, get him to the vet as soon as possible, i.e. immediately, not the day after; this is a medical emergency. The vet will carry out a manual examination and test your dog's eye pressure using a tonometer on the surface of the eye. The dog may lose sight in this eye, but the vet will have a much better chance of saving the second eye.

Treatment revolves around reducing pressure within the affected eye, draining the aqueous humour and providing pain relief. There are also surgical options for the long-term control of Glaucoma.

As yet it cannot be cured. A predisposition to Glaucoma can be detected by a test called a *gonioscopy*, which looks for an abnormality in the eye known as PLA (Pectinate Ligament Abnormality). This is recommended by the Kennel Club for all breeding dogs and is part of the BVA/KC eye testing scheme.

PRA (Progressive Retinal Atrophy)

PRA is the name for several progressive diseases causing degeneration of the retina that lead to blindness. First recognised at the beginning of the 20th century in Gordon Setters, this inherited condition has been documented in over 100 breeds, including English Springer Spaniels.

One type of PRA that can affect Springers is called **cord1-PRA,** which stands for Cone-Rod Dystrophy-PRA.

There is a relatively inexpensive DNA test for cord1-PRA, and it is compulsory for Assured Breeders and for Canine Health Information Center (CHIC) certification in the US.

Cord1-PRA first affects the cones in the retina, which are the photoreceptors that detect bright light or daylight. Then the rods, or low-light photoreceptors, begin to degenerate as well. Sadly, there is no cure as yet and most affected dogs eventually go blind.

Some dogs first show signs at around six months, though the average age of onset is around five years old. Some dogs never develop any symptoms.

Cord1-PRA is a genetic disorder associated with a *recessive* mutation in the RPGRIP1 gene. This means that the faulty gene must be inherited *from both parents* in order to cause disease in an offspring.

Entropion

English Springer Spaniels can be susceptible to Entropion. It occurs when the edge of the lower eyelid rolls inward, causing the dog's fur to rub the surface of the eyeball, or cornea. In rare cases the upper lid can also be affected, and one or both eyes may be involved. This painful condition is thought to have a hereditary link.

The affected dog scratches at his painful eye with his paws and this can lead to further injury. If your Spaniel suffers from it, he will usually show signs at or before his first birthday. You will notice that his eyes are red and inflamed and they will produce tears. He will probably squint.

The tears typically start off clear and can progress to a thick yellow or green mucus. If left untreated, Entropion causes corneal ulcers and you might also notice a milky-white colour develop. This is caused by increased fluid which affects the clarity of the cornea.

For your poor dog, the irritation is constant. Imagine how painful and uncomfortable it would be if you had permanent hairs touching your eyes. It makes my eyes water just thinking about it.

FACT It's important to get your dog to the vet as soon as you suspect Entropion before your dog scratches his cornea and worsens the problem.

A vet will make the diagnosis after a painless and relatively simple inspection of your dog's eyes. He or she will first have to rule out other issues, such as allergies. In mild cases, the vet may successfully prescribe eye drops, ointment or other medication. However, the most common treatment for more severe cases is a fairly straightforward surgical procedure to pin back the lower eyelid, *pictured.*

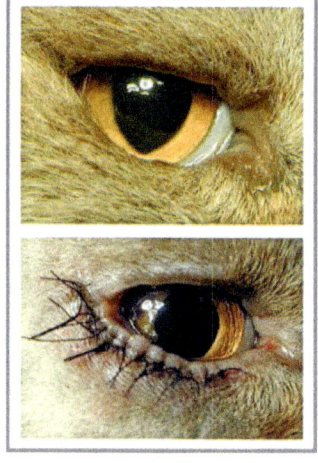

Some vets may delay surgery in affected young dogs and treat the condition with medication until the dog's face is fully grown. This avoids having to repeat the procedure later.

Ectropion

Ectropion is a condition where the lower lids turn outwards, causing the eyelids to appear droopy. One or both eyes may be involved and it can occur in any breed, but certain breeds, including Bulldogs, Cocker and Springer Spaniels, Saint Bernards, Mastiffs, Bassett Hounds, Newfoundlands, and Bloodhounds are more susceptible.

When the lower eyelid droops it exposes the conjunctiva and creates a pocket where pollens, grasses and dust can collect and rub against the sensitive conjunctiva. This is a consistent source of irritation to the dog and leads to increased redness of the conjunctiva and tears which flow over the lower lid and face, often causing a brownish staining of the fur below the eyes.

A thick mucus discharge may appear along the eyelid margin and the dog may rub or scratch his eyes if it becomes uncomfortable.

Vets normally make a diagnosis during a physical examination. Blood and urine tests may be performed on older dogs to search for an underlying cause. Your vet may also perform corneal staining to see if any ulcers are present.

Many dogs live normal lives with Ectropion. However, some develop repeated eye infections due to the collection of dirt and dust within the eye. Therefore, the risks are minor except in severe cases, where secondary eye infections may develop.

Some dogs require no treatment. But you should visit your vet if the eye is irritated. Mild cases can be treated with eye drops and ointments that prevent the cornea and conjunctiva from drying out. Special eye (ophthalmic) antibiotics are used to combat any corneal ulcers.

In severe cases surgery can remove excess tissue to tighten the lids and remove the abnormal pocket - the procedure has a high success rate.

'Acquired Ectropion' can occur in any dog at any age and it means that a reason other than genetics has caused the eyelid to sag, including:

- Facial nerve paralysis
- Hypothyroidism
- Scarring secondary to injury
- Chronic inflammation and infection of the tissues surrounding the eyes
- Surgical overcorrection of Ectropion
- Neuromuscular disease

Distichiasis

This occurs when eyelashes grow from an abnormal spot on the eyelid. (**Trichiasis** is ingrowing eyelashes and **Ectopic Cilia** are single or multiple hairs that grow through the inside of the eyelid - *cilia* are eyelashes).

With distichiasis, an eyelash or eyelashes abnormally grow on the inner surface or the very edge of the eyelid, and both upper and lower eyelids can be affected. The affected eye becomes red, inflamed, and may have a discharge.

The dog typically squints or blinks a lot, just like a human with a hair or other foreign matter in the eye. The dog can make matters worse by rubbing the eye against furniture, other objects or the carpet. In severe cases, the cornea can become ulcerated and it looks blue.

Often, very mild cases require no action, mild cases may require lubricating eye drops and in more severe cases, surgery may be the best option to remove the offending eyelashes and prevent them from regrowing. Left untreated, distichiasis can cause corneal ulcers and infection which can ultimately lead to blindness or loss of the eye.

Dry Eye (Keratoconjunctivitis sicca)

Keratoconjunctivitis sicca is the technical term for **Dry Eye**, which is caused by not enough tears being produced. With insufficient tears, a dog's eyes can become irritated and the conjunctiva appears red. It's estimated that as many as one in five dogs can suffer from Dry Eye at one time or another in their lives.

Dry Eye causes a dog to blink a lot, the eye or eyes typically develop a thick, yellowy discharge and the cornea develops a film. Infections are common as tears also have anti-bacterial and cleansing properties, and inadequate lubrication allows dust, pollen and other debris to accumulate. The nerves of these glands may also become damaged.

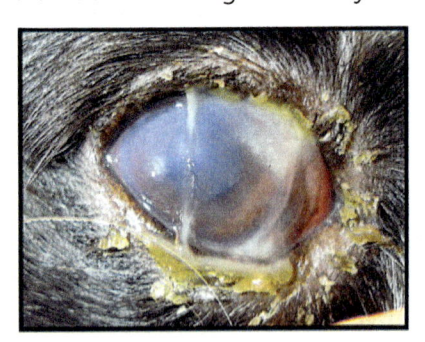

Dry eye is often associated with skin disorders, it may be due to increased rubbing and secondary infection in the eyes or it may be part of the immune disorder. It may also be caused by injuries to the tear glands, eye infections, disease such as distemper or reactions to drugs.

Left untreated, the dog will suffer painful and chronic eye infections, and repeated irritation of the cornea results in severe scarring, and even ulcers, which can lead to blindness. Early treatment is essential to save the cornea and usually involves drugs: cyclosporine, ophthalmic ointment or drops. In some cases, another eye preparation – Tacrolimus - is also used and may be effective when cyclosporine is not. Sometimes artificial tear solutions are also prescribed.

Treating Dry Eye involves commitment from the owner. Gently cleaning the eyes several times a day with a warm, wet cloth helps a dog feel better and may also help stimulate tear production. In very severe and rare cases, an operation can be performed to transplant a salivary duct into the upper eyelid, causing saliva to drain into and lubricate the eye.

Tip Any eye condition can be worsened by irritants and injury. Remove or fence off low, spiky plants in your garden or yard. And although your Springer may look like the canine version of Easy Rider with his head stuck out of the car window and ears flapping in the breeze, bear in mind that dust, insects and dirt particles can hit and damage those beautiful eyes.

Fucosidosis (Fuco)

This is a genetic metabolic disorder which strangely occurs only in humans and English Springer Spaniels. Sadly, there is no cure; it progresses over a period of weeks or months and is eventually fatal.

Fuco is caused by a faulty gene that regulates an enzyme called *alpha-fucosidase.* The lack of it causes complex molecules to accumulate in cells stopping them working properly, particularly in the central nervous system. Because it is an autosomal recessive inherited disease, **both** parents have to carry the faulty gene for a dog to be affected.

Although it is a very rare disease, it can be completely avoided by DNA testing, and both the AKC and Kennel Club recommend that **all** breeding Springers are screened for Fucosidosis. It is a simple DNA swab test. Symptoms, which usually show at between 18 months and four years of age, are:

- Ataxia (loss of control of movement)
- Change in behaviour
- Loss of learned behaviour
- Loss of balance
- Problems with swallowing
- Vomiting
- Loss of hearing
- Loss of vision
- Depression

Phosphofructokinase Deficiency (PFK)

This is a genetic metabolic disorder affecting Springers, as well as American Cockers. The lack of the phosphofructokinase enzyme prevents glucose metabolising into energy.

Symptoms vary depending on how serious the condition is, but typical signs are:

- Dark urine
- Pale or yellow gums
- Exercise intolerance

- 🐾 Lack of energy
- 🐾 Poor appetite
- 🐾 Fever
- 🐾 Depression

Symptoms can range from mild to life-threatening. Many dogs have persistent mild anaemia (low levels of red blood cells), but can usually compensate for this.

They may also have intermittent bouts of red blood cell breakdown (haemolysis), when they become lethargic and weak and may even bleed. This usually happens after intense exercise, excessive barking or panting.

The dog's gums are pale or jaundiced and he usually has a high fever. You may notice your dog's urine is brown, this is due to blood breakdown products in the urine and during these bouts the dog needs to see a vet.

It's important to see a vet at the outset to get the right diagnosis, which can be done by simple DNA swab. There is no cure, but the condition can be managed by owners with veterinary help. The main methods are to avoid stressful situations, strenuous exercise, hot conditions and any situations likely to cause stress, panting or lots of barking.

PFK is another autosomal recessive disease, which means that BOTH parents have to carry the faulty gene for the pup to be affected. DNA testing for PFK is recommended for UK Assured Breeders and the AKC in the US.

IMHA (Immune-Mediated Haemolytic Anaemia)

This is a rare and distressing disease, resulting in 40-60% of dogs losing their lives, either through the illness itself or by being put to sleep when treatment fails. It's more likely to occur in middle-aged dogs and to affect more females than males.

IMHA causes the body's immune system to destroy its own red blood cells. This often leads to severe anaemia and poor oxygen flow to the organs - kidneys, liver, brain, etc. Symptoms vary according to the severity of the disease.

In extreme cases a dog can collapse and be unable to stand. Gums are often very pale and there may be a yellow tinge in their eyes, mouth or skin due to staining with bilirubin. This is a yellow pigment normally excreted out of the body, but which gets released into the circulation when large numbers of red blood cells are destroyed.

Rapid breathing is another symptom, caused either by anaemia or blood clots in the lungs. In less severe cases, the only visible symptom might be a general lack of energy.

IMHA can be triggered by different factors including bacterial infection, tumours and even drugs. It's therefore very important to tell your vet about all medications your dog is receiving.

A vet will make a diagnosis after a physical examination of the dog and blood tests. Other tests will then be performed to differentiate **primary** IMHA from IMHA triggered by other diseases. If there is no other disease present, a diagnosis of **primary** or **idiopathic** IMHA will be made. This means that without an obvious underlying trigger, the dog's immune system has started destroying its own red blood cells.

Treatment and prognosis (outcome) depend on the cause and severity of the disease. With idiopathic or primary IMHA when a clear cause is not present, steroids are given to suppress the immune system, often alongside other drugs.

Severe cases may require blood transfusions to replace red blood cells, but the benefits can be short-lived if the new red blood cells are also destroyed by the immune system.

The cause of the disease is unknown, but it's thought there could be a genetic connection. UFAW (Universities Federation for Animal Welfare) says: "Those with affected close relatives (parents, siblings, grandparents and the siblings of parents and grandparents) may be more likely to develop or carry the disease than those from lineages in which the disease has not been detected or has been rare."

Epilepsy

Epilepsy means repeated seizures (also called fits or convulsions) due to abnormal electrical activity in the brain. Epilepsy affects around four or five dogs in every 100 across the dog population as a whole, with Springers being slightly more susceptible than some other breeds.

Epilepsy can be classified as **structural,** when an underlying cause can be identified in the brain, or *idiopathic,* when the cause is unknown. The type of epilepsy affecting most dogs of all breeds, including Springers, is *idiopathic epilepsy.* It often starts when the dog is aged between six months and three years.

In some cases, the gap between seizures is relatively constant, in others it can be very irregular with several occurring over a short period of time, but with long intervals between *"clusters."*

Affected dogs behave normally between seizures. If they occur because of a problem somewhere else in the body, such as heart disease (which stops oxygen reaching the brain), this is not epilepsy.

Seizures are not uncommon; however, many dogs only ever have one. If your dog has had more than one, it may be that he is epileptic.

Anyone who has witnessed their dog having a seizure knows how frightening it can be. The good news is that, just as with people, there are medications to control epilepsy in dogs, allowing them to live happy lives with normal lifespans.

Symptoms

Some dogs seem to know when they are about to have a seizure and may behave in a certain way. You will come to recognise these signs as meaning that an episode is likely. Often dogs just seek out their owner's company and come to sit beside them. There are two main types of seizure:

- **Petit Mal**, also called a Focal or Partial Seizure, which is the lesser of the two as it only affects one part of the brain. This may involve facial twitching, staring into space with a fixed glaze and/or upward eye movement, walking as if drunk, snapping at imaginary flies, and/or running or hiding for no reason. Sometimes this is accompanied by urination. The dog is conscious throughout

* **Grand Mal,** or Generalised Seizure, affects both hemispheres of the brain and is more often what we think of when we talk about a seizure. Most dogs become stiff, fall onto their side and make running movements with their legs. Sometimes they will cry out and may lose control of their bowels, bladder or both

FACT With Grand Mal the dog is unconscious once the seizure starts - he cannot hear or respond to you. While it is distressing to watch, the dog is not in any pain - even if howling.

It's not uncommon for an episode to begin as Petit Mal, but progress into Grand Mal. Sometimes, the progression is pretty clear - there may be twitching or jerking of one body part that gradually increases in intensity and progresses to include the entire body – other times the progression happens very fast.

Tip Most seizures last between one and three minutes - it is worth making a note of the time the seizure starts and ends - or record it on your phone because it often seems to go on for a lot longer than it actually does.

If you are not sure whether or not your dog has had a seizure, look on YouTube, where there are many videos of dogs having epileptic seizures.

Dogs behave in different ways afterwards. Some just get up and carry on with what they were doing, while others appear dazed and confused for up to 24 hours afterwards. Most commonly, dogs will be disorientated for only 10 to 15 minutes before returning to their old self.

FACT Most seizures occur while the dog is relaxed and resting quietly, often in the evening or at night; it rarely happens during exercise. In a few dogs, seizures can be triggered by particular events or stress.

They often have a set pattern of behaviour that they follow - for example going for a drink of water or asking to go outside to the toilet. If your dog has had more than one seizure, you may well start to notice a pattern of behaviour that is typically repeated.

The most important thing is to **STAY CALM**. Remember that your dog is unconscious during the seizure and is not in pain or distressed. It is probably more distressing for you than for him. Make sure that he is not in a position to injure himself, for example by falling down the stairs, but otherwise do not try to interfere with him.

NEVER try to put your hand inside his mouth during a seizure or you are very likely to get bitten.

It is very rare for dogs to injure themselves during a seizure. Occasionally, they may bite their tongue and there may seem to be a lot of blood, but it's unlikely to be serious; your dog will not swallow his tongue.

If it goes on for a very long time (more than 10 minutes), his body temperature will rise, which can cause damage to the liver, kidneys or brain. In very extreme cases, some dogs may be left in a coma after severe seizures. Repeated seizures can cause cumulative brain damage, which can result in early senility (with loss of learned behaviour and housetraining, or behavioural changes).

When Should I Contact the Vet?

Generally, if your dog has a seizure lasting more than five minutes or is having them regularly, you should contact your vet. When your dog starts fitting, make a note of the time. If he comes out of it within five minutes, allow him time to recover quietly before contacting your vet. It is far better for him to recover quietly at home rather than be bundled into the car right away.

If your dog does not come out of the seizure within five minutes, or has repeated seizures close together, contact your vet immediately, as he or she will want to see your dog as soon as possible. Call the vet before setting off to make sure there is someone who can help when you arrive.

Tip — If you can, record your dog's seizure on your mobile phone; it will help your vet.

The vet may need to run a range of tests to ensure that there is no other cause of the seizures. These may include blood tests, X-rays or an MRI scan of your dog's brain. If no other cause can be found, then a diagnosis of epilepsy may be made. If your English Springer Spaniel already has epilepsy, remember these key points:

- Don't change or stop any medication without consulting your vet
- See your vet at least once a year for follow-up visits
- Be sceptical of *"magic cure"* treatments

Treatment

As yet, it is not possible to cure epilepsy, so medication is used to control seizures – in some cases even a well-controlled epileptic may have occasional fits. There are many drugs available including Levetiracetam (brand names: Keppra, Elepsia, Spritam), Phenobarbital and Potassium Bromide; some may have side effects.

There are also a number of holistic remedies advertised, but we have no experience of them or any idea if any are effective.

Tip — Purina NeuroCare dog food, *pictured,* is reportedly helping to reduce seizure activity or severity in many affected dogs. Other factors useful in some cases are: avoiding dog food containing preservatives, adding vitamins, minerals and/or enzymes to the diet and ensuring drinking water is free of fluoride.

Each epileptic dog is an individual and a treatment plan will be designed specifically for yours, based on the severity and frequency of seizures and how he responds to different medications. Many epileptic dogs require a combination of one or more types of drugs for best results.

Keep a record of events in your dog's life, note down dates and times of episodes and record when you have given medication. Each time you visit your vet, take this diary along with you so he or she can see how your dog has been since his last check-up. If seizures are becoming more frequent, it may be necessary to change the medication.

Tip — Owners of epileptic dogs need patience and vigilance. Treatment success often depends on owners keeping a close eye on the dog and reporting any physical or behavioural changes to the vet.

It is also important that medication is given at the same time each day, as he becomes dependent on the levels of drug in his blood to control seizures. If a single dose of treatment is missed, blood levels can drop, which may be enough to trigger a seizure.

It is not common for epileptic dogs to stop having seizures altogether. However, provided your dog is checked regularly by your vet, *there is a good chance that he will live a full and happy life; most epileptic dogs have far more good days than bad ones.*

LIVE *WITH* EPILEPSY NOT *FOR* EPILEPSY.

Diabetes

Diabetes can affect dogs of all breeds, sizes and both genders - and overweight dogs are particularly susceptible. There are two types:

Diabetes insipidus (DI) is caused by a lack of vasopressin (ADH), a hormone that controls the kidneys' absorption of water. It gets its name from the fact that the urine of these patients is dilute enough to be tasteless or **insipid.**

Although relatively rare, symptoms are excessive drinking and the production of enormous volumes of extremely dilute urine. Some dogs may produce so much urine that they become incontinent.

Despite drinking large volumes of water, the dog can become dehydrated from urinating so much.

Once other causes have been ruled out, diagnosis is made by a complete blood count and there is also something called **a water deprivation test** which involves restricting the dog's water intake and then measuring the concentration of urine.

There are two types of DI, and they are treated either with synthetic ADH applied as eye drops or injection, or with diuretic tablets and a low-salt diet. Diabetes insipidus cannot be cured, but it can usually be successfully controlled.

Diabetes mellitus occurs when the dog's body does not produce enough insulin and therefore cannot successfully process sugars. This is the type overweight dogs get. Dogs, like us, get their energy by converting the food they eat into sugars, mainly glucose. This travels in the bloodstream and then, using a hormone called **insulin,** cells remove some of the glucose from the blood to use for energy.

Most diabetic dogs have Type 1 diabetes; their pancreas does not produce any insulin. Without it, the cells can't use the glucose that is in the bloodstream, so they *"starve"* while the glucose level in the blood rises.

Diabetes mellitus (sugar diabetes) is the most common form and affects mostly middle-aged and older dogs. Both males and females can develop it, although unspayed females have a slightly higher risk. Vets take blood and urine samples in order to diagnose diabetes. Early treatment helps to prevent further complications developing.

FACT ▶ The condition is treatable and need not shorten a dog's lifespan or interfere greatly with quality of life. Due to advances in veterinary science, diabetic dogs undergoing treatment now have the same life expectancy as non-diabetic dogs of the same age and gender.

Symptoms of Diabetes Mellitus:

- Extreme thirst
- Excessive urination
- Weight loss
- Increased appetite

- Coat in poor condition
- Lethargy
- Vision problems due to cataracts

If left untreated, diabetes can lead to cataracts or other ailments.

Treatment and Exercise

It is EXTREMELY IMPORTANT that English Springer Spaniels are not allowed to get overweight, as obesity is a major trigger for diabetes.

FACT Many cases of canine diabetes can be successfully treated with a combination of a diet low in sugar, fat and carbs recommended by your vet alongside a moderate and consistent exercise routine and medication. More severe cases may require insulin injections.

In the newly-diagnosed dog, insulin therapy begins at home after a vet has explained how to prepare and inject insulin. Normally, after a week of treatment, you return to the vet for a series of blood sugar tests over a 12 to 14-hour period to see when the blood glucose peaks and troughs.

Adjustments are made to the dosage and timing of the injections. You may also be asked to collect urine samples using a test strip of paper that indicates the glucose levels.

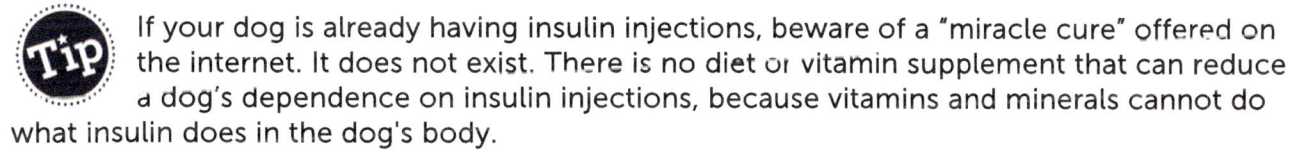

Tip If your dog is already having insulin injections, beware of a "miracle cure" offered on the internet. It does not exist. There is no diet or vitamin supplement that can reduce a dog's dependence on insulin injections, because vitamins and minerals cannot do what insulin does in the dog's body.

If you think that your dog needs a supplement, discuss it with your vet first to make sure that it does not interfere with any other medication.

Exercise burns up blood glucose the same way that insulin does. If your dog is on insulin, any active exercise on top of the insulin might cause him to have a severe low blood glucose episode, called *"hypoglycaemia."*

Keep your dog on a reasonably consistent exercise routine. Your usual insulin dose will take that amount of exercise into account. If you plan to take your dog out for some demanding exercise, such as running around with other dogs, you may need to reduce his usual insulin dose.

Tips

- Specially-formulated diabetes dog food is available from most vets
- Feed the same type and amount of food at the same times every day
- Most vets recommend twice-a-day feeding for diabetic pets (it's OK if your dog prefers to eat more often)
- Help your dog to achieve the best possible blood glucose control by NOT feeding table scraps or treats between meals
- Watch for signs that your dog is starting to drink more water than usual. Call the vet if you see this happening, as it may mean that the insulin dose needs adjusting

Food raises blood glucose - Insulin and exercise lower blood glucose - Keep them in balance

For more information visit www.caninediabetes.org

Cushing's Disease

This complex ailment, also known as **hyperadrenocorticism,** is caused when a dog produces too much Cortisol hormone. It develops over a period of time, which is why it is more often seen in middle-aged or senior dogs.

Cortisol is released by the adrenal gland near the kidneys. Normally it is produced during times of stress to prepare the body for strenuous activity. Think of an adrenaline rush. While this hormone is essential for the effective functioning of cells and organs, too much of it can be dangerous. The disease can be difficult to diagnose, as the most common symptoms are similar to those for old age. A dog may display one or more:

- A ravenous appetite
- Drinking excessive amounts of water
- Urinating frequently or urinary incontinence
- Hair loss or recurring skin issues
- Pot belly
- Thin skin
- Muscle wastage
- Insomnia
- Lack of energy, general lethargy
- Panting a lot

FACT Cushing's disease cannot be cured, but it can be successfully managed and controlled with medication, giving the dog a longer, happier life.

Some dogs with mild symptoms do not require treatment, but should be closely monitored for signs of them worsening.

Lysodren (mitotane) or Vetoryl (trilostane) are usually prescribed by vets to treat the most common pituitary-dependent Cushing's disease. Both can have a number of side effects - so your dog needs monitoring - and the dog remains on the medication for life.

The Heart

Just as with humans, heart problems are not uncommon among the dog population in general. The heart is a mechanical pump. It receives blood in one half and forces it through the lungs, then the other half pumps the blood through the entire body.

Two of the most common forms of heart failure in dogs are **Dilated Cardiomyopathy (DCM)**, also known as an enlarged heart, and **Degenerative Valvular Disease (DVD)**.

Cardiomyopathy is defined as degeneration of the heart muscle. As a result of this degeneration, the muscle becomes thinner, particularly the thick muscle wall of the left ventricle. The pressure of the blood inside the heart causes these thin walls to stretch resulting in a much larger heart. This condition is described as DCM.

In people, heart disease usually involves the arteries that supply blood to the heart muscle becoming hardened over time, causing the heart muscles to receive less blood than they need. Starved of oxygen, the result is often a heart attack.

FACT Although heart disease is quite common in dogs, hardening of the arteries (arteriosclerosis) and heart attacks are very rare. More often heart failure occurs, which means that the muscles *"give out"* after months or even years of heart disease.

This is usually caused by one chamber or side of the heart being required to do more than it is physically able to do. It may be that excessive force is required to pump the blood through an area, causing the muscles to eventually fail.

Symptoms of a heart condition:

- Tiredness
- Decreased activity levels
- Restlessness, pacing around instead of settling down to sleep
- Coughing – this is a classic system and an attempt to clear the lungs of fluid

As the condition worsens, other symptoms may appear:

- Lack of appetite
- Rapid breathing
- Abdominal swelling (due to fluid)
- Noticeable loss of weight
- Fainting (syncope)
- Paleness

A vet will carry out tests that may include listening to the heart, chest X-rays, blood tests, electrocardiogram (a record of your dog's heartbeat) or an echocardiogram.

If the heart problem is due to an enlarged heart or valve disease, the condition cannot be reversed

Treatment focuses on managing exercise and various medications, which may change over time as the condition progresses. The vet may also prescribe a special low salt diet, as sodium determines the amount of water in the blood.

Tip *Pay attention to your Spaniel's oral health, as dental problems can increase the risk of heart disease. There is evidence that fatty acids and other supplements may be beneficial for a heart condition; discuss this with your vet.*

Heart Murmurs

Heart murmurs are not uncommon in dogs - particularly older ones - and are one of the first signs that something may be amiss. One of our dogs was diagnosed with a Grade 2 murmur when he was five or six years old and, of course, your heart sinks when the vet gives you the terrible news.

But once the shock is over, it's important to realise that there are several different severities of the condition and, at its mildest, it is no great cause for concern. Our dog lived an active, healthy life and died at the age of 13.

Literally, a heart murmur is a specific sound heard through a stethoscope, which results from the blood flowing faster than normal within the heart itself or in one of the two major arteries. Instead of the normal *"lubb dupp"* noise, an additional sound can be heard that can vary from a mild *"pshhh"* to a loud *"whoosh."* The different grades are:

- **Grade 1** - barely audible
- **Grade 2** - soft, but easily heard with a stethoscope
- **Grade 3** - intermediate loudness; most murmurs that are related to the mechanics of blood circulation are at least Grade 3
- **Grade 4** - loud murmur that radiates widely, often including opposite side of chest
- **Grade 5 and Grade 6** - very loud, audible with the stethoscope barely touching the chest; the vibration is strong enough to be felt through the dog's chest wall

Murmurs are caused by a number of factors; it may be a problem with the heart valves or could be due to some other condition, such as hyperthyroidism, anaemia or heartworm.

In puppies, there are two major types of heart murmurs, often detected by a vet at the first or second vaccination visit. The most common type is called an innocent *"flow murmur."* This type of murmur is soft - typically Grade 2 or less - and is not caused by underlying heart disease. An innocent flow murmur typically disappears by four to five months of age.

However, if a puppy has a loud murmur - Grade 3 or louder - or if it is still easily heard with a stethoscope after four or five months of age, it's more likely that the pup has an underlying heart problem.

The thought of a puppy having congenital heart disease is worrying, but it is important to remember that the disease will not affect all puppies' life expectancy or quality of life.

Canine Cancer

This is the biggest single killer and will claim the lives of one in four dogs, regardless of breed. It is the cause of nearly half the deaths of all dogs aged 10 years and older, according to the American Veterinary Medical Association.

English Springer Spaniels live longer than many other breeds and may be therefore more prone to cancer in their golden years.

Mammary Cancer

One type of cancer not uncommon in female English Springer Spaniels is mammary tumours. These originate in the mammary glands - which each have a nipple - on a dog's chest and belly.

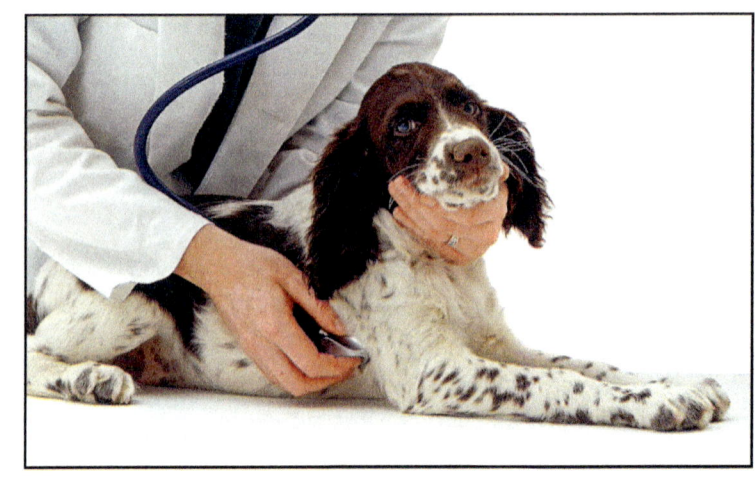

According to the UK English Springer Spaniel Health website: "Benign growths are often smooth, small and slow growing. Signs of malignant tumours include rapid growth, irregular shape, and firm attachment to the skin or underlying tissue, bleeding, and ulceration.

"Occasionally tumours that have been small for a long period of time may suddenly grow quickly and aggressively, but this is the exception, not the rule.

"There are multiple types of mammary tumours in (all) dogs. Approximately 50% of all mammary tumours in dogs are benign (not life threatening), and the other 50% are malignant (likely to spread and/or cause death).

"Mammary tumours are more likely to occur in unspayed, middle-aged female dogs - those between five and ten years of age.

"Spaying a female prior to two years of age significantly decreases risk for both benign and malignant mammary tumours. Spaying after this time reduces risk for benign tumours, but appears to have no advantage for prevention of malignant tumours.

"Interestingly, pregnancy and lactation appear to have no influence on mammary cancer risk. However, evidence suggests that females bred extensively, beginning at an early age, have a slightly lower risk for mammary cancer. The condition is extremely rare in male dogs."

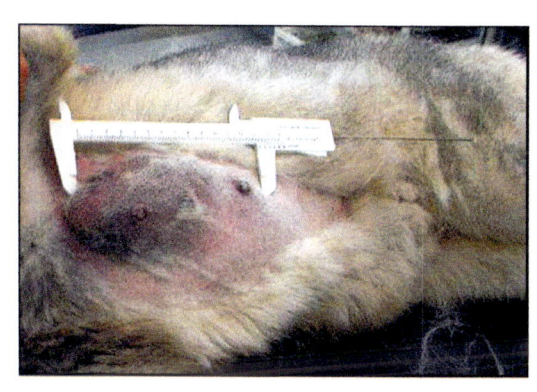

Recognising the Signs

The UK English Springer Spaniel Health website says: "Mammary tumours present as a solid mass or as multiple swellings. When they do arise in the mammary tissue, they are usually easy to detect by gently palpating (examine by feeling with the fingers) the mammary glands.

"When tumours first appear they will feel like small pieces of pea gravel just under the skin. They are very hard and are difficult to move around under the skin. They can grow rapidly in a short period of time, doubling their size every month or so.

"It is very difficult to determine the type of tumour based just on physical inspection. A consultation with your vet may lead to him or her deciding to perform a biopsy (removal of living tissue) or tumour removal, and analysis is almost always needed to determine if the tumour is benign or malignant, and to identify what type it is.

"Tumours that are more aggressive may metastasize (spread elsewhere in the body) and invade the surrounding lymph nodes or the lungs. A chest x-ray and physical inspection of the lymph nodes will often help in confirming this."

Treatment

The normal course of treatment is surgical removal – unless the dog is very old in which case the vet might decide against it.

English Springer Spaniel Health: "Some vets elect to first perform a fine needle aspiration to ascertain breast tumour classification. This gives them the opportunity to carry out cytology (examination of cells) on mammary tumours before surgery, in order to first rule out mast cell cancer and cystic disease.

"Should surgery be performed, the area excised (cut away) depends on the judgement and preference of the Vet performing surgery. Some choose to remove only the mass itself; others, taking into consideration how the cancer can spread, will remove the mass and the rest of the mammary tissue and lymph nodes that drain with the gland.

"It is important for you to discuss with your Vet all the options open to you, before deciding on what is best for your dog's future health and welfare."

Chemotherapy may be prescribed for cancer that has already spread to other areas of the body (metastatic disease), multi-site tumours or tumours that cannot be removed surgically. Chemotherapy may be used as the only treatment for certain cancers, or in conjunction with surgery and radiation therapy.

FACT There is evidence that the risk of mammary, uterine and testicular cancers decreases with neutering and spaying. See Chapter 15. The Facts of Life for more information.

Other Types of Cancer

As with humans, there are many types of cancer that can affect dogs. Typical symptoms of cancer (your dog may have one or more of these) include:

- Swellings anywhere on the body or around the anus
- Sores that don't heal
- Weight loss
- Lameness, which may be a sign of bone cancer, with or without a visible lump
- Laboured breathing
- Changes in exercise or stamina level
- Change in bowel or bladder habits
- Increased drinking or urination
- Bad breath, which can be a sign of oral cancer
- Poor appetite, difficulty swallowing or excessive drooling
- Vomiting

Treatment and Reducing the Risk

Just because your dog has a skin growth doesn't mean that it's serious. Many older dogs develop fatty lumps, or **lipomas,** which are often harmless, but it's still advisable to have the first one checked. Your vet will make a diagnosis following an X-ray, scan, blood test, biopsy or combination of these.

If your dog is diagnosed with cancer, there IS hope. Advances in veterinary medicine and technology offer various treatment options, including chemotherapy, radiation and surgery. Unlike with humans, a dog's hair does not fall out with chemotherapy.

We had a happy ending. We had a four-year-old dog develop a lump like a black grape on his anus. We took him down to the vet within a day or so of first noticing it and got the dreaded diagnosis of T-cell lymphoma, a particularly aggressive form of cancer.

The vet removed the lump a couple of days later and the dog went on to live a happy active life into his teens.

Tip Every time you groom your dog, get into the habit of checking his body for lumps and lift his top lip to check for signs of paleness or whiteness in the gums. As with any illness, early detection often leads to a better outcome.

We have all become aware of the risk factors for human cancer - stopping smoking, protecting ourselves from over-exposure to strong sunlight and eating a healthy, balanced diet all help to reduce cancer rates.

We know to keep a close eye on ourselves, go for regular health checks and report any lumps to our doctors as soon as they appear.

The same is true with your dog.

The outcome depends on the type of cancer, treatment used and, importantly, how early the tumour is found.

FACT > **The sooner the cancer is detected, diagnosed and treated, the greater the chances of success.**

While it is impossible to completely prevent cancer, the following points can help to reduce the risk:

- Feed a healthy diet with few or no preservatives
- Don't let your English Springer Spaniel get overweight
- Consider dietary supplements, such as antioxidants, Vitamins A, C, E, beta carotene, lycopene or selenium, or coconut oil – check compatibility with any other treatments
- Give your dog regular daily exercise
- Keep your dog away from chemicals, pesticides, cleaning products, etc. around the garden and home
- Avoid passive smoking
- Give pure, filtered or bottled water (fluoride-free) for drinking
- Consider natural flea remedies (check they are working) and avoid unnecessary vaccinations
- Check your dog regularly for lumps and any other physical or behavioural changes
- If you are buying a puppy, ask whether there is any history of early-age cancer in the bloodlines

Canine cancer research is currently being conducted all over the world and medical advances are producing a steady flow of new tests, treatments and cancer care.

Survival rates are improving year on year, giving owners lots of hope that if they catch the cancer early, their dog will go on to live a long and happy life.

With sincere thanks to Lesley Field and Louise Scott, UK English Springer Spaniel Breed Clubs' Joint Breed Health Co-ordinators, for their invaluable contributions to this chapter.

Excellent sources of further information on English Springer Spaniel health are:
English Springer Spaniel Health at www.englishspringerhealth.org.uk

The English Springer Spaniel Field Trial Association health pages at
https://essfta.org/english-springers/health-genetics-and-research-faq

Disclaimer: The author is not a veterinarian. This chapter is intended to give owners an outline of some of the main health issues and symptoms that may affect their English Springer Spaniels. If you have any concerns regarding your dog's health, our advice is always the same: consult a veterinarian.

13. Skin & Allergies

Visit any busy veterinary clinic these days — especially in spring and summer — and you'll see itchy dogs. Skin conditions, allergies and intolerances are on the increase in the canine world as well as the human one. While the English Springer Spaniel as a breed is not particularly prone to them, any individual dog can be affected.

How many children did you hear of having asthma or a peanut allergy when you were at school? Not too many, I'll bet. Yet allergies and adverse reactions are now relatively common — and it's the same with dogs. The reasons are not clear; it could be connected to genetics, diet, environment, over-vaccination — or a combination. As yet, there is no clear scientific evidence to back this up.

The skin is a complicated topic and a whole book could be written on this subject alone. While many dogs have no problems at all, some suffer from sensitive, itchy, dry or oily skin, hot spots, bald spots, yeast infections or other skin disorders, causing them to scratch, bite or lick themselves excessively. Symptoms vary from mild itchiness to a chronic reaction.

Canine Skin

The skin is the dog's largest organ. It acts as the protective barrier between your dog's internal organs and the outside world; it also regulates temperature and provides the sense of touch. Surprisingly, a dog's skin is actually thinner than ours, and it is made up of three layers:

1. **Epidermis** or outer layer, the one that bears the brunt of your dog's contact with the outside world.

2. **Dermis** is the extremely tough layer mostly made up of collagen, a strong and fibrous protein. This is where blood vessels deliver nutrients and oxygen to the skin, and it also acts as your dog's thermostat by allowing her body to release or retain heat, depending on the outside temperature and your dog's activity level.

3. **Hypodermis** is a dense layer of fatty tissue that allows your dog's skin to move independently from the muscle layers below it, as well as providing insulation and support for the skin.

FACT > Human allergies often trigger a reaction within the respiratory system, causing us to wheeze or sneeze, whereas allergies or hypersensitivities in a dog often cause a reaction in their SKIN.

- Skin can be affected from the INSIDE by things that your dog eats or drinks
- Skin can be affected from the OUTSIDE by fleas, parasites, or inhaled and contact allergies triggered by grass, pollen, man-made chemicals, dust, mould, etc.

Most Springers can run through fields, woodland and scrub and roll around in the grass with no after-effects at all - except for a muddy or tangled coat.

Others may spend less time in the countryside and have an excellent diet, but still experience itching, hot spots, bald patches or recurring ear infections. Some can eat anything and everything with no issues at all, while owners of others spend a lot of time trying to find the magic bullet – the ideal food for their Springer's sensitive stomach.

It's by no means possible to cover all of the issues and causes in this chapter. The aim here is to give a broad outline of some of the more common ailments and how to deal with them. We have also included remedies tried with some success by ourselves (we had a dog with skin issues) and other owners of affected dogs, as well as advice from a holistic specialist.

This information is not intended to take the place of professional help; always contact your vet if your dog appears physically unwell or uncomfortable. This is particularly true with skin conditions:

Tip SEEK TREATMENT AS SOON AS POSSIBLE. If you can find the cause(s) early, you reduce the chances of it taking hold and causing secondary issues and infections.

Whatever the cause, you'll have to give details of your dog's diet, exercise regime, habits, medical history and local environment before your vet can make a diagnosis. The vet will then carry out a physical examination, possibly followed by further tests, before a course of treatment can be prescribed. One of the difficulties with skin ailments is that the exact cause is often difficult to diagnose as the symptoms are similar to other ailments.

If environmental allergies are involved, specific and expensive tests are available. You'll have to take your vet's advice on this as the tests are not always conclusive. And if the answer is pollen, it can be difficult - if not downright impossible - to keep your Springer away from the triggers. There's no way you can keep a Springer permanently indoors, so it's often a question of managing rather than curing the condition.

There are many things you as an owner can do to reduce the allergen load – and many natural remedies and supplements that can help, as well as veterinary medications.

NOTE: Food allergies and intolerances are dealt with in Chapter 7. Feeding a Springer.

Types of Allergies

"Canine dermatitis" means inflammation of a dog's skin and it can be triggered by numerous things, but the most common is allergies. Vets estimate that as many as one in four dogs they see has some kind of allergy. Symptoms are (your dog may have one or more of these):

- Chewing, most commonly the feet or belly
- Itchy ears, head shaking
- Rubbing their face on the floor
- Scratching
- Scratching or biting the anus

- Hair loss
- Flaky or greasy skin, perhaps with sore or discoloured patches or hot spots
- The skin can smell of corn (tortilla) chips

Springers who are allergic to something show it through skin problems and itching; your vet may call this *"pruritus."* It may seem logical that if dogs are allergic to something inhaled, like certain pollen grains, their nose will run; if allergic to something eaten, they may vomit, or if allergic to an insect bite, they may develop a swelling. But in practice this is seldom the case.

Dogs with allergies often chew their feet until they are sore and red. You may see yours rubbing their face on the carpet or couch, or scratching their belly and flanks.

FACT > The ear glands then produce too much wax in response to the allergy, causing ear infections. Bacteria and yeast (which is a fungus) thrive in the excessive wax and debris.

Digestive health can play an important role. US holistic vet Dr Jodie Gruenstern says: "It's estimated that up to 80% of the immune system resides within the gastrointestinal system; building a healthy gut supports a more appropriate immune response. The importance of choosing fresh proteins and healthy fats over processed, starchy diets (such as kibble) can't be overemphasized.

"Grains and other starches have a negative impact on gut health, creating insulin resistance and inflammation."

Allergic dogs may cause skin lesions or **hot spots** by constant chewing and scratching. Sometimes they will lose hair, which can be patchy, leaving a mottled appearance, or the coat may change colour. The skin itself may be dry and crusty, reddened, swollen or oily, depending on the dog. It is common to get secondary bacterial skin infections due to these self-inflicted wounds.

An allergic dog's body is reacting to certain molecules called **allergens.** These may come from:

- Tree, grass or plant pollens
- Flea bites
- Grain mites
- Specific food or food additives, such as cooked or raw meat or poultry, grains, colourings or preservatives
- Milk products
- Fabrics, such as wool or nylon
- Rubber and plastics
- House dust and dust mites
- Mould
- Chemical products used around the home or garden

FACT > These allergens may be INHALED as the dog breathes, INGESTED as the dog eats, or caused by CONTACT with the dog's body when walking or rolling

Regardless of how they arrive, they all cause the immune system to produce a protein called IgE, which releases irritating chemicals like histamine inside the skin, hence the scratching.

Managing allergies is all about REDUCING THE ALLERGEN LOAD.

Inhalant Allergies (Atopy)

Some of the most common allergies are inhalant and seasonal - at least at first; some allergies may develop and worsen. Look at the timing of the reaction. Does it happen all year round? If so, this may be mould, dust or some other permanent trigger. If the reaction is seasonal, then pollens may well be the culprit.

There is a serum test called **VARL Liquid Gold** widely used in the USA. A simple blood sample is taken and tested for reactions to different types of pollen in your area, other environmental triggers and food. VARL claims it's at least as effective as the more intrusive *intradermal skin testing* (around 75%), which involves sedating the dog, injecting a small amount of antigen into the skin and then inspecting it for an allergic reaction.

They say a further advantage is that it does not give false positives. Depending on the results, treatment may involve avoidance or an immunotherapy programme consisting of a series of injections or tablets.

A similar serum test called **Avacta** is used by vets in the UK.

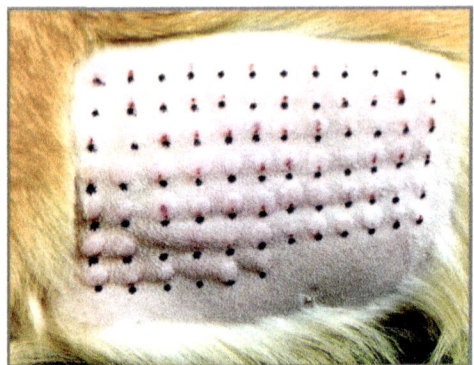

Our photo shows a Golden Retriever that has undergone intradermal skin testing. This dog was tested for over 70 allergens, which is a lot. The injections are in kits. If you consider this option, ask the vet or specialist how many allergens are in the kit.

Other blood tests work by checking for antibodies caused by antigens. The two standard tests are **RAST** and **ELISA**. Many vets feel that the ELISA test gives more accurate results, although both can give false positives.

Some owners of dogs with allergies consider changing to an unprocessed diet (raw or cooked) and natural alternatives to long-term use of steroids, which can cause other health issues.

Environmental or Contact Irritations

These are a direct reaction to something the dog physically comes into contact with, and the triggers are similar to inhalant allergies. If grass or pollen is the issue, the allergies are often seasonal.

An affected dog may be given treatments such as tablets, shampoo or localised cortisone spray for spring and summer – with a steroid injection to control a flare-up - but be perfectly fine the rest of the year. This was the case with our dog with allergies.

It's a bit of a nightmare if your dog does develop environmental or contact allergies as there's nothing Springers love more than running full tilt through the pollen-laden Great Outdoors. However, there's plenty you can do to reduce the symptoms.

Tip: If you suspect your Springer has outdoor contact allergies, hose them down after walks. Washing their feet and belly will get rid of some of the pollen and other allergens, which in turn reduces scratching and biting. Try them on a natural, unprocessed diet and reduce chemicals around the house and garden.

The problem may be localised - such as the paws or belly. Symptoms are a general skin irritation or specific hotspots - itching (pruritus) and sometimes hair loss. Readers of our website sometimes report that their dog will incessantly lick one part of the body, often the paws, anus, belly or back.

Flea Bite Allergy

This is a common allergy affecting lots of dogs. It's typically seasonal, worse during summer and autumn - peak time for fleas - and in warmer climates where fleas are prevalent. Unfortunately, some dogs with a flea allergy also have inhalant allergies.

This allergy is not to the flea itself, but to proteins in flea saliva left under the dog's skin when the insect feeds. Just one bite to an allergic dog will cause red, crusty bumps *(pictured)* and intense itching.

Affected dogs usually have a rash at the base of their tails and rear legs, and will bite and scratch the area. Much of the skin damage is done by the dog's scratching, rather than the flea bite, and can result in hair falling out or skin abrasions.

Some dogs also develop hot spots, often along the base of the tail and back.

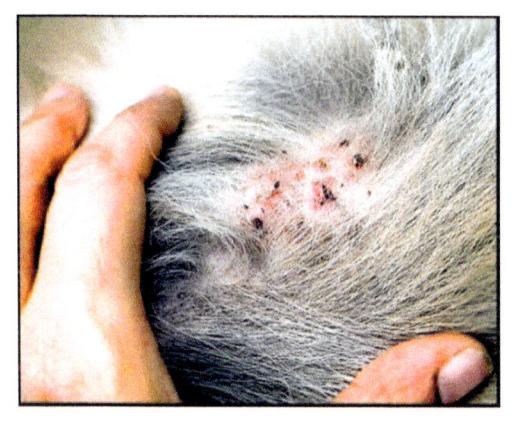

A vet can make a diagnosis with a simple blood test. If fleas are the cause, you'll also have to make sure your dog's bedding and your home are flea-free zones. Most flea bite allergies can be treated with medication, but they can only be totally prevented by keeping all fleas away from the dog. Various flea prevention treatments are available – see the section on **Parasites**.

Acute Moist Dermatitis (Hot Spots)

A hot spot can appear suddenly and is a raw, inflamed and often bleeding area of skin. The area becomes moist and painful and begins spreading due to continual licking and chewing. They can become large, red, irritated lesions in a short pace of time. The cause is often a local reaction to an insect bite.

Tip Some owners have had good results after dabbing hot spots, interdigital cysts and other skin irritations with an equal mixture of the amber-coloured Original Listerine *(pictured)*, baby oil and water. US owners have also reported success with Gold Bond Powder.

Once diagnosed and with the right treatment for the underlying cause, hot spots often disappear as soon as they appeared. Treatments may come in the form of injections, tablets or creams – or a combination of all three. The affected area is first clipped and cleaned by the vet.

Bacterial infection (Pyoderma)

Pyoderma literally means *pus in the skin* (yuk)! The offending bacteria is staphylococcus, and the condition may also be referred to as a *staph infection.* Early signs are itchy red spots filled with yellow pus, similar to pimples or spots in humans. They can sometimes develop into red, ulcerated skin with dry and crusty patches. Fortunately, the condition is not contagious.

Pyoderma is caused by several things: a broken skin surface, a skin wound due to chronic exposure to moisture, altered skin bacteria, or poor blood flow to the skin.

Allergies to fleas, food, parasites, yeast or fungal skin infections, thyroid disease, hormonal imbalances, heredity and some medications can all increase the risk. One of the biggest causes of infection is a dog with a skin disorder excessively licking or biting an itchy patch.

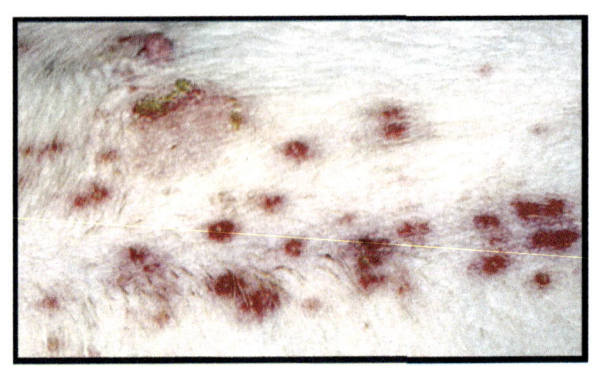

Puppies can develop **puppy pyoderma** in thinly-haired areas, such as the groin and underarms. If you notice symptoms, get to the vet quickly before the condition develops from **superficial pyoderma** into *severe pyoderma*, which is very unpleasant and takes a lot longer to treat.

Superficial and puppy pyoderma are usually successfully treated with a two to six-week course of antibiotic tablets or ointment. Severe or recurring pyoderma looks awful, causes your dog some distress and can take months to completely cure.

Medicated shampoos and regular bathing, as instructed by your vet, are also part of the treatment. It's also important to ensure your dog has clean, dry, padded bedding. Bacterial infection, no matter how bad it may look, usually responds well to medical treatment.

Seborrhoea

This is a common skin condition in dogs that occurs when either too much or too little of the protein **keratin** is produced. The result is flaky skin (dandruff) and greasiness of the skin and hair. Seborrhea also causes the dog's skin to give off a smelly, waxy substance that clumps in the ears, under the belly and armpits, elbows, and around the ankles.

Dogs may scratch at the affected areas causing bleeding, crusting, hair loss and secondary infections. There are two common types of seborrhea and most affected dogs have a combination of both:

- Oily (oleosa)
- Dry (sicca), which results in scaly skin

There are also two separate causes: **primary seborrhea** has a genetic base. The English Springer Spaniel is one of the breeds at a higher risk than average of suffering from primary seborrhoea, along with American Cockers, Bassett Hounds and Westies.

Secondary seborrhea results from injury to the skin caused by things such as parasites, allergies, food disorders and hormonal issues like hypothyroidism.

Symptoms:

- Very dry, dull coat
- Dandruff
- Greasy, oily skin with an unpleasant smell
- Rough and scaly skin lesions
- Itching - from mild to severe
- Lots of earwax and ear debris

All the skin is affected by seborrhea, but the folds of skin between the toes, in the armpits, on the belly, perineum (under a dog's tail) and at the base of the neck are often worse. A vet will make a diagnosis after a physical examination, which may be followed by a skin scraping and blood tests. Treatment depends on whether there is an underlying cause that needs to be dealt with first.

Treatment for the seborrhea itself may involve baths with an anti-seborrheic shampoo (which contains coal tar) every few days for two to three weeks until excess keratin is removed. Bathing continues less frequently for another two or three weeks until the skin improves.

You also need to clean your dog's ears with a medicated ear cleaner every two to three days. Your vet will prescribe an ear medication if the ears are infected.

Steroids (such as prednisone) may be prescribed to to decrease inflammation and debris build-up. Follow-up vet checks every one to three weeks are important to monitor treatment and progress.

Primary seborrhea cannot usually be cured, but treatment is often effective in managing the symptoms. Any underlying cause - such as allergies - also has to be tackled, along with any yeast or bacterial infections.

The vet might also recommend an omega-3 fatty acid supplement, which may seem odd as the dog often already has a greasy coat, but fatty acids are essential for normal skin cell function and do actually help.

Malassezia Dermatitis and Yeast Infections

Malassezia Dermatitis is a specific type of yeast infection that affects many dogs. **Malassezia** is a yeast, or fungus, that gets into the surface layers of the skin. These organisms cause no harm to the vast majority of animals, but cause inflammation in some dogs when numbers multiply.

Like all yeast infections, they like humid conditions - so climate can be a factor - and especially warm, damp areas on a dog's body like ear canals and skin folds. One trigger is saliva with repetitive licking – which explains why feet are often stained and itchy; saliva stains them and Malassezia grows.

FACT Dogs that already have poor skin condition, allergies or a hormonal disorder are more prone to Malassezia infection.

Symptoms are:

- Itchy, flaky skin at inflamed areas around the lips, ear canals, neck and armpits, between the toes and in skin folds on the face
- Greasy or flaky skin
- Unpleasant smell
- In long-term cases, the skin becomes thicker and darker
- Reddish-brown discolouration of the claws

The condition is easily diagnosed with a skin scraping and is often effectively treated with anti-fungal shampoos, wipes and creams, or tablets. If another skin disorder is causing the Malassezia to spread, this will have to be addressed.

Pemphigus Foliaceus

This is the name given to a rare autoimmune skin disease that can affect some breeds more than others, including Springers. It often starts at around four years of age and causes crusty scabs in otherwise healthy skin, and hair loss - usually on top of the nose and inside the ear flap. Some dogs also get it on their footpads and toenails.

Bacteria often finds its way into the damaged skin, so secondary skin infections are common.

Diagnosis is made with a skin scraping and while there is no cure for Pemphigus, there are a number of treatments that are often very effective. These include steroids and immunosuppressive drugs.

Viral infection and sunlight are known to make it worse, so avoid strong sunlight if possible and apply a zinc-free sunscreen to your dog's sensitive parts before heading out into bright sunshine if your dog is affected.

Interdigital Cysts

If your Springer gets a fleshy red lump between the toes that looks like an ulcerated sore or a hairless bump, then it's probably an interdigital cyst - or **interdigital furuncle**. These can be very difficult to cure as they are often not the main problem, but a symptom of some other ailment.

They are not cysts, but the result of **furunculosis**, a skin condition that clogs hair follicles and creates chronic infection. Causes include allergies, obesity, poor foot conformation, mites, yeast infections, ingrowing hairs or other foreign bodies.

FACT Bulldogs are the most susceptible breed, but any dog can get them - often the dog also has allergies.

These nasty-looking bumps are painful, will probably cause a limp and can be a nightmare to get rid of. Vets might recommend a whole range of treatments to get to the root cause, and it can be very expensive to have a barrage of tests or biopsies - even then you're not guaranteed to find the underlying cause.

Here are some remedies your vet may suggest:

- Antibiotics and/or steroids and/or mite killers
- Soaking the feet in Epsom salts
- Testing for allergies or thyroid problems
- Starting a food trial if food allergies are suspected
- Shampooing the feet
- Cleaning between the toes with medicated (benzoyl peroxide) wipes
- A referral to a veterinary dermatologist
- Surgery (this is a last-resort option)

If you suspect your Springer has an interdigital cyst, visit the vet as soon as possible for a correct diagnosis and to discuss the various options. A course of antibiotics may be suggested initially, along with switching to a hypoallergenic diet if a food allergy is suspected.

If the condition persists, many owners get discouraged, especially when treatment continues for several weeks.

Tip: Be wary of agreeing to a series of steroid injections or repeated courses of antibiotics, as this means that the underlying cause of the furuncle has not been diagnosed. In such cases, it is worth exploring natural diets and remedies – and trying to lower the overall allergen load on your dog.

Before you resort to any drastic action, first try soaking your Springer's affected paw in Epsom salts for five or 10 minutes twice a day. After the soaking, clean the area with medicated wipes, which are antiseptic and control inflammation.

Surgery is a drastic option. Although it can be effective in solving the immediate issue it doesn't deal with the underlying problem. Interdigital cysts are not simple to deal with and it's important to **get the right diagnosis as soon as possible.**

If your dog has a skin issue - or surgical procedure - she may have to wear an E-collar, which is very stressful for everybody. No dog likes the cone, but it's especially difficult for an energetic dog like the Springer.

Most Springers are resistant to the **"Cone of Shame"** - they may slump down like you've hung a 10-ton weight on their neck or sink into a depression. Even compliant dogs are miserable as they wander round banging into door frames and furniture.

Fortunately, they don't usually have to wear them for more than a few days.

If your dog is resistant and the problem is with the paws, try putting socks on the affected area instead. This works well while they sleep, but you have to watch them like a hawk when they are awake to stop them biting.

An alternative to prevent dogs licking damaged skin on their bodies is an **inflatable comfy collar, pictured.**

Parasites

Demodectic Mange (Demodex)

Also known as red mange, follicular mange or puppy mange, this skin disease is caused by the tiny mite Demodex canis, **pictured.** The mites actually live inside the hair follicles on the bodies of virtually every adult dog and most humans without causing any harm or irritation.

In humans, the mites are found in the skin, eyelids and the creases of the nose...try not to think about that!

The mite spends its entire life on the host dog. Eggs hatch and mature from larvae to nymphs to adults in 20 to 35 days and the mites are transferred directly from the mother to the puppies within the first week of life by direct physical contact.

Demodectic mange is not a disease of poorly-kept or dirty dogs or kennels. It is generally a disease of young dogs with inadequate or poorly-developed immune systems - or older dogs suffering from a suppressed immune system.

THE ENGLISH SPRINGER SPANIEL HANDBOOK Page **187**

Virtually every mother carries and transfers mites to her puppies, and most are immune to the mite's effects, but a few puppies are not and they develop full-blown mange. They may have a few (less than five) isolated lesions and this is known as *localised mange* – often around the head.

Puppy Mange is quite common, usually mild and often disappears on its own.

Generalised mange is more serious and covers the entire body or region of the body.

Bald patches are usually the first sign, usually accompanied by crusty, red skin which sometimes appears greasy or wet. Usually hair loss begins around the muzzle, eyes and other areas on the head. The sores may or may not itch.

Photo: Two healthy puppies with good coats.

In localised mange a few circular crusty areas appear, most frequently on the head and front legs of three to six-month-old puppies. Most self-heal as the puppy becomes older and develops their own immunity, but a persistent problem should be treated.

With generalised mange there are bald patches over the entire coat, including the head, neck, body, legs, and feet. The skin on the head, side and back is crusty, often inflamed and oozes a clear fluid.

The skin itself will often be oily to touch and there is usually a secondary bacterial infection. Some puppies can become quite ill and can develop a fever, lose their appetites and become lethargic.

If you suspect your puppy has generalised demodectic mange, get them to a vet straight away.

There is also a condition called **pododermatitis**, when the mange affects a puppy's paws. It can cause bacterial infections and be very uncomfortable, even painful. Symptoms include hair loss on the paws, swelling of the paws (especially around the nail beds) and red, hot or inflamed areas which are often infected. Treatment is always recommended and can take several rounds to clear it up.

Diagnosis and Treatment – The vet will make a diagnosis after he or she has taken a skin scraping or biopsy, in which case the mites can be seen with a microscope. As these mites are present on every dog, they do not mean that the dog necessarily has mange. Only when they are coupled with lesions will a diagnosis of mange be made. Treatment usually involves topical (on the skin) medication and sometimes tablets.

Traditional treatments for Demodex have included the FDA-approved heartworm drug Ivermectin, given at a higher dose as a tablet or liquid. For dogs that don't tolerate Ivermectin, including herding breeds, other treatments have included another heartworm medication, Milbemycin. Sometimes the anti-parasitic dip Mitaban has been dispensed as a last resort.

FACT ❯ All of these treatments can have side effects. Some dogs, especially Toy breeds, don't respond well to Mitaban as it can make them nauseous. Discuss treatment and other options fully with your vet.

The latest treatment to prove highly effective is *Bravecto*, given in chewable tablets. It not only gets rid of the mites, but also remains effective for 12 weeks following treatment. A bonus is that is also effective against ticks and fleas during those 12 weeks.

One UK veterinarian added: "One very effective treatment for Demodex is Bravecto, recently licensed for this, and now the best one available."

Dogs with generalised mange may have underlying skin infections, so antibiotics are often given for the first several weeks of treatment. Because the mite flourishes on dogs with suppressed immune systems, try to get to the root cause of immune system disease, especially if your Springer is older when she develops demodectic mange.

Sarcoptic Mange (Scabies)

Also known as canine scabies, this is caused by the parasite *Sarcoptes scabiei.* This microscopic mite can cause a range of skin problems, the most common of which is hair loss and severe itching. The mites can infect other animals such as foxes, cats and even humans, but prefer to live their short lives on dogs. Fortunately, there are several good treatments and it can be easily controlled.

In cool, moist environments, the mites live for up to 22 days. At normal room temperature they live from two to six days, preferring to live on parts of the dog with less hair. Diagnosing canine scabies can be somewhat difficult, and it is often mistaken for inhalant allergies.

The vet will take a skin scraping to make a diagnosis and there are a number of effective treatments, including selamectin (Revolution – again, some dogs can have a reaction to this), an on-the-skin solution applied once a month which also provides heartworm prevention, flea control and some tick protection. Various Frontline products are also effective – check with your vet for the correct ones.

One product used by some breeders is the **Seresto Flea Collar**, *pictured,* which provides full body protection for up to eight months against all fleas, ticks, sarcoptic mange, lice and other bloodsucking critters! The collar is waterproof, a big bonus with Springers. There are also holistic remedies for many skin conditions.

Because your dog does not have to come into direct contact with an infected dog to catch scabies, it is difficult to completely protect her. Foxes and their environment can also transmit the mite.

> Chemical flea and parasite treatments, such as Seresto, Bravecto, Comfortis, Nexgard, Frontline, Advantix, Tritexix, etc. can trigger epilespy, other disorders or strange behaviour in a very small percentage of dogs.
> Do your research, talk to your vet and consider all options, including natural alternatives.

Fleas

Most Springers spend a lot of time outdoors and so are more likely to pick up parasites such as fleas and ticks than couch potato breeds.

When you see your dog scratching and biting, your first thought is probably: *"She's got fleas!"* and you may well be right. Fleas don't fly, but they do have very strong back legs and they will take any opportunity to jump from the ground or another animal into your Springer's lovely, warm coat. You can sometimes see the fleas if you part your dog's hair.

And for every flea that you see on your dog, there is the stomach-churning prospect of hundreds of eggs and larvae in your home.... So, if your dog gets fleas, you'll have to treat your environment as well as the dog in order to completely get rid of them. **The best form of cure is prevention.**

Vets recommend giving dogs a preventative flea treatment every four to eight weeks – although the Seresto Flea Collar lasts for eight months. If you do give a regular skin treatment, the frequency depends on your climate, the season - fleas do not breed as quickly in the cold - and how much time your Springer spends outdoors.

To apply topical insecticides like Frontline and Advantix, part the skin and apply drops of the liquid on to a small area on your dog's back, usually near the neck. Some kill fleas and ticks, and others just kill fleas - check the details.

Tip It is worth spending the money on a quality treatment, as cheap brands may not rid your Springer completely of fleas, ticks and other parasites. There are also holistic and natural alternatives to insecticides, discussed later in this chapter.

Some breeders are opposed to chemical flea treatments. One added that when she found a flea, she simply washes all of her dogs, one after the other, and then washes every last piece of bedding.

Ticks

A tick is not an insect, but a member of the arachnid family, like the spider. There are over 850 types, some have a hard shell and some a soft one. Ticks don't have wings, they crawl. They have a sensor called Haller's organ that detects smell, heat and humidity to help them locate food, which in some cases is a Springer.

A tick's diet consists of one thing and one thing only – blood! They climb up onto tall grass and when they sense an animal is close, crawl on. Ticks can pass on a number of diseases to animals and humans, the most well-known of which is **Lyme Disease**.

Lyme Disease

This is a bacterial illness passed on to dogs by ticks once they have been on the dog's body for one to two days. The ticks that carry Lyme Disease are most likely to be found in woods, tall grasses, thick brush and marshy ground.

In the UK, Lyme Disease is more prevalent in wooded areas, and in the US almost all cases are from the Northeast, Upper Midwest and Pacific coast. Typical symptoms include:

- Fever
- Loss of appetite
- Reduced energy
- Lameness (can be shifting, intermittent, and recurring)
- Generalised stiffness, discomfort, or pain
- Swelling of joints

Treatment includes antibiotics, usually for at least 30 days, which often resolves the symptoms. But in severe cases Lyme Disease can progress to fatal kidney failure, and serious cardiac and neurological effects can also occur. Your dog can't pass Lyme Disease on to you or other pets, but a carrier tick could come into your house on your dog's fur and get on to you.

Tip If your Springer spends a lot of time outdoors in high-risk areas consider having them vaccinated against Lime Disease.

One breeder added: "If ticks are removed quickly, they're not harmful. We use a tick tool which has instructions in the packet. You put the forked end either side of the tick and twist it till it comes out."

If you do find a tick on your Springer's coat and are not sure how to get it out, have it removed by a vet or other expert. Inexpertly pulling it out yourself and leaving a bit of the tick behind can be detrimental to your dog's health.

Heartworm

Although heartworm does not affect the skin, we have included it in this section as it is a parasite. Heartworm is a serious and potentially fatal disease affecting pets in North America and many other parts of the world, but not the UK.

It is present in Mediterranean countries, so check with your vet if you're intending taking your dog there. **Leishmaniasis** is another parasitic disease that UK dogs can pick up in Europe. It's transmitted by a biting sand flea and causes skin lesions or organ infection.

The foot-long heartworms live in the heart, lungs and blood vessels of affected animals, causing severe lung disease, heart failure and damage to organs. The dog is a natural host for heartworms, enabling the worms living inside a dog to mature into adults, mate and produce offspring. If untreated, their numbers can increase; dogs have been known to harbour several hundred worms in their bodies.

Untreated heartworm disease causes lasting damage to the heart, lungs and arteries, and can affect the dog's health and quality of life long after the parasites are gone. For this reason, **prevention is by far the best option** and treatment - when needed - should be administered as early as possible.

When a mosquito *(pictured)* bites and takes a blood meal from an infected dog, it picks up baby worms that develop and mature into *infective-stage* larvae over 10 to 14 days. Then, when it bites another dog, it spreads the disease. Once inside a dog, it takes about six months for the larvae to develop into adult heartworms, which can then live for five to seven years in a dog. In the early stages, many dogs show few or no symptoms. The longer the infection persists, the more likely symptoms will develop, including:

- A mild persistent cough
- Reluctance to exercise
- Tiredness after normal activity
- Decreased appetite and weight loss

As the disease progresses, dogs can develop a swollen belly due to excess fluid in the abdomen and heart failure. Dogs with large numbers of heartworms can develop the life-threatening caval syndrome, which, without prompt surgery, is often fatal.

Although more common in the south eastern US, heartworm disease has been diagnosed in all 50 states. The American Heartworm Society recommends that you get your dog tested every year and give your dog heartworm preventive treatment for all 12 months of the year. If you live in a risk area, check that your tick and flea medication also prevents heartworm. In the UK, heartworm has only been found in imported dogs.

Ringworm

This is not actually a worm, but a fungus and is most commonly seen in puppies and young dogs. It is highly infectious and often found on the face, ears, paws or tail. This fungus is most prevalent in hot, humid climates but, surprisingly, most cases occur in autumn and winter. But it is not that common; in one study of dogs with active skin problems, less than 3% had ringworm.

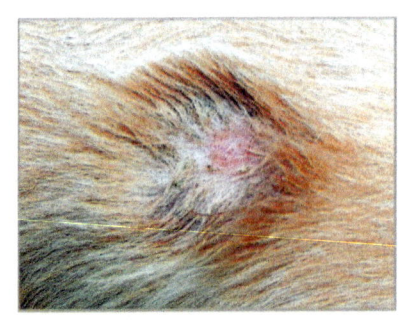

Ringworm, *pictured,* is transmitted by spores in the soil and by contact with the infected hair of dogs and cats, typically found on carpets, brushes, combs, toys and furniture.

Spores from infected animals can be shed into the environment and live for over 18 months, but most healthy adult dogs have some resistance and never develop symptoms. The fungi live in dead skin, hairs and nails - and the head and legs are the most common areas affected.

Tell-tale signs are bald patches with a roughly circular shape. Ringworm is relatively easy to treat with fungicidal shampoos or antibiotics from a vet.

FACT Humans can catch ringworm from pets, and vice versa. Children are especially susceptible, as are adults with suppressed immune systems and those undergoing chemotherapy. Hygiene is extremely important.

If your dog has ringworm, wear gloves when handling them and wash your hands well afterwards. And if a member of your family catches ringworm, make sure they use separate towels from everyone else or the fungus may spread.

As a teenager, I caught ringworm from horses at the local stables - much to my mother's horror - and was treated like a leper by the rest of the family until it cleared up!

Ear Infections

One of the English Springer Spaniel's many attractive features is their beautiful, luxuriant ears. All Spaniels have floppy (pendant) ears; they help them to trap a scent. But they also make them more susceptible to ear infections than short-haired dogs with pricked-up ears that allow air to circulate inside more easily.

FACT The fact that a dog has recurring ear infections does NOT necessarily mean that the ears are the issue – although they might be. If there is an underlying issue, it <u>must</u> be treated or the dog will continue to have ear infections.

Dogs can have ear problems for many different reasons, including:

- Allergies, such as environmental or food allergies
- Ear mites or other parasites
- Bacteria or yeast infections
- Injury, often due to excessive scratching
- Hormonal abnormalities, e.g. hypothyroidism
- The ear anatomy and environment, e.g. excess moisture
- Hereditary or immune conditions and tumours

In reality, many Springers have ear infections due to the structure of the ear. The long, hairy ears often prevent sufficient air flow inside the ear. This can lead to bacterial or yeast infections - particularly if there is moisture inside. These warm, damp and dark areas under the ear flaps provide an ideal breeding ground for bacteria.

Treatment depends on the cause and what – if any - other conditions your dog may have. Antibiotics are used for bacterial infections and antifungals for yeast infections. Glucocorticoids, such as dexamethasone, are often included in these medications to reduce the inflammation in the ear. Your vet may also flush out and clean the ear with special drops, something you may have to do daily at home until the infection clears.

A dog's ear canal is L-shaped, which means it can be difficult to get medication into the lower (horizontal) part of the ear. The best method is to hold the dog's ear flap with one hand and put the ointment or drops in with the other, if possible tilting the dog's head away from you so the liquid flows downwards **with gravity**.

Make sure you then hold the ear flap down and massage the medication into the horizontal canal before letting go of your dog, as the first thing she will do is shake her head – and if the ointment or drops aren't massaged in, they will fly out.

Tip When cleaning, plucking or trimming your Springer's ears, be very careful not to put anything too far down inside. Visit YouTube to see videos of how to correctly clean without damaging them. DO NOT use cotton buds inside the ear, they are too small and can cause injury.

Canine ear cleaning solution is widely available, or you can use a mixture of water and white vinegar.

Most Springers love splashing about in muddy water or swimming and it's a good idea to towel dry the insides of the ears afterwards - and after bathing at home. There is more information in **Chapter 14. Grooming.**

Nearly all ear infections can be successfully managed if properly diagnosed and treated. But if an underlying problem remains undiscovered, the outcome will be less favourable.

Deep ear infections can damage or rupture the eardrum, causing an internal ear infection and even permanent hearing loss. Closing of the ear canal (*hyperplasia* or *stenosis*) is another sign of severe infection. Most extreme cases of hyperplasia will eventually require surgery as a last resort; the most common procedure is called a 'lateral ear resection'.

Our dog with allergies had a lateral ear resection following years of recurring ear infections and the growth of scar tissue. It was surgery or deafness, the vet said. We opted for surgery and the dog has remained free of ear infections ever since. However, it is an **extremely** painful procedure for the animal and should only be considered as a very last resort.

To avoid or alleviate recurring ear infections, check your dog's ears and clean them regularly. Hair should be regularly plucked or trimmed from inside your Springer's ears – either by you or a groomer, or both.

Tip Consider buying elevated food and water bowls *(pictured)*. They have higher, narrower tops than normal dog dishes and help to keep your dog's ears out of his or her food and water.

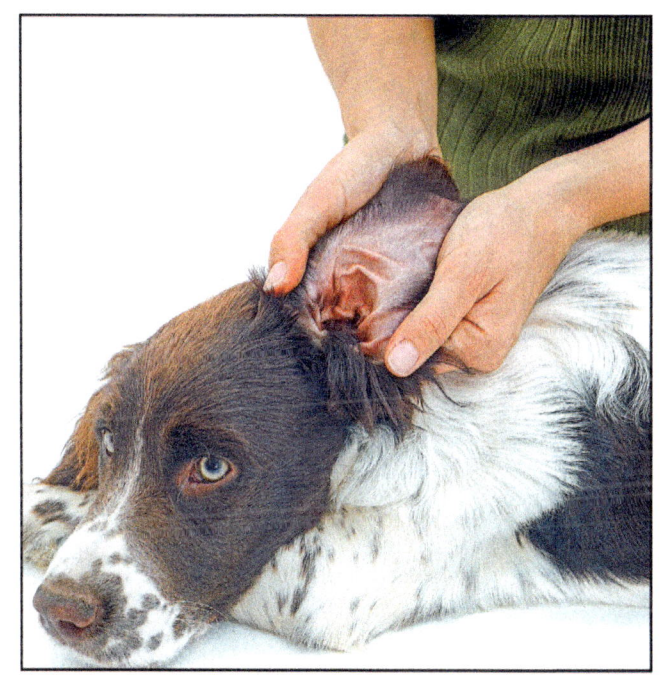

If your dog appears to be in pain, has smelly ears, or if their ear canals look inflamed, contact your vet straight away. If you can nip the first infection in the bud, there is a chance it will not return. If your dog has a ruptured or weakened eardrum, ear cleansers and medications could do more harm than good. Early treatment is the best way of preventing a recurrence.

Tip: Ear infections are notoriously difficult to get rid of once your dog's had one, so prevention is better than cure. Check your Springer's ears weekly when grooming, dry them after swimming and get the vet to check inside on routine visits.

If your dog appears to be in pain, has smelly ears, or if the inside of the ear looks red or sore, contact your vet straight away before the infection has a chance to become entrenched or recurring. If you can nip the first infection in the bud, you reduce the risk of it returning.

Some Allergy Treatments

Treatments and success rates vary tremendously from dog to dog and from one allergy to another, which is why it is so important to consult a vet at the outset. <u>Earlier diagnosis is more likely to lead to a successful treatment.</u>

Some owners of dogs with recurring skin issues find that a course of antibiotics or steroids works wonders for their dog's sore skin and itching. However, the scratching starts all over again shortly after the treatment stops.

Food allergies require patience, a change or several changes of diet and maybe even a food trial, and the specific trigger is notoriously difficult to isolate – unless you are lucky and hit on the culprit straight away.

With inhalant and contact allergies, blood and skin tests are available, followed by hyposensitisation treatment. However, these are expensive and often the specific trigger for many dogs remains unknown. So, the reality for many owners of Springers with allergies is that they manage the condition, rather than curing it completely.

FACT › While a single steroid injection is often highly effective in calming down symptoms almost immediately, frequent or long-term steroid use is not a good option as it can lead to serious side effects.

Our Experience With Max

According to our vet, Graham, more and more dogs are appearing in his waiting room with various types of allergies. Whether this is connected to how we breed or feed our dogs remains to be seen.

Our dog, Max, was perfectly fine until he was about two years old, when he began to scratch a lot. He scratched more in spring and summer, which meant that his allergies were almost certainly inhalant or contact-based and related to pollens, grasses or other outdoor triggers.

We decided not to have a lot of tests, not because of the cost (although they were not cheap), but because the vet said it was highly likely that he was allergic to pollens. Max was an active dog and if we'd had pollen allergy confirmed, we were not going to stop walking him two or three times a day.

Regarding medications, Max was at first put on to a tiny dose of Piriton *(pictured),* a cheap antihistamine manufactured in the millions for canine and human hay fever sufferers. For the first few springs and summers, this worked well.

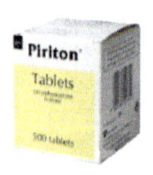

Allergies can change and a dog can build up a tolerance to a treatment, which is why they can be so difficult to treat. Max's symptoms changed from season to season, although the main ones were: general scratching, paw biting and ear infections.

One year he bit the skin under his tail a lot— he would jump around like he had been stung by a bee and bite frenetically. This was treated effectively with a single steroid injection, followed by spraying the area with cortisone once a day at home for a period. Localised spray can be very effective if the itchy area is small, but no good for spraying all over a dog's body.

Over the years we tried a number of treatments, all of which worked for a while, before he came off the medication in October when pollen levels fell. He was perfectly fine the rest of the year without any treatment at all.

Not every owner wants to treat his or her dog with chemicals, nor feed a diet that includes preservatives, which is why this book includes alternatives. Also, 16 years ago, when we were starting out on the *"Allergy Trail,"* there were far fewer options than there are now.

We fed Max a high quality hypoallergenic dry food. If we were starting again from scratch, knowing what we know now, I'd look into a raw or home-cooked diet (which is what we fed him as he neared the end of his life in his teens), if necessary, in combination with holistic remedies.

One spring the vet put him on a short course of steroids, which were effective for a season, but steroids are not a long-term solution. Another year we were prescribed the non-steroid Atopica. The active ingredient is **cyclosporine**, which suppresses the immune system - some dogs can get side effects, although ours didn't.

The daily tablet was expensive, but initially extremely effective — so much so that we thought we had cured the problem completely. However, after a couple of seasons on cyclosporine he developed a tolerance to the drug and started scratching again. A few years ago, he went back on the antihistamine Piriton, a higher dose than when he was two years old, and this was effective.

Other Options

In 2013 the FDA approved **Apoquel** (oclacitinib) - *pictured* - to control itching and inflammation in allergic dogs. Like most allergy drugs, it acts by suppressing the immune system, rather than addressing the root cause.

It has, however, proved to be highly effective in treating countless thousands of dogs with allergies. We used Apoquel with excellent results. There was some initial tweaking to get the daily dose right, but it proved highly effective. The tablets are administered according to body weight — it's not cheap, but Apoquel can be a miracle worker for some dogs, including ours.

FACT Side effects have been reported in some dogs, and holistic practitioners, Dogs Naturally magazine and others believe it can be harmful to the dog. Do your research.

Cytopoint is another recent option that's proved to be highly effective for many dogs. It is given as an injection every four to eight weeks and starts working almost immediately. Dogs with seasonal allergies may only need the injections for part of the year.

One added advantage of Cytopoint is that it is a biological therapy, not pharmaceutical, and does not suppress the dog's immune system. It contains engineered antibodies, similar to a dog's natural antibodies, which fight viruses and bacteria.

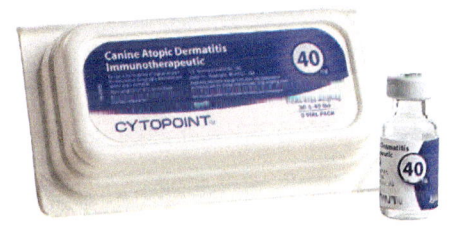

These antibodies have been specifically designed to target and neutralise a protein that sends itch signals to a dog's brain. This in turn helps to minimise scratching, giving the irritated skin chance to heal.

Allergies are often complex and difficult to treat; you should weigh up the pros and cons in the best interests of your own dog. Max's allergies were manageable; he loved his food, was full of energy and otherwise healthy, and lived a happy life to the age of 13. The Apoquel definitely helped him, but it's not for every dog.

Add fish oils, which contain Omega-3 fatty acids, to a daily feed to keep your dog's skin and coat healthy all year round – whether or not she has problems. A liquid supplement called Yuderm, *pictured,* (formerly Yumove Itchy Dog), which contains Omegas 3 and 6, golden flax and borage, is a good choice to add to your dog's daily feeds all year round.

When the scratching got particularly bad, we also bathed Max in an antiseborrheic shampoo twice a week for a limited time. This helped, although was not necessary once on Apoquel. Here are some other suggestions from owners:

Use an astringent such as witch hazel or alcohol on affected areas. We have heard of zinc oxide cream being used to some effect on dogs as well as babies' bottoms! In the human world, this is rubbed on to mild skin abrasions and acts as a protective coating.

Zinc oxide works as a mild astringent and has some antiseptic properties and is safe to use on dogs, *as long as you do not allow the dog to lick it off!*

Vitamins A and E also help to make a dog's skin healthy, and one breeder added: "A couple of mine tend to have itchy legs and feet. I feed them a grain-free food and use anti-itch herbal remedies."

Coconut oil was widely recommended for dogs, but the latest research shows that it may contribute to inflammation and leaky gut.

....

Massage

Anybody can do it – we do – and your Springer will love the attention! There are many videos on YouTube explaining techniques and showing very relaxed Springers enjoying a massage from their owners.

Tip: Massage can stimulate your dog's immune system and help to prevent or reduce allergies. It's also good for improving your dog's circulation and flexibility, reducing muscle and arthritis pain and other age-related problems.

Holistic practitioners also believe that *acupressure* can specifically help dogs with allergies. Type *"Acupressure for Dogs"* into Google to learn about the theory behind it and how to apply pressure at specific points on your dog's body.

Acupressure can also help nervous and elderly dogs.

....

The Holistic Approach

Many owners of dogs with sensitivities find that their dog does well for a time with injections or medication, but then the symptoms slowly start to reappear. More owners are now considering natural foods and remedies. A holistic practitioner looks at finding and treating the root cause of the problem, rather than just treating the symptoms.

Dr Sara Skiwski is an American holistic vet. She writes here about canine environmental allergies: "Here in California, with our mild weather and no hard freeze in Winter, environmental allergens can build up and cause nearly year-round issues for our beloved pets. Also, seasonal allergies, when left unaddressed, can lead to year-round allergies. Unlike humans, whose allergy symptoms seem to affect mostly the respiratory tract, seasonal allergies in dogs often take the form of skin irritation/inflammation."

Recurring Problems

"Allergic reactions are produced by the immune system. The way the immune system functions is a result of both genetics and the environment: Nature versus Nurture. Let's look at a typical case. A puppy starts showing mild seasonal allergy symptoms, for instance a red tummy and mild itching in Spring. Off to the vet!

"The treatment prescribed is symptomatic to provide relief, such as a topical spray. The next year when the weather warms up, the patient is back again - same symptoms but more severe this time.

"This time the dog has very itchy skin. Again, the treatment is symptomatic - antibiotics, topical spray (hopefully no steroids), until the symptoms resolve with the season change.

"Fast forward to another Spring…on the third year, the patient is back again but this time the symptoms last longer, (not just Spring but also through most of Summer and into Fall).

"By Year Five, all the symptoms are significantly worse and are occurring year-round. This is what happens with seasonal environmental allergies.

"The more your pet is exposed to the allergens they are sensitive to, the more the immune system over-reacts and the more intense and long-lasting the allergic response becomes. What to do?"

Root Cause

"In my practice, I like to address the potential root cause at the very first sign of an allergic response, which is normally seen between the ages of six to nine months old. I do this to circumvent the escalating response year after year.

"Since the allergen load your environmentally-sensitive dog is most susceptible to is much heavier outdoors, I recommend two essential steps in managing the condition. They are vigilance in foot care as well as hair care. What does this mean? A wipe down of feet and hair, especially the tummy, to remove any pollens or allergens is key. This can be done with a damp cloth, but my favorite method is to get a spray bottle filled with Witch Hazel *(pictured)* and spray these areas.

"First, spray the feet then wipe them off with a cloth, and then spray and wipe down the tummy and sides. This is best done right after the pup has been outside playing or walking. This will help keep your pet from tracking the environmental allergens into the home and into their beds. If the feet end up still being itchy, I suggest adding foot soaks in Epsom salts."

Dr Sara also stresses the importance of keeping the immune system healthy by avoiding unnecessary vaccinations or drugs: "The vaccine stimulates the immune system, which is the last thing your pet with seasonal environmental allergies needs.

"I also will move the pet to an anti-inflammatory diet. Foods that create or worsen inflammation are high in carbohydrates. An allergic pet's diet should be very low in carbohydrates, especially grains. Research has shown that 'leaky gut,' or dysbiosis, is a root cause of immune system overreactions in both dogs and cats (and some humans).

"Feed a diet that is not processed, or minimally processed; one that doesn't have grain and takes a little longer to get absorbed and assimilated through the gut. Slowing the assimilation assures that there are not large spikes of nutrients and proteins that come into the body all at once and overtax the pancreas and liver, creating inflammation.

"A lot of commercial diets are too high in grains and carbohydrates. These foods create inflammation that overtaxes the body and leads not just to skin inflammation, but also to other inflammatory conditions, such as colitis, pancreatitis, arthritis, inflammatory bowel disease and ear infections. Also, these diets are too low in protein, which is needed to make blood. This causes a decreased blood reserve in the body and in some of these animals this can lead to the skin not being properly nourished, starting a cycle of chronic skin infections which produce more itching."

Supplements

"After looking at diet, check that your dog is free from fleas and then these are some of Dr Sara's suggested supplements:

- ✓ **Raw (Unpasteurised) Local Honey** - an alkaline-forming food containing natural vitamins, enzymes, powerful antioxidants and other important natural nutrients, which are destroyed during the heating and pasteurisation processes.

    Raw honey has anti-viral, anti-bacterial and anti-fungal properties. It promotes body and digestive health, is a powerful antioxidant, strengthens the immune system, eliminates allergies, and is an excellent remedy for skin wounds and all types of infections. Bees collect pollen from local plants and their honey often acts as an immune booster for dogs living in the locality.

    Dr Sara says: "It may seem odd that straight exposure to pollen often triggers allergies, but that exposure to pollen in the honey usually has the opposite effect. But this is typically what we see. In honey, the allergens are delivered in small, manageable doses and the effect over time is very much like that from undergoing a whole series of allergy immunology injections."

- ✓ **Mushrooms** - make sure you choose the non-poisonous ones! Dogs don't like the taste, so you may have to mask it with another food. Medicinal mushrooms are used to treat and prevent a wide array of illnesses through their use as immune stimulants and modulators, and antioxidants. The most well-known and researched are reishi, maitake, cordyceps, blazei, split-gill, turkey tail and shiitake.

Histamine is what causes much of the inflammation, redness and irritation in allergies. By helping to control histamine production, the mushrooms can moderate the effects of inflammation and even help prevent allergies in the first place.

WARNING! Mushrooms can interact with some over-the-counter and prescription drugs, so do your research as well as checking with your vet first.

- ✓ **Stinging Nettles -** contain biologically active compounds that reduce inflammation. Nettles can reduce the amount of histamine the body produces in response to an allergen. Nettle tea or extract can help with itching. Nettles not only help directly to decrease the itch, but also work overtime to desensitise the body to allergens.

- ✓ **Quercetin -** is an over-the-counter supplement with anti-inflammatory properties. It is a strong antioxidant and reduces the body's production of histamines.

- ✓ **Omega-3 Fatty Acids -** help decrease inflammation throughout the body. Adding them into the diet of all pets - particularly those struggling with seasonal environmental allergies - is very beneficial. If your dog has more itching along the top of her back and on her sides, add in a fish oil supplement. Fish oil helps to decrease the itch and heal skin lesions.

- ✓ The best sources of Omega 3s are krill oil *(pictured),* salmon oil, tuna oil, anchovy oil and other fish body oils, as well as raw organic egg yolks. If using an oil alone, it is important to give a vitamin B complex supplement.

Dr Sara adds: "Above are but a few of the over-the-counter remedies I like. In non-responsive cases, Chinese herbs can be used to work with the body to help to decrease the allergy threshold even more than with diet and supplements alone. Most of the animals I work with are on a program of Chinese herbs, diet change and acupuncture.

"So, the next time Fido is showing symptoms of seasonal allergies, consider rethinking your strategy to treat the root cause instead of the symptom."

With thanks to Dr Sara Skiwski, of the Western Dragon Integrated Veterinary Services, San Jose, California, for her kind permission to use her writings as the basis for *The Holistic Approach*.

Remember:

- ❖ A high-quality diet
- ❖ Maintaining a healthy weight
- ❖ Regular grooming and check-overs, and
- ❖ Attention to cleanliness

all go a long way in preventing or managing skin problems in Springers.

If your Springer does have a skin issue, seek a professional diagnosis as soon as possible before attempting to treat it yourself and it becomes entrenched. Even if a skin condition cannot be completely cured, almost all can be successfully managed, allowing your dog to live a happy, pain-free life.

14. Grooming

Springers have many advantages over other breeds: they adapt to a variety of roles, from family pet to working gundog to sniffer dog. They generally get along with everybody and other dogs, they are intelligent, eager to please their owners and easier than many breeds to train and housetrain.

However, they are not low maintenance when it comes to grooming! Keeping your Springer clean and tidy requires commitment.

Springers are hard-wired to flush birds, rabbits and other small critters out of the undergrowth, and love nothing better than running through anything that is likely to stick to or get tangled in their coats. Their second favourite hobby is splashing about in muddy water.

All of this adds up to a dog that may not be the best choice if your home is your palace!

The English Springer Spaniel has a double coat. The undercoat is short, dense and soft, while the topcoat is medium to long with longer hairs on the legs, chest, belly, ears and tail called **feathering**. The feathers look attractive, but they are also very good at trapping and holding dirt.

The topcoat is flat or wavy and comprises fine, tougher hairs designed to give the dog some in-built waterproofing.

It also gives some protection against brambles, thorns, burrs, etc. - but doesn't stop any of these getting tangled in the fur and helping it to become matted (knotted).

Photo: Living the dream: this American Springer has run through a bog, making his coat nice and sticky, before rolling in the ash of an old bonfire!

As with all things Springer, there's a difference between the field (working) type and the show type. Springers from show lines have longer, more luxuriant coats and longer ears than working Springers - and US show-type Springers have even longer coats.

Show Springers have a heavy undercoat which requires hand-stripping – either by the owner or a groomer. They *"blow"* or shed their dense undercoat twice a year, usually in spring and autumn (Fall), when you'll remove copious amounts of hair during grooming.

When the coat is blowing, Springers with long, dense coats need grooming almost daily. Unless you want to disappear inside a giant fluff ball, we recommend doing it outdoors! Working Springers have a shorter coat.

Factors affecting shedding are:

- Bloodlines
- Age
- Sudden changes in temperature

- Nutrition
- Allergies
- Whether the dog has been neutered. In some cases, more often reported in females, this can lead to a loss of sheen and coat condition, wooliness or increased shedding

There are three different coat colour combinations:

- Liver-and-white (the most common)
- Black-and-white
- Either of these with tan markings, usually on the cheeks and eyebrows

Working Springers tend to have more white in their coats for visibility. European dogs have ticking (flecks of colour in the white), whereas this has largely been bred out of show Springers in the US.

Photo: A beautiful American show-type ("bench-bred" in the US) English Springer Spaniel, note the lack of ticking.

A healthy coat is silky with a sheen and a joy to behold; it's one of the breed's many attractive features. Regular brushing - once or twice a week, and every other day in shedding season helps to keep the coat in tiptop condition and is recommended for owners of pet Springers.

It also removes dirt and dead hair, stimulates blood circulation - which in turn helps to keep the skin healthy - and spreads natural oils throughout the coat.

A high-quality diet also helps, and some owners have found that feeding hypoallergenic kibble, or a raw or home-cooked diet can improve skin health and reduce shedding. Adding a daily squirt or spoonful of Omega 3 oil to a feed can also be beneficial.

Given the Springer's innate love of all things muddy, many owners have an outdoor tap fitted and give the dog a hose down underneath and quick dry with a towel before letting them into the house – particularly on rainy days. Rinsing your Springer's paws and under his belly is also effective in reducing contact allergies.

FACT If your Springer is smelly, he needs a bath! A healthy Springer coat should not have an unpleasant smell or any matting. Mats have to be cut out, which ruins the coat. Regular grooming - with possibly the occasional trip to a groomer - will stop mats and reduced the chances of him picking up an ear infection.

NOTE: If you do notice an unpleasant smell (in addition to your Springer's normal gassy emissions) and he hasn't been rolling in something unmentionable, then he may have a yeast infection or his anal glands may need squeezing.

Lisa Cardy, who breeds working line Springers, says: "They need brushing at least once a week and I send mine to be professionally groomed twice a year. Their ears do need brushing often to check for mats, etc. They are also prone to ear infections, so it is important to keep an eye on them.

"Springers' coats vary greatly, some are long-coated with lots of feathering while others are smoother coated, so be guided by your own dog's coat for grooming."

Lynne Lucas adds: "My intact girls are only properly bathed twice a year. Obviously, they are hosed off when back from a muddy walk with just warm water - that keeps the oils in their coats.

"They are not clipped, except Calamity. Once spayed the coat tends to become woolly, so Calamity needs a trip to the groomer's for clipping every eight weeks."

"I am proud to say (touch wood) that none of my girls have ever had an ear infection. I just wipe their inner ear lobe with a damp cloth if they are dirty after a run. I also trim their nails."

Photo: HELP!! Stella putting on a not-very-brave face while Lynne trims her nails. Stella is a working-type Springer.

Routine grooming sessions also allow you to examine your Springer's ears, tail, teeth, eyes, paws and nails for signs of problems. Older Springers may need more regular personal attention and checks from their owners.

Time spent grooming is also time spent bonding with your English Springer Spaniel. This physical and emotional inter-reliance helps bring us closer to our dogs.

Tip: Springers are lively and some can be stubborn, so it's important to get your puppy used to being handled; a wilful adult will not take kindly to being groomed if he's not used to it. And some English Springer Spaniels are notorious cowards when it comes to nail trimming (see photo!), so start early. Many groomers offer reduced puppy rates.

Hand Stripping or Trimming?

If you have a working Springer, you will probably be able to groom your dog yourself at home. There are, however, other tasks that you may not want to do, which a groomer will. These include removing hair from inside the ear flaps, trimming hair between the foot pads, nail trimming and anal gland squeezing.

Clipping (trimming or shaving with electric clippers) the whole body of a Springer is frowned upon by breed purists as it damages the natural texture of the topcoat. Although some specific areas of the coat may be clipped for the show ring, especially in the US, show dogs are normally hand stripped. However, if your Springer is a pet, you could consider clipping. Some active working gundogs are clipped for the summer.

Other circumstances when a Springer might be clipped are if you live in a hot climate and the dog has a particularly thick coat, if the coat has already lost its condition (perhaps with an older dog) and you want an easy way of keeping it tidy, or if it has become so matted that shaving it off is the only option.

Clipping the coat will not harm your dog, but the topcoat will become softer and lose some of its natural properties, such as an element of waterproofing. Show-type Springers have a thick, denser undercoat that needs regularly stripping out to keep it in good condition.

Hand stripping involves removing dead hairs from the coat by hand, particularly in the main shedding seasons of spring and autumn. This also speeds up the natural process of shedding and new growth.

The process does not hurt the dog, but he may not like it to begin with. If you have a show Springer and don't want the expense of a grooming parlour, you'll have to learn to do it yourself and invest in a stripping knife and stone to help remove the dead and loose hair. Hand stripping is not necessary with working Springers as they have a lot less coat.

Southern English Springer Spaniel Society (SESSS) has this advice: "For a more professional look, try using finger and thumb to pull the coat out, rather than using scissors or clippers. Often called the "Coronation Street" trim, sit the dog on your lap and let them settle.

"Once all is calm lay the dog down on its side and gently pull the coat starting just behind the shoulder, working down the side of the dog. Do this for 30 minutes whilst watching your favourite soap. You will be surprised just how much coat you will remove in just a week!"

Grooming Techniques and Equipment

Your puppy's coat starts to change at around six months, getting thicker and longer, and requiring attention. Hopefully, before then you will have got your puppy used to being handled and groomed.

Here in a nutshell are a few basic tasks involved in regular maintenance of a pet Springer:

1. Checking your dog's coat for tangles and mats (and ticks if he's often in woods).
2. Checking the insides of the ears are clean and not red or smelly (which could be a sign of infection).
3. Regular brushing to remove dead hair and stop the coat becoming matted
4. Trimming the ears, chest and throat, legs and feet, including hair between the toes.
5. Keeping your dog's teeth clean.
6. Nail trimming.
7. Hand stripping if you have a show-type Springer.

Photo: An English-bred show-type Springer.

Some useful equipment for basic grooming is

- A pair of straight-edged grooming scissors
- Steel comb or "spaniel comb"
- A bristle brush
- A slicker brush with steel pins
- Two rubber thumbs (the kind cashiers use to count notes!) or a rubber glove
- Thinning shears for the feathers and ears

The English Springer Spaniel Club recommends this grooming technique:

1. Use the combs and brushes to remove all dust, dirt, tangles and dead hair from the coat. The close-toothed spaniel comb and the slicker brush are particularly effective on the ear feathering. Don't be rough with your dog when you are grooming - remember there's real live skin under the hair!

2. Inside the ear around the entrance to the ear canal, the hair should be **carefully** trimmed quite short to allow air to circulate freely into the ear. Use the thinning scissors; they can also be used to trim the hair on the outside of the earflap.

   The hair from the top of the ear to about a third of the way down should be thinned out. After thinning, use the spaniel comb, **pictured,** to remove all loose hair from the ear.

3. The hair on top of your dog's head is likely to go a lighter shade and stick up when it is dead and therefore, needs to be trimmed out. All you need to do here is pluck the dead hair out.

   This is where the rubber thumbs, **pictured,** or a rubber glove are useful as they give you a better grip on the hair. You can use this action to remove any dead hair from other parts of the dog's coat.

4. Use a brush to remove dust and dirt from the coat. Gently tease out any tangles and knots.

5. The hair on the chest and throat will, at some stage, need thinning out and you will once again do this with the thinning scissors and a comb.

6. The feet should be trimmed using a pair of straight edge scissors; the aim is to make each foot look tight and rounded. This also means trimming flat any hair growing up between the toes, and any growing underneath the foot. The hair on the hocks (ankle joint on back legs) should be trimmed close using the thinning scissors.

7. Comb through the feathering on the chest carefully, teasing out any knots.

NOTE: As with any aspect of trimming always work against the natural lie of the hair.

On the following page is an excellent Guide to Trimming Your ESS, reproduced with kind permission of Southern English Springer Spaniel Society (SESSS)

Ear Cleaning

Ear infections (otitis externa) are not an uncommon problem with all types of Spaniels.

The Springer has pendulous (droopy), hairy ears, which make it difficult for air to circulate inside, compared to dogs with pricked-up ears. Underneath the ear flap is warm and sometimes moist, creating a haven for bacteria.

Ear infections are painful for your dog and notorious for recurring once they have taken hold. In very severe cases they can cause deafness, so it pays to check your dog's ears regularly while grooming. Many Springers love swimming, which can also result in ear infections if the area inside the ear remains damp for long periods. Get into the habit of towel-drying your dog's ears after swimming.

Never put anything sharp or narrow - like a small cotton bud - inside your dog's ears, as you can cause damage.

Typical signs of an ear infection are:

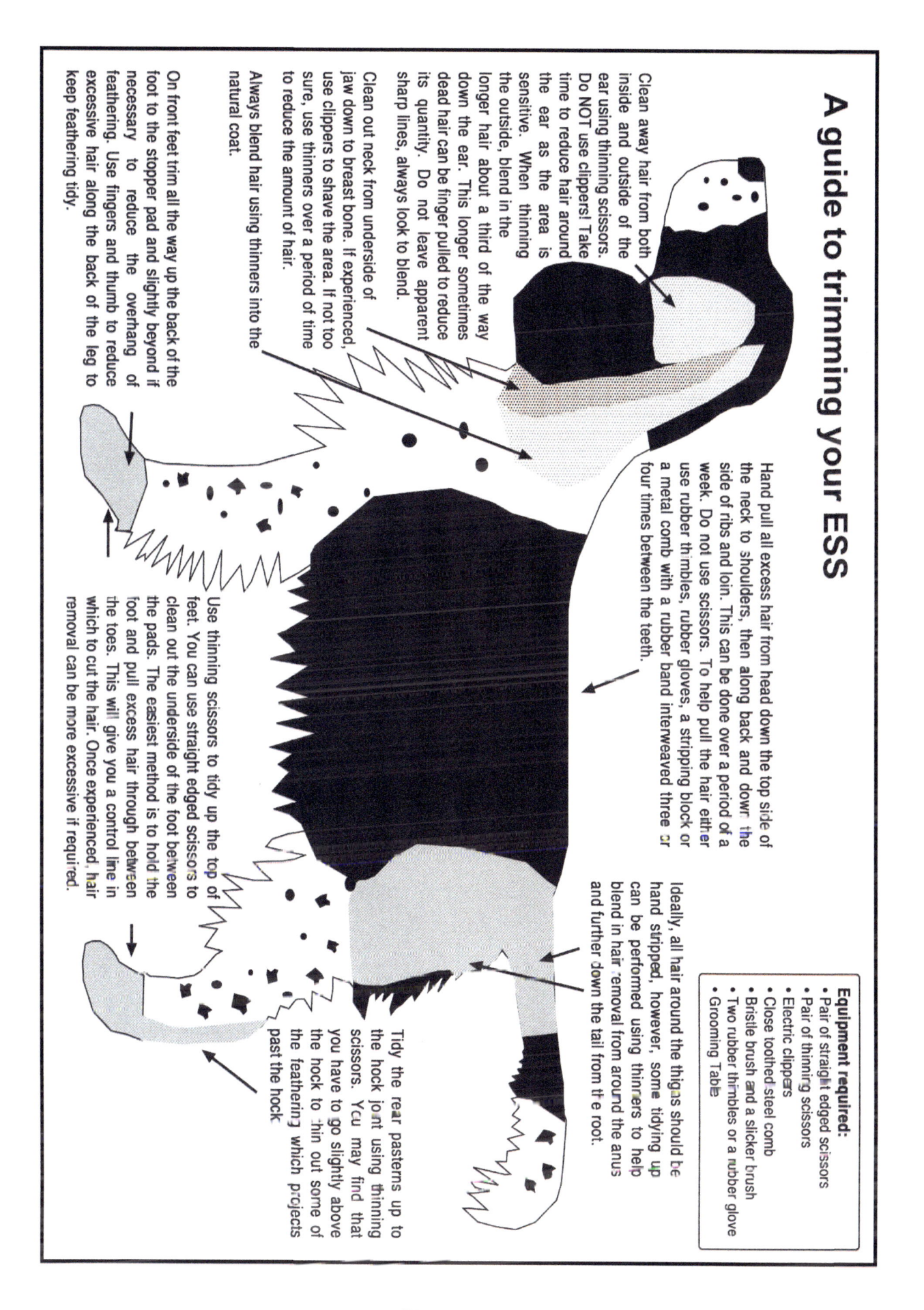

A guide to trimming your ESS

Clean away hair from both inside and outside of the ear using thinning scissors. Do NOT use clippers! Take time to reduce hair around the ear as the area is sensitive. When thinning the outside, blend in the longer hair about a third of the way down the ear. This longer dead hair can be finger pulled to reduce its quantity. Do not leave apparent sharp lines, always look to blend.

Clean out neck from underside of jaw down to breast bone. If experienced, use clippers to shave the area. If not too sure, use thinners over a period of time to reduce the amount of hair.

Always blend hair using thinners into the natural coat.

On front feet trim all the way up the back of the foot to the stopper pad and slightly beyond if necessary to reduce the overhang of feathering. Use fingers and thumb to reduce excessive hair along the back of the leg to keep feathering tidy.

Hand pull all excess hair from head down the top side of the neck to shoulders, then along back and down the side of ribs and loin. This can be done over a period of a week. Do not use scissors. To help pull the hair either use rubber thimbles, rubber gloves, a stripping block or a metal comb with a rubber band interweaved three or four times between the teeth.

Use thinning scissors to tidy up the top of feet. You can use straight edged scissors to clean out the underside of the foot between the pads. The easiest method is to hold the foot and pull excess hair through between the toes. This will give you a control line in which to cut the hair. Once experienced, hair removal can be more excessive if required.

Ideally, all hair around the thighs should be hand stripped, however, some tidying up can be performed using thinners to help blend in hair removal from around the anus and further down the tail from the root.

Tidy the rear pasterns up to the hock joint using thinning scissors. You may find that you have to go slightly above the hock to thin out some of the feathering which projects past the hock.

Equipment required:
- Pair of straight edged scissors
- Pair of thinning scissors
- Electric clippers
- Close toothed steel comb
- Bristle brush and a slicker brush
- Two rubber thimbles or a rubber glove
- Grooming Table

THE ENGLISH SPRINGER SPANIEL HANDBOOK Page **205**

- The dog shaking his head a lot
- Scratching his ears
- Rubbing his ears on the floor
- An unpleasant smell coming from the ears, which is a sign of a yeast or other infection
- Redness and/or inflammation inside the ears
- Lots of wax inside the ears

If your dog has any of these signs, consult your vet ASAP, as simple routine cleaning won't solve the problem.

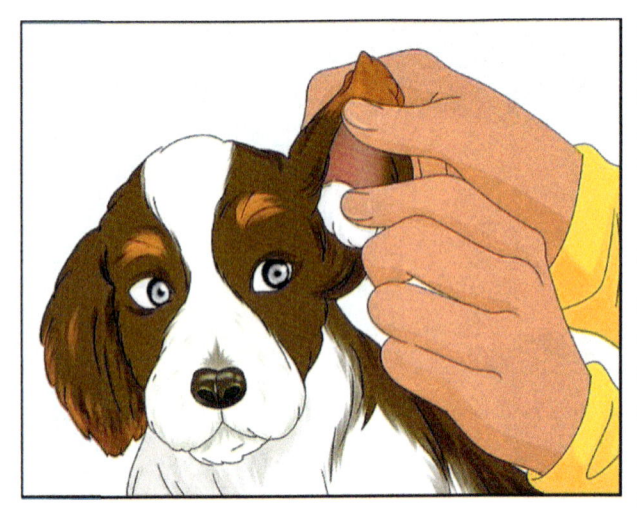

If your dog has a lot of dense hair, you can regularly pluck - or ask your groomer to pluck - some of the hair inside the ear flap. Do it gently and keep an eye out for redness or inflammation of the ear flap or inner ear.

If your dog is not being shown, you can trim - or ask your groomer to trim - the inside of the ear.

Check and clean the inside of your Springer's ears regularly - once every week or two weeks. Use a ball of damp cotton wool or baby wipe regularly to gently remove dirt and wax, *pictured*.

From time to time you can also consider using an ear cleansing solution. Squeeze a few drops of cleanser into the ear canal. If you can, tilt your dog's head so the ear canal is pointing downwards, allowing gravity to help distribute the solution.

Massage the base of the ear for 15 seconds before allowing him to shake his head. Then dry the inside of the ear flap with cotton wool and **gently** wipe out any dirt and waxy build-up in the ear canal with cotton wool.

In both cases it is important to only clean as far down the ear canal as you can see to avoid damaging the eardrum. Keep your dog's ears clean and free from too much hair right from puppyhood and hopefully he will never get an ear infection.

Bathing

Too much bathing can rid the coat of its natural oils, so don't bathe your Springer unless you think it necessary; a regular hosing down after a walk will suffice most of the time.

However, if the coat and skin get too dirty it can cause irritation, leading to scratching and excessive shedding - it's all a question of getting the balance right.

FACT If you do decide your Springer needs a proper bath, only use a canine shampoo. A dog's coat has a different pH to human hair and shampoos made for humans can cause skin irritation.

If your Springer has skin problems or allergies, select a *medicated* shampoo with antibacterial, antifungal or anti-itching properties with antihistamines. It will help to get rid of bacteria and fungi without damaging the coat. Your vet will be able to recommend a suitable shampoo. They are also widely available in pet stores and online. Before you bathe your Springer, give him a good brush to remove all the dead hair.

> **Tip:** To help prevent ear infections, put cotton wool inside the ears while bathing and towel them dry afterwards. Don't force the cotton wool into the ear canal, do it gently. And don't forget to remove them afterwards or your Springer may be even deafer than usual to your commands!

You also have to be extremely careful with the eyes. Some owners put a drop or two of artificial tears in each eye to offer some limited protection against soap or chemicals in the shampoo.

Photo: A show Springer

There is a wide variation on how your Springer will react to having a bath – some love the attention, while others are not so keen.

Make sure you get everything ready before you start and, if your dog is resistant, keep the collar on so you have something to hold on to.

Use **lukewarm** water and spray it from the neck down to the tail until the coat is completely soaked, avoid wetting the face if you can, but gently wash the ear flaps without getting water in the ear canals.

Work the shampoo into your dog's body and legs, not forgetting the underneath, and if it's a medicated shampoo, you may have to leave it on for a few minutes.

This is not easy with a lively Springer, so keep a firm hold or better still, have an accomplice hold the dog! It does get better as they get more used to it – especially if they get a treat at the end of the ordeal.

Rinse your dog thoroughly on top, underneath, on the legs, etc., making sure that all of the soap is out of the coat. Use your hand to squeegee excess water off the coat before putting him on an old towel on the floor and towelling him dry - again, be careful with the eyes.

Then stand back as he gets his revenge by shaking and soaking you too! Dry the coat as much as possible, a double-coated dog like the Springer may take a while to dry naturally. You may want to put the heating on to help him dry out or find him a sunny spot. Don't forget to remove the cotton wool.

One not uncommon reaction after a bath is for a Springer to run around like a lunatic afterwards doing the *Zoomies* - as though they have just miraculously escaped the most horrific ordeal!

....

Teeth Cleaning

Veterinary studies show that by the age of three, 80% of dogs show signs of gum or dental disease. Symptoms include yellow and brown build-up of tartar along the gum line, red inflamed gums and persistent bad breath (halitosis). And if your dog suddenly stops eating his food, check his mouth and teeth.

Many owners keep their dogs' teeth clean by giving them an occasional raw bone (not chicken as it splinters), or regularly feeding bully sticks, Nylabones, Dentastix, etc.

However, it is important to take time to take care of your English Springer's teeth - regular dental care greatly reduces the onset of gum and tooth decay and infection. If left, problems can quickly escalate.

Without cleaning, plaque coats teeth and within a few days this starts to harden into tartar, often turning into gingivitis (inflammation of the gums). Gingivitis is regularly accompanied by periodontal disease (infections around the teeth).

This can be serious as, in the worst cases, it can lead to infections of the vital organs, such as heart, liver and kidneys. Even if the infection doesn't spread beyond the mouth, bad teeth are very unpleasant for a dog, just as with a human, causing painful toothache and difficulty chewing.

If your English Springer Spaniel needs a deep clean, remedial work or teeth removing, he will have to be anaesthetised, a procedure which is to be avoided unless it is absolutely necessary. Prevention is better than cure.

Tip: If your dog has to be anaesthetised for something else, ask the vet to check and clean your dog's teeth while he's under.

One option is to brush your dog's teeth. There are also various tools owners can buy to control plaque, such as dental picks and scrapers.

Start while still a puppy and take things slowly in the beginning, giving lots of praise.

Once used to the process, many dogs love the attention - especially if they like the flavour of the toothpaste!

Use a pet toothpaste, as the human variety can upset a dog's stomach.

Photo: A working Springer

The real benefit comes from the actual action of the brush on the teeth, and various brushes, sponges and pads are available for dogs - the choice depends on factors such as the health of your dog's gums, the size of his mouth and how good you are at teeth cleaning.

Get him used to the toothpaste by letting him lick some off your finger when he is young. If he doesn't like the flavour, try a different one. Continue this until he enjoys licking the paste - it might be instant or it might take days.

Put a small amount on your finger and gently rub it on one of the big canine teeth at the front of his mouth. Then get him used to the toothbrush or dental sponge for several days - praise him when he licks it. The next step is to actually start brushing.

Lift his upper lip gently and place the brush at a 45° angle to the gum line. Gently move the brush backwards and forwards. Start just with his front teeth and then gradually do a few more. Do the top ones first.

Regular brushing shouldn't take more than five minutes - well worth the time and effort when it spares your English Springer Spaniel the pain and misery of serious dental or gum disease.

Nail Trimming

If your English Springer Spaniel is regularly exercised on grass or other soft surfaces, his nails may not be getting worn down sufficiently, so they may require clipping or filing.

FACT › Nails should be kept short for the paws to remain healthy. Overly-long nails interfere with a dog's gait, making walking awkward or painful and putting stress on elbows, shoulder and back. They can also break easily, usually at the base of the nail where blood vessels and nerves are located.

Be prepared: many Springers dislike having their nails trimmed - especially if they are not used to it - so it requires patience and persistence if you do it yourself.

Get your dog used to having his paws inspected from puppyhood; it's also a good opportunity to check for other problems, such as cracked pads or interdigital cysts. (These are swellings between the toes, often due to a bacterial infection).

To trim your dog's nails, use a specially designed clipper. Most have safety guards to prevent you cutting the nails too short. Do it before they get too long.

Tip If you can hear the nails clicking on a hard surface, they're too long. Trim only the ends, before *"the quick,"* which is a blood vessel inside the nail. You can see where the quick ends on a white nail, but not on a dark nail.

Clip only the hook-like part of the nail that turns down. Start trimming gently, a nail or two at a time, and your dog will learn that you're not going to hurt him. If you accidentally cut the quick, stop the bleeding with some styptic powder.

Another option is to use a nail grinder tool, also called a Dremel, **pictured.** Some dogs have tough nails that are harder to trim and this may be less stressful for your dog, with less chance of cutting the quick. The grinder is like an electric nail file and only removes a small amount of nail at a time. Some dogs prefer them to a clipper, although others don't like the noise.

If you find it impossible to clip your dog's nails, or you are at all worried about doing it, take him to a vet or groomer and have it done as part of a routine visit - and check if your dog's anal sacs need squeezing, or "expressing," while he's there!

Anal Glands

While we're discussing the less appealing end of your English Springer Spaniel, let's dive straight in and talk about anal sacs. Sometimes called **scent glands,** these are a pair of glands located inside your dog's anus that give off a scent when he has a bowel movement. You won't want to hear this, but problems with impacted anal glands are not uncommon in dogs!

When a dog passes firm stools, the glands normally empty themselves, but watery poop can mean that not enough pressure is exerted to empty the glands, causing discomfort. If they get infected, they become swollen and painful. In extreme cases, one or both anal glands can be removed – we had a dog that lived happily for many years with one anal gland.

If your dog drags himself along on his rear end - *"scooting"* - or tries to lick or scratch his anus, he could well have impacted anal glands that need squeezing, either by you if you know how to do it, your vet or a groomer. (Scooting is also a sign of worms).

Either way, it pays to keep an eye on both ends of your dog!

15. The Facts of Life

Judging by the number of questions our website receives, there is a lot of confusion about the canine facts of life. Some ask if, and at what age, they should have their dog spayed or neutered, while others want to know whether they should breed from their dog.

Owners of females ask when and how often she will come on heat and how long this will last. Sometimes they want to know how you can tell if a female is pregnant or how long a pregnancy lasts. So here, in a nutshell, is a chapter on the birds and bees as far as English Springer Spaniels are concerned.

Females and Heat

The female English Springer Spaniel has an oestrus (*estrus* in the US) cycle which is similar to the human menstrual cycle. This is when she is ready (and willing!) for mating and is more commonly called *heat*, being *in heat*, *on heat* or *in season*.

Springers usually have their first cycle any time between 9 and 15 months old, with some bloodlines being slightly later. All dogs are different; Kennel Club Assured Breeder Chris Brandon-Lodge has bred Springers for 40 years and says: "All of mine have come into season for the first time before eight months, sometimes as early as five months."

Fellow Assured Breeder Lynne Lucas, of Traxlerstarr Spaniels, Surrey, says: "My girls' first season has been anytime between eight to 15 months. My first girl Elsie was the latest at 15 months, but they are usually around nine months old.

"The girls usually season every eight months - sometimes to the day - but Agatha was early this last season at 6 months. The heat is around 21 days' duration, but I am always careful for the following week as well, with the optimum time for breeding from about day 10 to 21, depending on the bitch.

"Elsie was so clean I would never know that she was in season as she cleaned herself impeccably, but she was the only one! The others don't seem to care about being clean, but my girls are quite light in season compared to other breeds, I believe.

"One thing that definitely does happen is that if you keep more than one bitch in close-living, they tend to synchronise their seasons. Once one starts, within a week the others will start."

Pictured is Elsie (Boo's Misty Lady at Traxlerstarr), aged 4.

Lisa Cardy, also an Assured Breeder, of CallisWold Springer Spaniels, North Yorkshire, added: "Mine generally come into season for the first time at around eight to nine months. A typical season is twice a year, so six months apart, and it lasts on average 21 days - but, like people, all dogs are different! Some are very clean so you don't even notice; but others aren't!"

Tip: Females often follow the patterns of their mother, so ask the breeder at what age the dam had her first heat and how often they occur.

Springers typically have two cycles every year, although they can be up to every nine months.

There is no time of the year that corresponds to a breeding season, so heat could occur during any month.

When a young bitch comes in season, it is normal for her cycles to be somewhat irregular - it can take up to two years for regular cycles to develop. The timescale also becomes more erratic with older, unspayed females.

A heat cycle normally lasts 18 to 21 days, the last days might be lighter in terms of blood loss - you might not even know that she is still in heat.

FACT: Unlike with women, the reproductive cycle does not stop when dogs reach middle age, although the heat becomes shorter and lighter. However, a litter takes a heavy toll on older females.

NOTE: Women cannot get pregnant during their period, while female dogs can ONLY get pregnant during their heat.

Here are some typical physical signs of heat;

- The pink bit under her tail (external sex organ called the vulva) becomes swollen and sometimes darker
- She loses some blood - the amount of blood varies from one dog to another - from "spotting," which is very light, to heavier bleeds
- She tries to lick the area under her tail
- She may urinate more frequently

The canine heat cycle is a complex mix of physical, hormonal and behavioural changes. Here are some behaviour changes to look out for - your Springer may display none, one or several of these:

- Some dogs become more needy around you - or irritable, e.g. being less tolerant of other dogs and people, or more possessive with toys or food.
- Others seem a little depressed and retire to their beds
- She may go off her food
- Some shed more hair when on heat
- Her hormones are raging and she may try to mount you, other dogs or even the furniture!

Some dogs clean themselves regularly, while others are less scrupulous on the personal hygiene front. If your girl has "heavy days" and is constantly on and off your furniture, put covers on your bed or sofa during her heat - or invest in a couple of pairs of washable doggie pants for her heaviest days, *pictured.*

A Springer requires either Medium or Large depending on her weight and waist measurement. Manufacturers' sizes vary, but Medium typically fits up to around 35lb or 25" (63.5cm) waist.

THE ENGLISH SPRINGER SPANIEL HANDBOOK Page **211**

Even with pants on, leakages occasionally occur and a few females will even take advantage and poo(p) in them. One breeder added: "I have one dog that can get out of them in about two seconds by rubbing on the carpet or underneath a chair! Please also tell owners that those panties are not chastity belts!"

The Cycle

There are four stages of the heat cycle (a female's season is proestrus plus oestrus):

Proestrus - this is when the bleeding starts and lasts around nine days. Male dogs are attracted to her, but she is not yet interested, so she may hold her tail close to her body. Her vulva becomes swollen. The blood is usually light red or brown, turning more straw-coloured or even colourless when she's ready to mate.

Tip: If you're not sure if she's in heat, hold a tissue against her vulva or put a white sheet or cloth underneath when she lies down. Does any of it turn pink or red?

Oestrus - this is when eggs are released from ovaries and the optimum time for breeding. Males are extremely interested in her and the feelings are often very much reciprocated - her hormones are raging!

If there is a male around she may stand for him and *"flag"* her tail (or move it to one side) to allow him to mount her. Oestrus is the time when a female CAN get pregnant and usually lasts around nine days, so roughly from Day 10-19.

Dioestrus - this is the two-month stage when her body produces the hormone progesterone whether or not she is pregnant. During this stage she is no longer interested in males. These hormones can sometimes lead to what is known as a *"false pregnancy."*

Anoestrus - this the period of rest when reproductive organs are inactive. It is the longest stage of the cycle and lasts around five-and-a-half months. If she normally lives with a male dog, they can return to living together again - neither will be interested in mating and she cannot get pregnant.

FACT: When a female is on heat, she produces pheromones that attract male dogs. Because dogs have a sense of smell several hundred times stronger than ours, your girl on heat is a magnet for all the neighbourhood males. It is believed that they can detect the scent of a female on heat up to two miles away!

They may congregate around your house or follow you around the park - if you are brave or foolish enough to venture out there while she is in season - waiting for their chance to prove their manhood (or mutthood in their case).

It is amazing the lengths to which some entire (uncastrated) males will go to impregnate a female on heat. Travelling great distances to follow her scent, digging under fences, jumping over barriers, chewing through doors or walls and sneaking through hedges are just some of the tactics employed by canine Casanovas on the loose.

Love is a powerful thing - and canine lust even more so. A dog living in the same house as a female in heat has even been known to mate with her through the bars of a crate!

To avoid an unwanted pregnancy, you must keep a close eye on her throughout her heat and not allow her to wander unsupervised - and that includes the garden or yard unless you 100% know it is safe. Determined male dogs can jump and scramble over high fences.

Keep her on a lead if you go out on walks and whatever you do, don't let her run free anywhere that you might come across other dogs. If you have a large garden or yard, you may wish to restrict her to that during her heat. You can compensate for the restrictions by playing more games at home to keep her mentally and physically active.

Tip: The instinct to mate will trump all of her training. Her hormones are raging and, during her most fertile days (the oestrus), she is ready, able and ... VERY willing! If you do have an entire male, you need to physically keep him in a separate place or kennel.

The desire to mate is all-consuming and can be accompanied by howling or "marking" (urinating) indoors from a frustrated Romeo.

You can also buy a spray that masks the natural oestrus scent. Marketed under such attractive names as "*Bitch Spray,*" these lessen, but don't eliminate, the scent.

They may reduce the amount of unwanted attention, but are not a complete deterrent.

There is no canine contraceptive, so if your female is unspayed, you need to keep her under supervision during her heat cycle - which may be up to three or even four weeks.

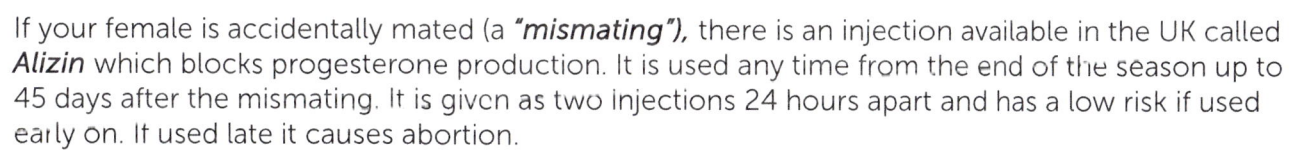

If your female is accidentally mated (a *"mismating")*, there is an injection available in the UK called **Alizin** which blocks progesterone production. It is used any time from the end of the season up to 45 days after the mismating. It is given as two injections 24 hours apart and has a low risk if used early on. If used late it causes abortion.

NOTE: Females tend to come back into season quite soon after the Alizin injections - usually 1-3 months, so take care not to get "caught out" at the next season. Alizin is also quite a painful injection for your girl.

Neutering - Pros and Cons

This is currently a hot potato in the dog world and there is a lot to think about before you make a decision on what's best for your Springer. Show dogs are not spayed or neutered, neither are most working Springers, whereas dogs kept purely as pets often are.

There is already too much indiscriminate breeding of dogs in the world. However, there's mounting scientific evidence that spaying or neutering young dogs while they are still growing can have a detrimental effect on their future health. Then there is the very real threat of mammary cancer in unspayed Springers, as well as the life-threatening Pyometra in unspayed middle-aged bitches of all breeds.

As you will read in **Chapter 16. Springer Rescue**, it is estimated that 1,000 dogs are put to sleep every hour in the USA alone. Rescue organisations in North America, the UK and Australia routinely neuter all dogs that they rehome. The RSPCA, along with most UK vets, also promotes the benefits of neutering; it's estimated that more than half of all dogs in the UK are spayed or castrated.

THE ENGLISH SPRINGER SPANIEL HANDBOOK Page **213**

Another point is that you may not have a choice. Some breeders' Puppy Contracts may stipulate that, except in special circumstances, you agree to neuter your English Springer Spaniel as a Condition of Sale. Others may state that you need the breeder's permission to breed your dog.

While early spay/neuter has been traditionally recommended, there is scientific evidence that it is better to wait until the dog is through puberty if you decide to spay or neuter – whatever your vet might recommend.

The Science

Regardless of how big young English Springer Spaniels look, their skeletons take a full 12 months to mature.

Based on the latest scientific studies, we recommend waiting until your Springer Spaniel is at least one year old before considering spaying or neutering.

This is because we now realise that the sex hormones play an important role in normal growth and development.

Veterinarian and a Health Co-ordinator for the Kennel Club, Dr Samantha Goldberg, says: "Testosterone and oestrogen are involved in some of the long bone formations in the body, so removing this too early can affect correct growth leading to prolonged growth and poorer quality bone with abnormal mechanical behaviours of the joints.

"Early neutering – i.e. before skeletal growth has finished - results in taller, leggier hounds as the closure of the plates in the long bones is helped by release of puberty hormones. There is also increased risk of cranial cruciate rupture, intervertebral disc disease (IVDD), hip dysplasia and patella luxation being cited in some breeds. The number of breeds listed as affected is likely to increase as we know more.

"Bitches may be sexually mature before the body has finished developing physically and mentally. Although they may be able to come into season, they have not finished growing if under 12 months and will certainly not have finished maturing mentally.

"Many vets will try to influence owners to spay their bitch at six months and often before a season. It is best to be patient and not just neuter to suit the human family."

Dr Goldberg added: "There is a lot of work looking at behavioural issues with dogs in rescues and when they were neutered. So far it seems likely that more dogs ending up in rescue with behavioural issues were neutered early – i.e. under 12 months.

"Neutering reduces metabolic rate and this means they need fewer calories or more exercise to balance it. Often neutering is carried out without the vet warning the owner of this.

"Thus we hear: 'She is overweight because she is spayed.' Actually not true - being overweight is caused by eating more calories than are expended.

"Overweight dogs have higher risks from many health conditions, e.g. Diabetes Mellitus and joint issues…and obvious things such as heart disease due to increased workload.

"Neutering male dogs directly reduces risks of increased prostate size due to testosterone (not the same as tumours) and in bitches removes the risk of Pyometra, a life-threatening uterine condition, and ovarian cancers. These effects are very positive.

"To summarise: Neutering should be carried out at the correct time to maximise health in your dog and afterwards their lifestyle may be changed a little, e.g. calorie control. Neuter to reduce risks of many health conditions, but do it at the right time to maximize the lifespan of your dog."

Spaying

Spaying is the term traditionally used to describe the sterilisation of a female dog so that she cannot become pregnant. This is normally done by a procedure called an *"ovariohysterectomy"* and involves the removal of the ovaries and uterus, or womb. Although this is a routine operation, it is major abdominal surgery and she has to be anaesthetised.

One less invasive option offered by some vets is an *"ovariectomy,"* which removes the ovaries, but leaves the womb intact. It requires only a small incision and can even be carried out by laparoscopy, or keyhole surgery.

The dog is anaesthetised for a shorter time and there is less risk of infection or excess bleeding during surgery.

One major reason often given for not opting for an ovariectomy is that the female still runs the risk of **Pyometra** later in life. However, there is currently little or no scientific evidence of females that have undergone an ovariectomy contracting Pyometra afterwards. Pyometra affects females of all breeds.

However, unspayed middle-aged (over five years old) English Springer Spaniels have a higher risk of getting *mammary cancer* (the equivalent of breast cancer in humans) than many other breeds.

One study (Rivera et al 2009) involving 366 Springers in Scandinavia and the UK stated: "The English Springer Spaniel has been shown to have a median age of onset at seven years of age in the Swedish dog population and 32% of the female dogs are affected at ten years of age in this high-risk breed."

The English Springer Spaniel Club says: "Approximately 50% of all mammary tumours in dogs are benign (not life threatening), and the other 50% are malignant (likely to spread and/or cause death).

"Mammary tumours are more likely to occur in unspayed, middle-aged female dogs (those between five and ten years of age). Spaying a female prior to two-and-a-half years of age significantly decreases risk for both benign and malignant mammary tumours.

"Spaying after this time reduces risk for benign tumours, but appears to have no advantage for prevention of malignant tumours. Interestingly, pregnancy and lactation appear to have no influence on mammary cancer risk."

One study, Beauvais (2012), stated "There is some evidence to suggest that neutering bitches before the age of 2·5 years is associated with a considerable reduction in the risk of malignant mammary tumours."

FACT Spaying is a much more serious operation for females than neutering is for males. It involves an internal abdominal operation, whereas the neutering procedure is carried out on the male's testicles, which are outside his abdomen. Both procedures require a full general anaesthetic.

As with any major procedure, there are pros and cons.

Pros:

- Spaying eliminates the risk of Pyometra and significantly reduces the risk of mammary cancer. It also reduces hormonal changes that can interfere with the treatment of diseases like diabetes or epilepsy
- Spaying also prevents infections and other diseases of the uterus and ovaries
- You no longer have to cope with any potential mess caused by bleeding inside the house during heat cycles
- You don't have to guard your female against unwanted attention from males
- Spaying can reduce behaviour problems, such as roaming, aggression towards other dogs, anxiety or fear (not all canine experts agree)
- A spayed dog does not contribute to the pet overpopulation problem

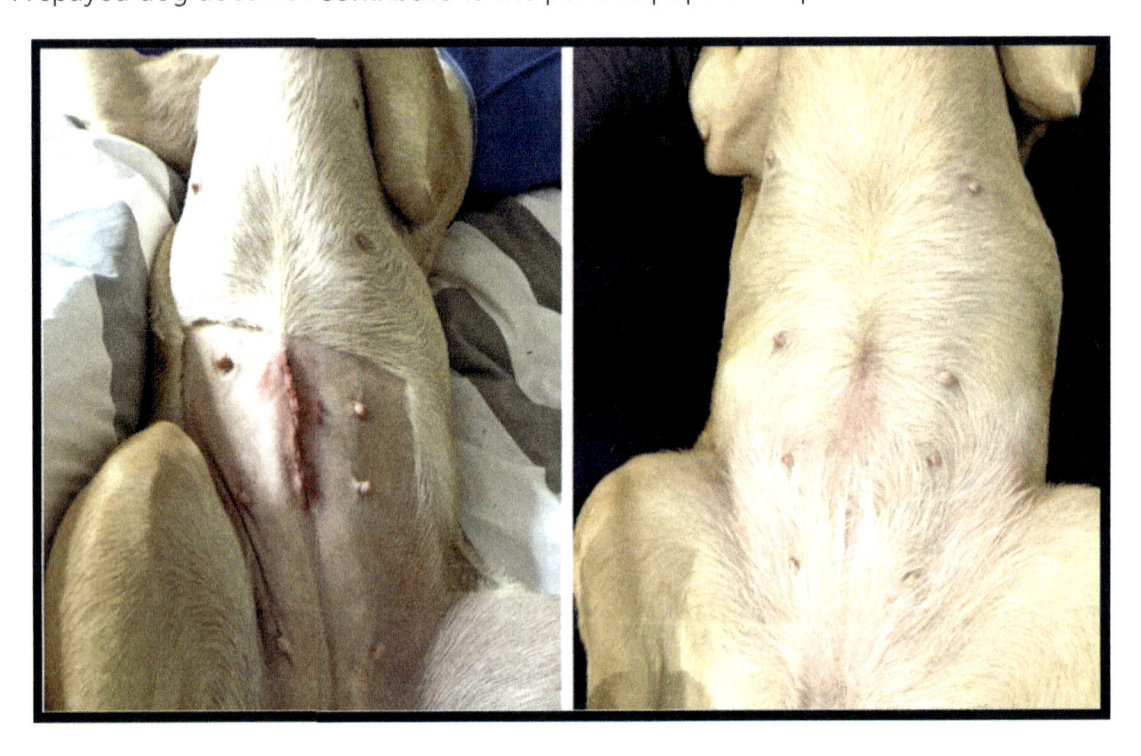

These photographs are reproduced courtesy of Guy Bunce and Chloe Spencer, of Dizzywaltz Labrador Retrievers, Berkshire, England. The left image shows four-year-old Disney shortly after a full spay (ovariohysterectomy). The right one shows Disney several weeks later.

Cons:

- Early spay can lead to an increased risk of joint and other diseases
- Complications can occur, including an abnormal reaction to the anaesthetic, bleeding, stitches breaking and infections; these are not common
- Occasionally there can be long-term effects connected to hormonal changes. These include weight gain or less stamina, which can occur years after spaying
- Cost. This can range from £100 to £250 in the UK, more for keyhole spaying, and anything from $150 to over $1,000 at a vet's clinic in the USA, or from around $50 at a low-cost clinic, for those that qualify

- Urinary incontinence is more common in neutered females, especially if spayed early. One study found that urinary incontinence was not diagnosed in intact females, but was present in 7% of females neutered before one year old

Spaying during a heat cycle results in a lot of bleeding during the operation, which makes things messy for the vet and can make the operation more risky for the female.

Neutering

Neutering male dogs involves castration, or the removal of the testicles. This can be a difficult decision for some owners, as it causes a drop in the pet's testosterone levels, which some humans - men in particular! - feel affects the quality of their dog's life. Fortunately, dogs do not think like people, and male dogs do not miss their testicles or the loss of sex.

FACT Dogs working in the Services or for charities are often neutered and this does not impair their ability to perform any of their duties. NOTE: All male show Springers and most working Springers are unneutered (entire).

Technically, neutering can be carried out at any age over eight weeks provided both testicles have descended. However, as you've read, recent scientific studies are undoubtedly coming down on the side of waiting until the dog is one year or older.

Surgery is relatively straightforward, and complications are less common and less severe than with spaying. Although he will feel tender afterwards, your dog should return to his normal self within a couple of days.

When a dog comes out of surgery, his scrotum, or sacs that held the testicles, will be swollen and it may look like nothing has been done. It is normal for these to shrink slowly in the days following surgery.

Here are the main pros and cons:

Pros:

- Castration is a relatively straightforward procedure
- Unwanted sexual behaviour, such as mounting people or objects, is usually reduced or eliminated
- You cannot have an uncastrated male and unspayed female together when the female is on heat. A castrated male can live alongside a female all year round – although be aware he can still get a female pregnant up to three or four weeks after castration due to residual sperm in his tubes!
- Behaviour problems such as aggression, marking and roaming can be reduced
- Testicular problems such as infections, cancer and torsion (painful rotation of the testicle) are eradicated
- Benign prostatic hyperplasia is much less likely after castration
- A neutered dog is not fathering unwanted puppies

Cons:

- Studies indicate that males neutered before one year old may be more susceptible to joint problems later in life than those neutered after two years old

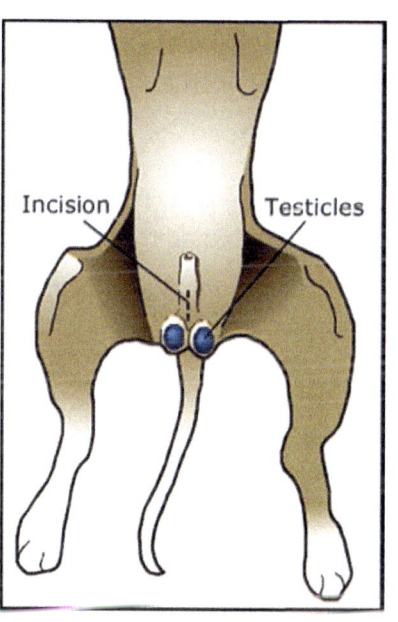

- As with any surgery, there can be swelling and redness around the wound. It's fairly routine for dogs to need 10 days of anti-inflammatory medication and to have to wear an E-collar afterwards
- Some prostate cancers are more likely after neutering
- In some cases castration can make behaviour problems worse. Pain, trips to the clinic and having testosterone removed can lead to a reduction in the dog's confidence
- There is evidence that some dogs' coats may be affected; this also applies to spaying
- Cost - this starts at around £120 in the UK. In the USA this might cost anything from $150 to $1,000 at a private veterinary clinic, depending on your state, or less at a low cost or Humane Society clinic

Urban Myths

Neutering or spaying will spoil the dog's character - There is no evidence that any of the positive characteristics of your dog will be altered. He or she will be just as obedient, playful and loyal as before. Neutering may reduce aggression or roaming in male dogs, because they are no longer competing to mate with a female.

A female needs to have at least one litter - There is no proven physical or mental benefit to a female having a litter.

Mating is natural and necessary - We tend to ascribe human emotions to our dogs, but they do not think emotionally about sex or having and raising a family.

Unlike humans, their desire to mate or breed is entirely physical, triggered by the chemicals called hormones within their body.

Without these hormones – i.e. after neutering or spaying – the desire disappears or is greatly reduced.

Male dogs will behave better if they can mate - This is simply not true; sex does not make a dog behave better. In fact, it can have the opposite effect. Having mated once, a male may show an increased interest in females.

He may also consider his status elevated, which may make him harder to control or call back.

✓ *Do your own research. Many vets still promote early spay and neuter.*

Pregnancy

Regardless of how big or small the dog is, a canine pregnancy lasts for 58 to 65 days; 63 days is average. This is true of all breeds of dog from the Chihuahua to the Great Dane. Sometimes pregnancy is referred to as *"the gestation period."*

A female should have a pre-natal check-up after mating. The vet should answer any questions about type of food, supplements and extra care needed, as well as informing the owner about any physical changes likely to occur in your female.

Photo of Poppy (Jarailstar Sole of CallisWold) with her litter, courtesy of Lisa Cardy.

There is a blood test available that measures levels of **relaxin**. This is a hormone produced by the ovary and the developing placenta, and pregnancy can be detected by monitoring relaxin levels as early as 22 to 27 days after mating.

The levels are high throughout pregnancy and then decline rapidly after the female has given birth.

A vet can usually see the puppies (but not how many) using Ultrasound from around the same time.

Signs of Pregnancy

After mating, many females become more affectionate. However, a few may become uncharacteristically irritable and maybe even a little aggressive!

- She may produce a slight mucous-like discharge from her vagina one month after mating
- Three or four weeks after mating, some females experience morning sickness – if this is the case, feed little and often. She may seem more tired than usual
- She may seem slightly depressed or show a drop in appetite. These signs can also mean there are other problems, so you should consult your vet
- Her teats will become more prominent, pink and erect 25 to 30 days into the pregnancy. Later on, you may notice a fluid coming from them. This first milk (colostrum) is the most important milk a puppy gets on Day One as it contains the mother's immunity.
- Her body weight will start to increase about 35 days after mating
- Abdominal swelling may be just about noticeable from Day 40 and becomes more obvious from around Day 50, although first-time mums and females carrying few puppies may not show as much
- Many pregnant females' appetite will increase in the second half of pregnancy
- Her nesting instincts will kick in as the delivery date approaches. She may seem restless or scratch her bed or the floor - she may even rip and shred items like your comforter, curtains or carpeting!
- During the last week of pregnancy, females often start to look for a safe place for whelping. Some seem to become confused, wanting to be with their owners and at the same time wanting to prepare their nest. If the female is having a C-section, she should still be allowed

to nest in a whelping box with layers of newspaper, which she will scratch and dig as the time approaches

✓ *If your English Springer Spaniel becomes pregnant - either by design or accident - your first step should be to consult a vet.*

The size of Springer litters varies. Very occasionally a huge litter of a dozen or more puppies is born, but three or four to seven or eight is typical.

The number depends on factors such as bloodlines, the age of the dam and sire (young and older dogs have smaller litters), the health and diet of the dam, and the size of the gene pool; the lower the genetic diversity, the smaller the litter.

False Pregnancies

Occasionally, unspayed females may display signs of a false pregnancy. Before dogs were domesticated, it was common for female dogs to have false pregnancies and to lactate (produce milk). She would then nourish puppies of the Alpha bitch or puppies who had lost their mother in the pack.

False pregnancies occur 60 to 80 days after the female was in heat - about the time she would have given birth - and are generally nothing to worry about for an owner. The exact cause is unknown; however, hormonal imbalances are thought to play an important role. Some dogs have shown symptoms within three to four days of spaying; these include:

- Making a nest
- Mothering or adopting toys and other objects
- Producing milk (lactating)
- Appetite fluctuations
- Barking or whining a lot
- Restlessness, depression or anxiety
- Swollen abdomen
- She might even appear to go into labour

Under no circumstances should you restrict your Spaniel's water supply to try and prevent her from producing milk. This is dangerous as she can become dehydrated.

Occasionally, an unspayed female may have a false pregnancy with each heat cycle. Spaying during a false pregnancy may actually prolong the condition, so better to wait until it is over to have her spayed.

FACT False pregnancy is not a disease, but an exaggerated response to normal hormonal changes. Even if left untreated, it almost always resolves itself.

However, if your dog appears physically ill or the behavioural changes are severe enough to worry about, visit your vet. He or she may prescribe *Galastop*, which stops milk production and quickly returns the hormones to normal. In rare cases, hormone treatment may be necessary.

Generally, dogs experiencing false pregnancies do not have serious long-term problems, as the behaviour disappears when the hormones return to their normal levels in two to three weeks.

Pyometra

One exception is *Pyometra*, a serious and potentially deadly infection of the womb, caused by a hormonal abnormality. It normally follows a heat cycle in which fertilisation did not occur and the dog typically starts showing symptoms within two to four months. It occurs most often in middle-aged females.

Commonly referred to as *"pyo,"* there are *open* and *closed* forms of the disease. Open pyo is usually easy to identify with a smelly discharge, so prompt treatment is easy.

Closed pyo is often harder to identify and you may not even notice anything until your girl becomes feverish and lethargic. When this happens, it is very serious and time is of the essence.

Typical signs of Pyometra are excessive drinking and urination, vomiting and depression, with the female trying to lick a white discharge from her vagina. She may also have a temperature. If the condition becomes severe, her back legs will become weak, possibly to the point where she can no longer get up without help.

Pyometra can be fatal and needs to be dealt with promptly by a vet. Standard treatment is emergency spay soon after starting intravenous fluids and antibiotics. In some milder cases, the vet may recommend Alizin injections plus antibiotics and (if needed) IV fluids, then spay as soon as possible after the pyo resolves.

Should I Breed From My English Springer Spaniel?

The short and very simple answer is: **NO!** Not unless you do a lot of research, find a mentor for expert advice and then a good vet, preferably one experienced with English Springers.

Breeding healthy English Springer Spaniel puppies with good temperaments is a messy, complex, time-consuming and expensive process and should not be approached lightly.

The risk of breeding puppies with health issues is very real if you don't know what you are doing. Today's responsible breeders are continually looking at ways of improving the health of the English Springer Spaniel through selective breeding. See **Chapter 12. Springer Health** for a list of recommended health tests.

FACT According to an in-depth UK study published in the Journal of Small Animal Practice, over 10% of English Springer Spaniel litters were born by Caesarean, or C-Section.

Typical veterinary fees for a C-section are in four figures and are not covered by normal pet insurance - and even then, a good outcome is not guaranteed. We know of several breeders who have lost beloved dogs during or following C-sections.

English Springer Spaniel genetics are a complicated business that cover a multitude of traits, including health, coat colour, temperament and natural instinct.

Well-bred Springer puppies fetch a high price. But despite this, you may be surprised to hear that many dedicated breeders make little money from the practice, due to the high costs of veterinary fees, health screening, stud fees and expensive special nutrition and care for the female and her pups.

Responsible breeding is backed up by genetic information and screening as well as a thorough knowledge of the desired traits of the English Springer Spaniel. It is definitely not an occupation for the amateur hobbyist.

✓ **Breeding is not just about the look or colour of the puppies; health and temperament are at least as important.**

Many dog lovers do not realise that the single most important factor governing health and certain temperament traits is genetics. Top breeders have years of experience in selecting the right pair for mating after they have considered the ancestry, health, temperament, size and physical characteristics of the two dogs involved.

They may travel hundreds of miles to find the right mate for their dog. Some of them also show or work their Springers.

Teasel (Cottonstones Walnut), right, with her nine-day-old litter. Grandmother Millie, left, moved in from time to time to help with the pups.

Photo courtesy of Chris Brandon-Lodge, of Cottonstones Springers, Shropshire. Chris added: "Millie was brilliant with all of the puppies; a real granny."

Anyone considering mating their dog must first ask themselves these questions:

- **Did you get your English Springer Spaniel from a good, ethical breeder?** Dogs sold in pet stores and on general sales websites are seldom good specimens and can be unhealthy

- **Does your dog conform to the Breed Standard?** Do not breed from a Springer that is not an excellent specimen in all respects, hoping that somehow the puppies will turn out better. They won't. Talk with experienced breeders and ask them for an honest assessment of your dog

- **Do you understand COI and its implications?** COI stands for Coefficient of Inbreeding. It measures the common ancestors of a dam and sire and indicates the probability of how genetically similar they are

- **Have your dog and his or her mate both been screened** for genetic Springer health issues that can be passed on to the puppies?

- **Have you researched his or her lineage** to make sure there are no problems lurking in the background? Puppies inherit traits from their grandparents and great-grandparents as well as from their mother and father

- **Are you 100% sure that your Springer has no temperament issues** which could be inherited by the puppies?

- Are you positive that the same can be said for the dog you are planning on breeding yours with?
- **Do you have the finances** to keep the mother healthy through pregnancy, whelping, and care of her and the puppies after birth – even if complications occur?
- **Is your female two years old or older and at least in her second heat cycle?** Female Springers should not be bred until they are physically mature, have had their joints screened, and are robust enough to whelp and care for a litter. Even then, not all females are suitable
- **Giving birth takes a lot out of a female - are you prepared to put yours through that?** And, as you've read, it's not without risk
- **Some females are poor mothers,** which means that you have to look after the puppies 24/7. Even if they are not, they need daily help from the owner to rear their young
- Can you care for lots of lively puppies if you can't find homes for them?

- **Will you be able to find good homes for all the puppies?** Good breeders do not let their precious puppies go to just any home. They want to be sure that the new owners will take good care of their dogs for their lifetime
- Would you take back, or help to rehome, one of your dogs if circumstances change?

Having said that, experts are not born, they learn their trade over many years. Anyone who is seriously considering getting into the specialised art of breeding English Springer Spaniels should first spend time researching the breed and its genetics.

Make sure you are going into breeding for the right reasons and not primarily to make money - ask yourself how you intend to improve the breed. Make contact with established breeders, visit dog shows or talk to owners and breeders of working Springers. Find yourself a mentor, somebody who is already very familiar with the breed.

To find a good breeder:

- ✓ **In the UK**, The English Springer Spaniel Club has a full list of regional clubs and contacts on their website at www.englishspringer.org/english-springer-spaniel-uk-breed-clubs/ or visit the Kennel Club website and find a Kennel Club **Assured Breeder** in your county.
- ✓ **In the USA,** visit the English Springer Spaniel Field Trial Association website for a list of all regional ESS clubs at:

https://essfta.org/resources/regional-clubs/akc-licensed-english-springer-spaniel-specialty-clubs/ or visit the AKC website for a **Breeder of Merit,** or one who is a member of the **Bred with H.E.A.R.T.** programme.

If you are determined to breed from your English Springer Spaniel - and breed properly - do your research. Read as much as you can; one useful resource is *"Book of the Bitch"* by J. M. Evans and Kay White.

....

You may have the most wonderful Springer in the world, but don't enter the world of dog breeding without knowledge and ethics. Don't do it for the money, the cute factor, to show the kids "The Miracle of Birth!" or because you want to breed the best show/working Spaniel ever - you can't!

Breeding poor examples only brings heartache in the long run when health or temperament issues develop.

Our strong advice is: When it comes to breeding Springers, leave it to the experts - or set out to become one yourself.

Photo: Five working English Springer Spaniel puppies aged seven weeks.

....

With sincere thanks to Dr Marianne Dorn, "The Rehab Vet," https://TheRehabVet.com for her assistance with this chapter.

16. Springer Rescue

Not everyone who wants a Springer gets one as a puppy from a breeder. Some people prefer to give a rescue dog a second chance for a happy life.

What could be kinder and more rewarding than giving a poor, abandoned dog a loving home for the rest of his life?

Not much really; adoption saves lives and gives unfortunate dogs a second chance of happiness. The problem of homeless dogs is truly depressing. It's a big issue in Britain, but even worse in the US, where the sheer numbers in kill shelters are hard to comprehend. In *"Don't Dump The Dog,"* Randy Grim states that 1,000 dogs are being put to sleep every hour in the States.

Reasons for Rescue

A Springer is a lively, athletic breed with a high drive and a desire to be with people or other dogs.

That velvety little puppy with the floppy ears looked so cute. But later down the line, owners who don't put in enough time and effort can find they have a challenging adolescent or adult dog that's too much to handle.

Behaviour is a common reason for Springers ending up in rescue. They may have become too vocal, demanding, anxious or badly-behaved - quite surprising for a dog whose greatest wish is to please his owner.

The reason they end up like this is almost always due to a lack of socialisation, training or exercise, or all three - all of which are part of the bargain when you decide to get an energetic, people-loving breed like the Springer.

Other reasons for English Springers being put into rescue include:

- The dog develops health issues
- A change in work patterns, so the dog is left alone for long periods
- The dog has way too much energy and needs a lot more exercise and attention than the owner is able or prepared to give
- A change in family circumstance, such as divorce or a new baby
- Moving into smaller or rented accommodation
- He is growling or biting
- He chews things he shouldn't
- He makes a mess in the house (housetraining requires time and patience from the owner)
- He costs too much to keep

Not For the Faint-Hearted!

Cynthia Turvey rescued her first English Springer nearly four decades ago and went on to found the UK's Northern English Springer Spaniel Rescue (NESSR) over 30 years ago.

Cynthia says: "Nearly all of the dogs that come into us are working-stream Springers. Maybe they should come with a health warning because people just don't do their research.

"I recently took back a three-month-old working-stream Springer with a full docking certificate and all the paperwork from a family who had an autistic child. Of course, the family was devastated at giving the dog up. This was clearly an unsuitable match; they hadn't done their research.

"People see pretty pictures and want a Springer. Unfortunately, Springer puppies are beautiful and people fall in love with their teddy bear face.

"I love Springers dearly, but they are not for the faint-hearted! I live rurally and if I'm out, they are out with me. They require a lot of exercise and attention - a young Springer requires a lot of energy from its owner.

"They love to run away with socks or tea towels and, yes, if the guinea pig or rabbit is in a run in the garden, they think it's easy prey! They also love mud and snow and going for walks in all weathers. If you can do Agility or Flyball with them, it helps to fulfil their natural instincts."

NESSR adds: "It is an unfortunate fact of life that, whilst arguably among the most cuddly of puppies, some young Springers find their welcome disappears as fast as their youth. After Christmas, Cynthia receives a nightmare number of calls from people whose puppy from Santa has turned into the dog from hell."

NESSR has some excellent insights into the pros and cons of the breed for potential owners: "The English Springer represents perhaps the greatest divergence between working and show lines of any breed of dog. A field-bred dog (working) and a show-bred dog appear to be different breeds, but are registered together. In fact, the gene pools are almost completely segregated and have been for at least 70 years.

"A field bred dog would not be even remotely competitive in a modern dog show while a show dog would be unlikely to have the speed or stamina to succeed in a field trial (Fergus, 2002).

"The Springer is an affectionate and easy-going family dog, and its alertness and attentiveness make it the ideal hunting companion. An intelligent dog and eager to please, a Springer is easily incorporated into a family setting.

"Although good with children, it tends to have a moderate to high energy level. Its long-legged build makes it among the fastest of the Spaniels. It has unlimited stamina and needs plenty of activity, as much as two hours per day, to focus its mind and to provide substantial exercise.

"Like any breed described as 'good with children,' a Springer Spaniel must be accustomed to children. Any dog that is not well socialised with children will not behave predictably around them. Unless trained, Springers do have a tendency to jump up at people and this can lead to them knocking smaller children over.

"English Springer Spaniels are playful animals; many owners find humour in their play. As with many playful dogs or hunting dogs bred as retrievers, these dogs will play with things as simple as empty plastic bottles, socks, or towels.

"These Spaniels easily remember where such things are kept and are good at getting them out.

"English Springer Spaniels need a lot of regular exercise and mental stimulation for optimum mental health.

"Some people say that English Springer Spaniels are like Velcro, because they want to be in the immediate vicinity of their owner. If the owner walks to the other side of a room, so does the English Springer Spaniel.

"Unless trained from a young age, some may become agitated and whine if they cannot get near people that they know are nearby.

"Walks alone are not enough to satisfy a Springer Spaniel; they must get mental stimulation through training and games. Like most other breeds of dogs, if a Springer becomes bored or stressed, they can become destructive in the home environment.

"Young pups when teething are also known to chew household items if they are not given teething toys. A destructive Springer can chew chairs, walls, skirting boards, door frames and doors... kitchen units, shoes, cuddly toys, handbags, etc. etc., the list is endless. You need to keep them stimulated.

"Springer Spaniels are natural mud magnets. They love nothing better than swimming in stagnant ponds, throwing themselves through muddy puddles and rolling in unmentionable things!! Springer Spaniels are not for the houseproud, they moult and can create a lot of muddy paw prints and dust.

"Having said the downsides of owning a Springer Spaniel, they can't be all bad as a lot of people don't stop at owning one ... they go on to own two, three, four or even more at one time! Beware, Springer Spaniels are addictive!"

The Dog's Point of View...

If you are serious about adopting a Springer, do so with the right motives and with your eyes wide open. If you're expecting a perfect dog, you could be in for a shock. Rescue Springers can and do become wonderful companions, but much depends on you and how much effort you are prepared to put in.

If you can, look for a rescue organisation specialising in English Springer Spaniels - and preferably one where the dog has been fostered out. If a dog has picked up bad habits, the foster parents have probably started to work on some of them.

Springers are extremely loyal to their owners. Sometimes those that end up in rescue centres are traumatised, others may have behaviour or health problems. They don't understand why they have been abandoned, neglected or badly treated by their owners and may arrive at your home with "baggage" of their own until they adjust to being part of a loving family again.

This may take time. Patience is the key to help the dog to adjust to new surroundings and family and to learn to love and trust again. Ask yourself a few questions before you take the plunge and fill in the adoption forms:

- Are you prepared to accept and deal with any problems - such as bad behaviour, aggression, timidity, chewing, jumping up or eliminating in the house - that a rescue dog may display when initially arriving in your home?
- Just how much time do you have to spend with your new Springer to help him integrate back into normal family life?
- Are you prepared to take on a new addition to your family that may live for another decade?
- Will you guarantee that dog a home for life - even if he develops health issues later?

What could be worse for the unlucky dog than to be abandoned again if things don't work out between you?

Other Considerations

Adopting a rescue dog is a big commitment for all involved. It is not a cheap way of getting a Springer. It could cost you several hundred pounds - or dollars.

Depending on the adoption centre, you may have to pay adoption fees, vaccination and veterinary bills, as well as worm and flea medication and spaying or neutering. Make sure you're aware of the full cost before committing.

Many rescue dogs are older and some may have health or temperament issues. You may even have to wait a while until a suitable dog comes up. One way of finding out if you are suitable is to become a foster home for a rescue centre. Fosters offer temporary homes until a forever home comes along. It's shorter-term, but still requires commitment and patience.

And it's not just the dogs that are screened! Rescue groups make sure that prospective adopters are suitable. They also want to make the right match - placing an energetic dog in a household of couch potatoes, a lively young Springer with an elderly couple, or an anxious dog in a noisy household - would be storing up trouble. It would be a tragedy for the dog if things did not work out again.

Most rescue groups ask a raft of personal questions - some of which may seem intrusive. But you'll have to answer them if you are serious about adopting. Here are some typical questions:

- Name, address, age
- Details, including ages, of all people living in your home
- Type of property you live in
- Size of your garden or yard and height of the fence around it
- Extensive details of any other pets

- Your work hours and amount of time spent away from the home each day
- Whether you have any previous experience with dogs or Springers
- Your reasons for wanting to adopt
- Whether you have any experience dealing with canine behaviour or health issues
- Details of your vet
- If you are prepared for aggression/destructive behaviour/chewing/fear and timidity/soiling inside the house/medical issues
- Whether you are willing to housetrain and obedience train the dog
- Your views on dog training methods
- Whether you are prepared for the financial costs of dog ownership
- Where your dog will sleep at night
- Whether you are prepared to accept a Springer cross
- Two personal references

If you go out to work, it is useful to know that UK rescue organisations will not place dogs in homes where they will be left alone for more than four to five hours at a stretch.

After you've filled in the adoption form, a chat with a representative from the charity usually follows. There will also be a home inspection visit - and even your vet may be vetted! If all goes well, you will be approved to adopt and when the right match comes along, a meeting will be arranged with all family members and the dog. You then pay the adoption fee and become the proud new owner of a Springer.

It might seem like a lot of red tape, but the rescue groups have to be as sure as they can that you will provide a loving, forever home for the dog. It would be terrible if things didn't work out and the dog had to be placed back in rescue again.

All rescue organisations will neuter the dog or, if he or she is too young, specify in the adoption contract that the dog must be neutered and may not be used for breeding. Some Springer rescue organisations have a lifetime rescue back-up policy, which means that if things don't work out, the dog must be returned to them.

NESSR has this advice: "A rescue dog is certainly not an easy option: they require a lot of patience and understanding. Some of them can have behavioural difficulties, such as Separation Anxiety, destructiveness or just odd behaviour that is hard to explain. (If only they could tell us what has happened to them in the past! I am sure we would be shocked).

"In most cases, these problems can be worked out, but it can take many months of hard work on your part. If you persevere, you'll be rewarded with one of the most loving and faithful dogs you can imagine.

"No dog ever comes into your home with a guarantee of good behaviour. Whether it's a puppy or an adult dog it still has to understand the difference between conduct you find acceptable or less acceptable as an owner.

"If you have children, we insist you bring them to meet the dog, to make sure both parties like each other - the same goes for any other dogs in the household.

"The first stages of having a rescue dog can be compared to having a foster child - the dog feels insecure, in a strange environment, with strange people and neither of you knows what to expect. Handled correctly though, you'll get lots of lovely surprises!

"There's loads of sources of good advice and ideas - check out your local library, pet store or the internet, talk to other people who've taken on a rescue dog and consider some gentle training or obedience classes. Above all enjoy your new-found friend."

Training a Rescue Dog

Some Springers are in rescue because of behavioural problems, which often develop due to lack of training and attention from the previous owner.

As one rescue group put it: **"Rescue dogs are not damaged dogs; they have just been let down by humans, so take a little while to unpack their bags and get familiar with their new owners and surroundings before they settle in."**

If you approach rescue with your eyes wide open, if you're prepared to be patient and devote plenty of time to your new arrival, then rescuing a Springer is incredibly rewarding. They are such loyal and eager-to-please dogs, you'll have a friend for life.

Organisations with experience of Springers are more likely to be able to assess the dog and give you an idea of what you might be letting yourself in for. Often, lack of training or exercise is the root cause of any issues - but how this manifests itself depends on the individual dog's temperament and experiences.

Ask as many questions as you can about the background of the dog, his natural temperament and any issues likely to arise. You are better having an honest appraisal than simply being told the dog is wonderful and in need of a home.

Training methods for a rescue Springer are similar to those for any adult Springer, but it may take longer as the dog first has to unlearn any bad habits.

If the dog you are interested in has a particular issue, such as indiscriminate barking or lack of housetraining, it is best to start right back at the beginning with training. Don't presume the dog knows anything and take each step slowly. See **Chapter 9. Basic Training** for more information.

Tips

- Start training the day you arrive home, not once he has settled in
- He needs your attention, but, importantly, he also needs his own space where he can chill out. Put his bed or crate in a quiet place; you want your dog to learn to relax. The more relaxed he is, the fewer hang-ups he will have

- Show him his sleeping and feeding areas, but allow him to explore these and the rest of his space in his own time
- Using a crate may help speed up training, but it's important he first learns to regard the crate as a safe place, and not a prison. See **Chapter 6. Crate and Housetraining** for the best way of achieving this
- If you have children or other animals, introduce them quietly and NEVER leave them alone with the dog for the first few months – you don't know what his triggers are
- Maintain a calm environment at home
- Never shout at the dog - even if he has made a mess in the house - it will only stress him and make things worse
- Don't give treats because you feel sorry for him. Only give him a treat when he has carried out a command. This will help him to learn quicker and you to establish leadership
- Set him up to SUCCEED and build confidence - don't ask him to do things he can't yet do
- Socialisation is extremely important - introduce him to new places and situations gradually and don't over-face him. You want him to grow in confidence, not be frightened by new things. Talk reassuringly throughout any new experience
- Mental stimulation as well as physical exercise is important for Springers, so have games, toys or challenges to keep your new dog's mind occupied
- Don't introduce him to other dogs until you are confident he will behave well - and then not while he is on a lead (leash), when the *"flight or flight"* instinct might kick in
- Getting an understanding of your dog will help to train him quicker - is he by nature submissive or dominant, anxious or outgoing, fearful or bold, aggressive or timid? If he shows aggressive tendencies, such as barking, growling or even biting, he is not necessarily bold. His aggression may be rooted in fear, anxiety or lack of confidence

> The aim of training a rescue Springer is to have a relaxed dog, comfortable in his surroundings, who respects your authority and responds well to your positive training methods.

Rescue Organisations

Rescue organisations are usually run by volunteers who give up their time to help dogs in distress. They often have a network of foster homes, where a Springer is placed until a permanent new home can be found.

There are also online Springer forums where people sometimes post information about a dog that needs a new home.

THE ENGLISH SPRINGER SPANIEL HANDBOOK Page **231**

UK

English Springer Spaniel Welfare www.essw.co.uk

Just Springers Rescue www.justspringersrescue.co.uk

English Springer Spaniel Rescue – North West England www.englishspringerrescue.co.uk

Northern English Springer Spaniel Rescue (NESSR) www.nessr.net

South Yorkshire English Springer Spaniel Rescue www.syessr.co.uk

Springer Rescue For Scotland www.springerrescuescotland.org

USA

English Springer Rescue (ESRA) www.springerrescue.org

If you visit these websites, you cannot presume that all descriptions are 100% accurate. They are given in good faith, but ideas of what constitutes a "lively" or "challenging" dog may vary.

Some dogs advertised may have other breeds in their genetic make-up. It does not mean that these are worse dogs, but if you are attracted to the Springer for its handsome looks, easy-going temperament, loyalty and other assets, make sure you are looking at a Springer.

If you haven't been put off with all of the above...

Congratulations, you may be just the person that poor homeless Springer is looking for!

If you can't spare the time to adopt - and adoption means forever - you might consider fostering. Or you could help by becoming a home inspector or fundraiser to help keep these very worthy rescue groups providing such a wonderful service.

How ever you decide to get involved, Good Luck!

With thanks to Cynthia Turvey and Northern English Springer Spaniel Rescue (NESSR) www.nessr.net for help with this article.

Saving one dog will not change the world,
But it will change the world for one dog.

17. Caring for Older Springers

The English Springer Spaniel has a longer lifespan than lots of other breeds. If all goes well you can expect your puppy to live well over a decade and even into his mid-teens if you're lucky.

Lifespan is influenced by genetics and also by owners; how you feed, exercise and generally look after your dog will all have an impact on his life. Generally, Springers are fitter and more active in old age compared to many other dogs, but eventually all of them – even energetic English Springer Spaniels – slow down.

Approaching Old Age

After having got up at the crack of dawn as a puppy, you may find your old Springer now enjoys a lie-in in the morning. He may be slower on his walks, stopping to sniff every blade of grass, and probably won't want to go as far. Joints often become stiffer and organs, such as heart, kidneys or liver, may not function quite as effectively. On the mental side - just as with humans - your dog's memory, ability to learn and awareness will all start to dim.

Photo of Jake still enjoying life aged 14. Photographer: Stephen Davies.

Your faithful companion might become a bit grumpier, stubborn or a little less tolerant of lively dogs and children. You may also notice that he doesn't see or hear as well as he used to.

On the other hand, your old friend might not be hard of hearing at all. He might have developed that affliction common to many older dogs of *"selective hearing."*

Our 12-year-old Max had bionic hearing when it came to the word *"Dinnertime"* whispered from 20 paces, yet seemed strangely unable to hear the commands *"Come"* or *"Down"* when we were right in front of him!

FACT We normally talk about dogs being old when they are in the last third of their life. Dogs are classed as a "Veteran" at seven years old in the show ring - although Springers usually stay fitter for longer.

You can help ease a mature dog into old age gracefully by keeping an eye on him, noticing the changes and taking action to help him as much as possible. This might involve:

- Slowly reducing the amount or intensity of daily exercise
- A change of diet
- Modifying your dog's environment – perhaps with an extra blanket, a warmer place and thicker bed for those aching joints
- A visit to the vet for supplements and/or medications

Ageing varies greatly from dog to dog and bloodline to bloodline. However, it's very important to keep all Springers at an optimum weight as they get older.

Their metabolisms slow down, making it easier for them to pile on the pounds. Extra weight places additional, unwanted stress on their joints, back and organs, making them all have to work harder than they should.

Physical Signs of Ageing

Here are some signs of Springers feeling their age - they may have a couple or more of these symptoms:

- Grey hairs are appearing, particularly around the muzzle, and coat colour fades
- They get up from lying down and move more slowly
- They generally slow down and are no longer as keen to go for long walks - and often less keen to go out in bad weather
- They put on a bit of weight - or lose weight
- They urinate more frequently
- They drink more water
- Hearing deteriorates
- They may have the occasional "accident" (incontinence) inside the house
- They have bouts of constipation or diarrhoea
- They shed more hair
- The foot pads thicken and nails may become more brittle
- One or more lumps or fatty deposits (lipomas) develop on the body

  One of our old dogs developed two small bumps on top of his head aged 10 and we took him straight to the vet, who performed minor surgery to remove them. They were benign (harmless), but always get the first one checked out ASAP in case they are an early form of cancer - they can also grow quite rapidly, even if benign
- They can't regulate body temperature like they used to and so feel the cold and heat more
- Bad breath (halitosis), which could be a sign of dental or gum disease. If the bad breath persists, get it checked out by a vet
- If inactive, they may develop callouses on the elbows, especially if lying on hard surfaces
- Eyesight may also deteriorate – if eyes appear cloudy they may be developing cataracts, so see your vet if you notice the signs. Most older dogs live quite well with failing eyesight, particularly as English Springer Spaniels have an incredible sense of smell

Here is the story of Abbey, a Springer who started to develop cataracts in middle age and lived happily until the ripe old age of 17½:

Photos: Two pictures of Abbey (Romaline Perfect Dream At Goldcliffe) aged 16.

Owner Louise Scott, UK English Springer Spaniel Breed Clubs' Breed Health Co-ordinator, said: "I'd say Abbey's eyes started to look cloudy at around the age of eight or nine and we started to see signs of some sight impairment at around 12.

"She probably lost her sight completely at around 15 years old, along with much of her hearing, but she coped incredibly well.

"Of course it's never ideal for a dog to go blind, but it's quite remarkable how their noses make up for the loss of other senses. As long as they feel secure and are in a familiar environment, they just get on with it.

"The fact that Abbey was by then old and moved around pretty sedately meant that we didn't have to worry about her running into things at pace and hurting herself – if she bumped into anything it was at worst a gentle nudge!

"Abbey went on to live until the age of 17½. For the last couple of years, she lost interest in going for walks and was happy to just potter around the garden.

"Losing her sight also didn't stop her from being first in the queue for any food donations **(bottom photo)** and, as you can see, she still looked good and her coat remained beautiful. We have wonderful memories of her."

Mental Signs of Ageing

It's not just your dog's body that may deteriorate; his mind may too. Your dog may display none, some or all of these signs of **Canine Cognitive Dysfunction:**

- Sleep patterns change, older dogs may be more restless at night and sleepy during the day. They may start wandering around the house at odd times, causing you sleepless nights
- They bark more, sometimes at nothing or open spaces
- Forgetting or ignoring commands or habits they once knew well, such as the Recall and sometimes toilet training
- They stare at objects, such as walls, hide in a corner, or wander aimlessly around the house or garden
- Increased anxiety or aggression
- Some dogs may become clingier and more dependent, resulting in Separation Anxiety. They may seek reassurance that you are near as faculties fade and they become a bit less confident and independent. Others may become a bit disengaged and less interested in human contact

Understanding the changes happening to your dog and acting on them compassionately and effectively will help ease your dog's passage through his senior years.

Your dog has given you so much pleasure over the years, now he needs you to give that bit of extra care for a happy, healthy old age. You can help your Springer to stay mentally active by playing gentle games and getting new toys to stimulate interest.

Helping Your Dog To Age Gracefully

There are many things you can do to ease your dog's passage into his declining years.

As dogs age they need fewer calories and less protein, so some owners feeding kibble switch to one specially formulated for older dogs. These are labelled **Senior, Ageing** or **Mature.**

Check the labelling; some are specifically for dogs aged over eight, others may be for 10 or 12-year-olds. If you are not sure if a Senior diet is necessary for your English Springer Spaniel, talk to your vet on your next visit. Remember, if you do change brand or switch to a wet food, do it gradually over a week or so. Unlike with humans, a dog's digestive system cannot cope with sudden changes of diet.

Years of eating the same food, coupled with less sensitive taste buds can result in some dogs going off their food as they age.

If you feed a dry food, try mixing a bit of gravy with it; this works well for us, as has feeding two different feeds: a morning one of kibble with gravy and the second tea-time feed of home-cooked rice and boiled chicken or fish. Rice, white fish and chicken – all cooked – can be particularly good if your old dog has a sensitive stomach.

If you are considering a daily supplement, Omega-3 fatty acids are good for the brain and coat, and glucosamine and various other supplements help joints. Yumega Omega 3, Yumove and Joint Aid are used by lots of breeders with older dogs.

Photo: Fit for function. Jule (Deb's Cortina), aged nine years and nine months, owned by Svenja Arendt. Photographer Claudia Bruhn.

We had one dog that became very sensitive to loud noises as he got older and the lead up to Bonfire Night was a nightmare. (November 5th in the UK, when the skies are filled with fireworks and loud bangs). Some dogs become more stressed by grooming or trips to the vet as they age.

Tip: There are medications, homeopathic remedies, such as melatonin, and various DAP (dog appeasing pheromone) products that can help relieve anxiety. Check with your vet before introducing any new medicines.

One of the most important things throughout your English Springer Spaniel's life is **dental care** - either by regular tooth brushing or feeding bones, bully sticks or antlers, etc. to gnaw on.

Not only is toothache painful and unpleasant, but they may lose weight due to being unable to eat properly. It can also be traumatic for dogs to have teeth removed under anaesthetic.

If your old friend has started to ignore your verbal commands when out on a walk – either through *"switching off"* or deafness - try a whistle to attract his attention and then use an exaggerated hand signal for the Recall. Once your dog is looking at you, hold your arm out, palm down, at 90 degrees to your body and bring it down, keeping your arm straight, until your fingers point to your toes.

Hand signals worked very effectively with our old Max. He looked, understood ... and then decided if he was going to come or not - but at least he knew what he should be doing! More often than not he did come back, especially if the visual signal was repeated while he was still making up his mind.

Weight - no matter how old your English Springer Spaniel is, he still needs a waist! Maintaining a healthy weight with a balanced diet and regular, gentler exercise are two of the most important things you can do for an old dog.

Some Springers can also lose weight when they get older. In such cases, try and tempt your dog with white fish, chicken and rice, which are all gentle on the stomach, or add tasty warm gravy to his meals.

Tip If your dog loses or gains weight rapidly or without any obvious reason, it's important to consult your vet promptly to rule out any underlying medical issues.

Environment - Make sure your dog has a nice soft place to rest his old bones, which may mean adding extra padding to his bed. This should be in a place that is not too hot or cold, as he may not be able to regulate his body temperature as well as when he was younger.

He also needs plenty of undisturbed sleep and should not be pestered and/or bullied by younger dogs, other animals or young children.

If his eyesight is failing, move obstacles out of his way or use pet barriers to reduce the chance of injuries.

Jumping on and off furniture or in or out of the car should definitely NOT be allowed. It's high impact for old joints and bones. He may need a helping hand to get on to the couch (if he's allowed on there) or a ramp to get into the car.

We bought an expensive plastic ramp to get one old dog into the car, but it proved to be a complete waste of money as dogs are tactile and he didn't like the feel of the non-slip surface under his paws.

After a few tentative attempts, he steadfastly refused to set a paw on it and we donated the ramp to a canine charity! I have heard of breeders carpeting ramps to (successfully) persuade their dogs to use them to get into the car.

Exercise - Take the lead from your dog, if he doesn't want to walk as far, then don't force him to go further. But if your dog doesn't want to go out at all, you will have to coax him out.

ALL old dogs need exercise, not only to keep their joints moving, but also to keep their heart, lungs and joints exercised, and their minds engaged with different places, scents, etc.

Ears - Sometimes older dogs produce more ear wax, so regularly checking inside your Springer's ears is important. Keeping the hair under the ear flap short and clean allows good air circulation, reduces moisture in the ear and lessens the wax and yeast build-up.

If necessary, use clean damp cotton wool to clean out the inner ear and pluck extra ear hair if it's getting waxy.

Coat - Some Springer Spaniels' coats thicken with age and they require grooming more often.

Time to Get Checked Out

If your dog is showing any of these signs, get him checked out by a vet:

- Drinking and/or urinating far more frequently than normal, which could be a sign of diabetes, Cushing's disease or a kidney complaint
- Constipation or not urinating regularly, a possible symptom of a digestive system or organ problem
- Incontinence, which could be a sign of mental or physical deterioration
- Watery poo(p) or vomiting
- Cloudy eyes, possibly cataracts
- Decreased appetite - this is often one of the first signs of an underlying problem
- Lumps or bumps on the body - often benign, but can occasionally be malignant (cancerous)
- Excessive sleeping or a lack of interest in you and his surroundings
- A darkening and dryness of skin that never seems to get any better, which can be a sign of hypothyroidism
- Any other out-of-the-ordinary behaviour for your dog. A change in patterns or behaviour is often your dog's way of telling you that all is not well

What the Experts Say

Lesley Field and Louise Scott, UK English Springer Spaniel Breed Clubs' Joint Breed Health Co-ordinators: "Typical lifespan for an English Springer Spaniel is 11 to 13 years, but many can live to 14 or 15. Louise had one who lived to 17½, one 16½ and one nearly 16! Our 2013 ESS Health Survey included one Springer aged 20.

"Ageing obviously depends on the individual dog, but we'd generally say an English Springer Spaniel enters what we'd call old age at around nine to 10 years.

"The visible signs are grey around the muzzle, being less active and sleeping for longer periods, stiffness getting up or moving around due to arthritis, hearing loss, less interest and desire to explore new things or run around. They might have cataracts so eyes become cloudy and vision may be impaired.

"General health issues for older Springers, as mentioned, are sight and hearing impairment and stiffness/lack of mobility. They may also need to go to the toilet more often – and may have a few more 'accidents' or sometimes even become incontinent.

"As with dogs of all breeds, cancer, heart/liver/kidney failure, stroke and other diseases all become much more likely as they get older.

"There may be some behavioural changes, such as less engagement, no longer responding to their name or familiar commands. Also, other signs of confusion, increased or inappropriate vocalisation (howling, barking or whining), which could indicate dementia, but could also be due to disorientation if they can't see or hear very well.

"Reduced exercise and general slowing down mean that weight and food need to be monitored and, yes, we change to a Senior diet. We also add joint supplements, such as Yumove.

"In terms of exercise, do shorter walks two or three times a day, rather than one very long walk. Be more cautious about walking them far on very warm days - and certainly not when the weather is hot.

"Other advice is to keep a close eye on them so as not to miss any developing health issues as they get older. Be patient with them and just enjoy the fact that they have slowed down a bit and are probably even more likely to revel in all your love and attention!"

UK Assured Breeder Chris Brandon-Lodge has bred Cottonstones English Springer Spaniels for 40 years and adds: "Ageing depends very much on the individual. My late Spaniel granny Millie lived to be two weeks off 17 and did not show much sign of aging before 12. Her daughter Teasel had a nasty illness at around 10 and is now aging noticeably. She has gone very grey about the face and has slowed down.

"Signs of ageing are some stiffening of the joints and possibly an inclination to sleep more. There is a deterioration in quality in the coats of older dogs, particularly if neutered, and they do need extra grooming to keep them respectable. There can be a general loss of weight, particularly at the flanks and back end when the hindquarters lose muscle; the dog will start to look thinner.

"Eyes will also start to deteriorate and you may see the clouding that indicates the start of cataracts. Old dogs will often go deaf in their teens, but this is rarely a big problem because they respond very well to hand signals such as the beckoning movement.

"I keep mine on the same Adult food unless I feel they need something different.

"I don't change my exercise habits, but the older dogs can choose whether to come or not – it is best left to them to decide.

"My advice for owners is to make sure they don't get cold, especially if they've been wet – and give them a bit of extra TLC and cuddles."

Photo: Millie (right) with granddaughter Tawny Cottonstones Walnut.

The Last Lap

Huge advances in veterinary science have meant that there are countless procedures and medications that can prolong the life of your dog, and this is a good thing. But there comes a time when you do have to let go.

If your dog is showing all the signs of ageing, has an ongoing medical condition from which he cannot recover, is showing signs of pain, anxiety or distress and there is no hope of improvement, then the dreaded time has come to say goodbye. You owe it to your English Springer Spaniel.

There is no point keeping an old dog alive if all that lies ahead is pain and death. We have their lives in our hands and we can give them the gift of passing away peacefully and humanely at the end when the time is right.

Losing our beloved companion, our best friend, a member of the family, is truly heart-breaking. But one of the things we realise at the back of our minds when we got that gorgeous, lively little puppy that bounded up to meet us like we were the best person in the whole wide world is the pain that comes with it.

We know we will live longer than them and that we'll probably have to make this most painful of decisions at some time in the future.

It's the worst thing about being a dog owner.

If your English Springer Spaniel has had a long and happy life, then you could not have done any more. You were a great owner and your dog was lucky to have you. Remember all the good times you had together.

Try not to rush out and buy another dog straight away. Assess your current life and lifestyle and, if your situation is right, only then consider getting another dog and all that that entails in terms of time, commitment, exercise and expense over the next decade and more.

Whatever you decide to do, put the dog first.

Twilight Years: Jake and Lady, both aged 14.

We'll end on a positive note with a comment from Lesley: "The memories and gratitude you feel to an old dog who has travelled the road with you for so many years is a special reward that only owners of old dogs experience."

Contributors

Lynne Lucas, Kennel Club Assured Breeder, Traxlerstarr Spaniels, Surrey.

Chris Brandon-Lodge, Kennel Club Assured Breeder, Cottonstones English Springer Spaniels and Gordon Setters, Shrewsbury, Shropshire.

Lisa Cardy, Kennel Club Assured Breeder, CallisWold English Springer Spaniels, Kirby Underdale, North Yorkshire. Website: www.thecottagecanines.co.uk

Lesley Field and Louise Scott, UK English Springer Spaniel Breed Clubs' Joint Breed Health Co-ordinators www.englishspringerhealth.org.uk

Dr Marianne Dorn, MRCVS, "The Rehab Vet," https://TheRehabVet.com

Dr Vicky Payne, MRCVS, Quincegrove Working Springer Spaniels, East Sussex

http://workingspringerspaniels.uk

Haja van Wessem, (English) Cocker Spaniels www.spegglewaggel.com

Francie Nelson, Vice President, International Relations, US English Springer Foundation, Fanfare English Springer Spaniels, Minneapolis, Minnesota, USA.

Cynthia Turvey and **Northern English Springer Spaniel Rescue (NESSR)** www.nessr.net

Dr Sara Skiwski, DVM, The Western Dragon holistic veterinary practice, San Jose, California, USA www.thewesterndragon.com

Cover shot: Warren Photographic www.warrenphotographic.co.uk

Back Cover: Adobe Stock https://stock.adobe.com

Useful Contacts

The English Springer Spaniel Club (UK) www.englishspringer.org

ESSFTA (English Springer Spaniel Field Trial Association (USA) https://essfta.org

English Springer Spaniel Health for the most up-to-date information on English Springer Spaniel health, www.englishspringerhealth.org.uk

Southern English Springer Spaniel Society (SESSS) www.sesss.org

Kennel Club (UK) Assured Breeders www.thekennelclub.org.uk/search/find-an-assured-breeder

AKC (American Kennel Club) www.akc.org/dog-breeds/english-springer-spaniel

RSPCA Puppy Contract https://puppycontract.rspca.org.uk/home

AKC Preparing a Puppy Contract www.akc.org/expert-advice/dog-breeding/preparing-a-contract-for-puppy-buyers

AKC Canine Good Citizen www.akc.org/products-services/training-programs/canine-good-citizen

KC Good Citizen Scheme www.thekennelclub.org.uk/training/good-citizen-dog-training-scheme

Association of Pet Dog Trainers UK www.apdt.co.uk

Association of Pet Dog Trainers US www.apdt.com

Canadian Association of Professional Pet Dog Trainers www.cappdt.ca

Useful info on dog foods (US) www.dogfoodadvisor.com (UK) www.allaboutdogfood.co.uk

Helps find lost or stolen dogs in the US: register your dog's microchip at www.akcreunite.org and www.petmicrochiplookup.com to trace a registered microchip

English Springer Spaniel internet forums and Facebook groups are also a good source of information from other owners.

Disclaimer

This book has been written to provide helpful information on English Springer Spaniels. It is not meant to be used, nor should it be used, to diagnose or treat any medical condition. For diagnosis or treatment of any animal medical problem, consult a qualified veterinarian.

The author is not responsible for any specific health or allergy conditions that may require medical supervision and is not liable for any damages or negative consequences from any treatment, action, application or preparation, to any animal or to any person reading or following the information in this book.

The views expressed by contributors to this book are solely personal and do not necessarily represent those of the author. References are provided for informational purposes only and do not constitute endorsement of any websites or other sources.

Pet Care Tracker

Vet's Name: _ _ _ _ _ _ _ _ _ _ _ _   Groomer's Name: _ _ _ _ _ _ _ _ _ _ _ _

Vet's Phone: _ _ _ _ _ _ _ _ _ _ _ _   Groomer's Phone: _ _ _ _ _ _ _ _ _ _ _ _

Day Care: _ _ _ _ _ _ _ _ _ _ _ _   Holiday Sitter: _ _ _ _ _ _ _ _ _ _ _ _

Pet's Name	Date	Vet Visit	Groomer	NOTES

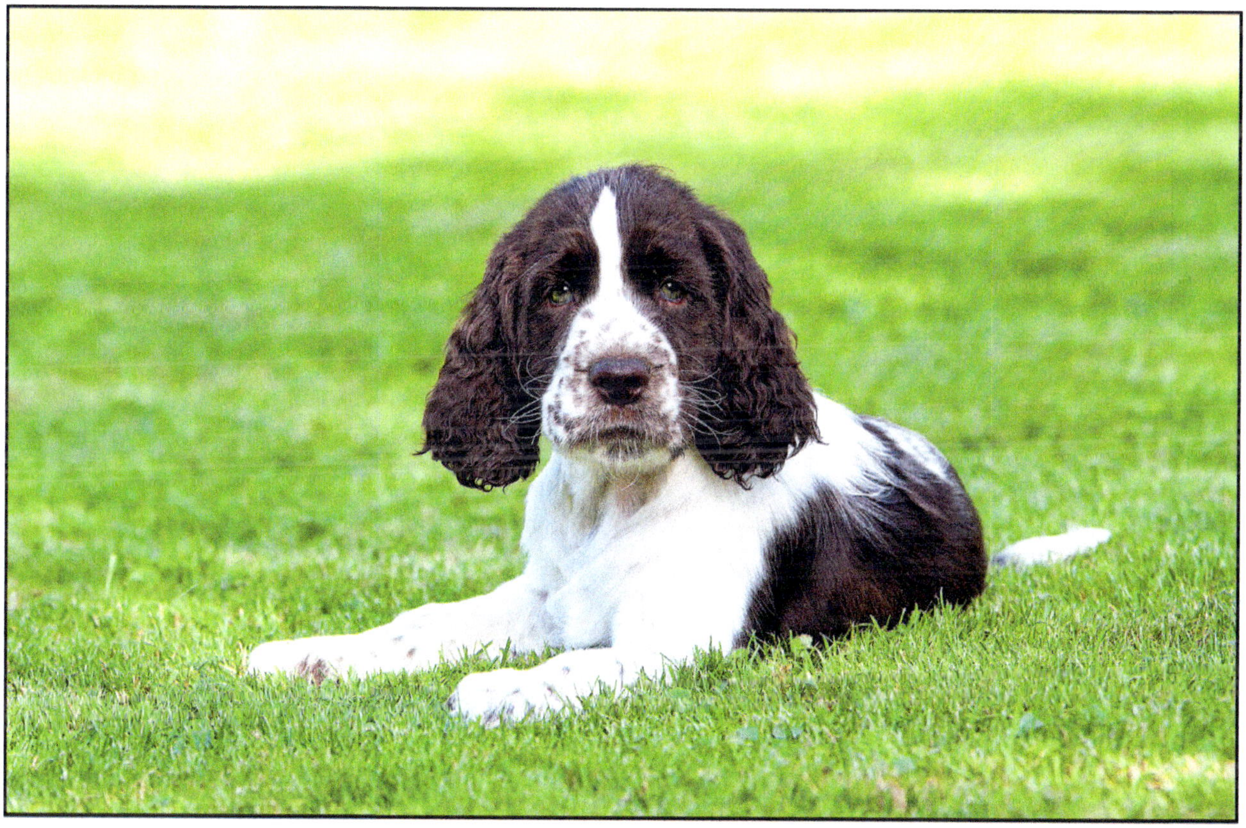

Printed in Great Britain
by Amazon